WILDFLOWERS
of WASHINGTON

WILDFLOWERS
of WASHINGTON

by C.P. Lyons

The Publisher: **Lone Pine Publishing**

1901 Raymond Avenue SW, Suite C	206, 10426 - 81 Avenue	202A, 1110 Seymour Street
Renton, Washington	Edmonton, Alberta	Vancouver, British Columbia
USA 98055	Canada T6E 1X5	Canada V6B 3N3

Canadian Cataloguing in Publication Data
Lyons, C.P. (Chester Peter), 1915-
   Wildflowers of Washington

   Includes index.
   ISBN 1-55105-092-7

   1. Wildflowers—Washington (State)—Identification. I. Title.
QK192.L96 1997   582'.13'09797   C97-910770-9

Senior Editor: *Nancy Foulds*

Editors: *Roland Lines, Heather Markham*

Production Manager: *David Dodge*

Design and Layout: *Beata Kurpinski, Gregory Brown*

Photography: *Chess Lyons, Bill Merilees*

Black and White Drawings: *Chess Lyons*

Cartography: *Volker Bodegom*

Separations and Film: *Elite Lithographers, Ltd., Edmonton, Alberta, Canada*

Printing: *Select Colour Press, Edmonton, Alberta, Canada*

Caution: Although this guide mentions medicinal and culinary uses of plants, it is not a "how to" reference for using traditional, plant-derived medicines or foods. We do not recommend experimentation by readers, and we caution that many plants in our region, including some with traditional, medical or food use—or look-alikes—can be poisonous or harmful.

The publisher gratefully acknowledges the support of Alberta Community Development and the Department of Canadian Heritage.

CONTENTS

PREFACE

AN AUTHOR MUST BELIEVE quite strongly that there is a purpose for a book, or one wouldn't suffer through the countless items of toil and frustration. At the beginning, the concept can appear deceptively simple. Produce a book that is small and light enough to invite inclusion during a walk or hike. It should be easily understood and priced attractively. Then the problems start. How small is "small"? What do you put in and what do you leave out? Some people prefer the clarity of black and white drawings. For others it is color, and in today's world that seems to be the most preferable. But identification is the most important issue, so use whichever is best.

Then slipping in sideways comes a new factor. Many plant names are related to Lewis and Clark— the leaders of the daring expedition that crossed to the Pacific Ocean in 1805 and returned to St. Louis the following year. Lewis and Clark traversed Washington twice and left colorful records of what they saw and experienced. Two decades later, the botanist-explorer David Douglas (the Douglas-fir bears his name) traveled thousands of miles by foot, horseback and canoe in the Pacific Northwest and added greatly to the knowledge of our flora. Could some of their adventures and observations be integrated into the book material? Why not give it a try?

Wildflowers of Washington is adapted from my original flora book, *Trees, Shrubs and Flowers to Know in Washington* (1956), and the major revision I made over several years with the help of Bill Merilees, *Trees, Shrubs and Flowers to Know in Washington and British Columbia* (1995). This newest guide adds color photographs of most plants and frequent references to the travels and collections of Archibald Menzies, the Lewis and Clark Expedition and David Douglas. I hope that being able to relate the early explorers to some of the flora of Washington will lead to a better appreciation of these early endeavors. There is still a thrill of discovery yourself when you chance for the first time to find a floral gem in a forest glade or high on a mountain side.

Bill Merilees has helped with photos from his extensive collection. Andy MacKinnon has given freely of his botanical knowledge, and he had helpful advice on format. Adolf Ceska has used his botanical skill to rectify errors and make suggestions. Ruth Kirk has used her professional editing skill to check from cover to cover. However, the author takes full responsibility for all aberrations. Trish Ellison has gamely tackled another session of transcribing my abominably written notes into computer format.

To these and others who have helped in various ways, your efforts have been much appreciated.

WHO WRITES PLANT BOOKS?

FROM THE TIME OF Aristotle (384–322 BC), people have recorded their perceptions of plants, but it wasn't until the 13th century that these early works reached the Medieval world. Several centuries later there was a surge of interest in botanical exploration based largely on a search for plants with medicinal values. Several illustrated volumes were published in the 1500s. All used the system of listing all the plants in alphabetical order along with whatever descriptive notes were thought pertinent.

In 1539, Hieronymus Bock made a major change by publishing his plant descriptions under a breakdown into "trees," "shrubs" and "herbs." Later attempts at organization saw plants divided by leaf designs, another on reproductive structures. As more and more data was accumulated, it accentuated the need for a systematic means of classification.

One enthusiast, Georg Everhard Ruinpf, devoted many years to studying the flora of the Dutch West Indies. This resulted in the much delayed publication in the mid-1700s of a 12-volume work with nearly 700 plates and descriptions of some 1200 species—the first work on tropical flora. Considering the rather primitive means of printing and illustrating, this was a stupendous achievement.

Several prominent botanists were working toward a system of classifying plants, but it remained for Carl Linnaeus (1707-78), a Swedish naturalist and physician, to instigate a system and be credited as "The Father of Botany." In 1753, he proposed a two-name system (binomial nomenclature). A Latin or Greek name would be used for the genus, such as *Pinus*, *Vacinnium* and *Rosa*, followed by a specific diagnostic term, such as *ovalifolium*, *tridentata*, *densiflora* and *sulphureus*, or the name of the discoverer or someone to be honored, such as *douglasii* and *menziesii*. Linnaeus also introduced a standard botanical terminology so every botanist could record his findings and be understood by other botanists.

Today, any person who writes about plants—anywhere in the world—has a framework of technical names and descriptive terminology to follow. Many flora books follow this organization, but others, like this field guide, attempt to provide identification without following technical descriptive terminology.

EXPLORER-BOTANISTS

Archibald Menzies • 1792

Archibald Menzies

ON CAPTAIN George Vancouver's voyage to the western coast of North America in 1792, Archibald Menzies (1754-1842) was the expedition's surgeon and botanist. His instructions: "to investigate the whole of the natural history of the countries visited." And that was only a start! His was the first scientific mind to fully appreciate the floral wonders. As he came ashore near Port Townsend on May 1 he saw "a variety of wild flowers in full bloom but what chiefly dazzles our eyes... Was a species of wild Valerian [sea blush]." The same flood of pink can dazzle our eyes today.

Captain Vancouver was intent on charting the convoluted shoreline of Puget Sound and its islands. Menzies went ashore at every opportunity, but he was never able to get very far inland and away from the more or less typical coastal flora. Nevertheless, he was a master craftsman at his trade of collection, preservation and description, which included fine drawings from this "botanical draughtsman." On May 17, he was busy "... in getting on aboard some live plants which were new... & in planting them on the frame on the Quarter Deck." It was his fine collection of flora from an unknown land that intrigued botanists and horticulturists in Great Britain. They supported new explorations and were in large part responsible for David Douglas' travels.

Menzies' specimens were studied by prominent botanists, the most famous being Sir William Hooker, whose findings were published in various ways and avidly studied.

Menzies epitomized the creed of the scientific botanist: "seek, find, collect and share with others." The travels and collections by Lewis and Clark, and later by David Douglas, have to be correlated to this pioneer. How could Lewis or Clark put a name to many plants seen for the first time without some prior knowledge, sketchy as it may have been? Douglas went ashore on this faraway land and wrote on April 8, 1825, "On stepping on the shore *Gaultheria shallon* [salal] was the first plant I took in my hands." Strange as it may seem, he had seen this plant in the Botanical Gardens in Glasgow, raised from seed brought back by Menzies in 1792.

Two other names of botanical significance are John Scouler and Thomas Nuttall. The former was a geologist-surgeon-naturalist who accompanied David Douglas on his first trip to the Northwest. Nuttall was a "botanical explorer" who ventured into areas of western North America.

The Lewis and Clark Expedition • 1804 to 1806

Both Meriwether Lewis (1774-1809) and William Clark (1770-1838) made extensive botanical collections. A number of today's popular plants bear witness to this in the suffixes to botanical names, such as clarkii *and* lewisii.

Meriwether Lewis

BACKGROUND

Thomas Jefferson, President of the United States, was well aware that Alexander Mackenzie had crossed Canada to the Pacific Ocean in 1793. Mackenzie later proposed the 45th Parallel as the Canadian border. This line would pass about 160 km (100 miles) south of the lower Columbia River and ensure an ocean port and river access to the interior. To Jefferson, it seemed imperative that an exploration of the far west should be carried out before the British laid claim to the land. There also was a strong incentive to see what wonders of natural history might be found in this wilderness to the west. Jefferson, an amateur naturalist, had pondered whether dinosaurs and mastodons might still exist. He chose an army captain to lead this great trek—Lewis—who was "brave, prudent, habituated to the woods, and familiar with Native American manners and character."

Clark also had a military background. He was an "Indian fighter" and experienced in forest and river travel. He was skilled in map-making and his artistic ability proved valuable as he made sketches to record new features. Both men studied celestial navigation and used it constantly in their map-making. Among Lewis' supplies was a book, Barton's *Elements of Botany,* and a large package of purple blotting paper for pressing plant specimens. Both men were to perform an unbelievably wide scope of duties: among the "objects worthy of notice" were "the soil and face of this country, its growth and vegetable production."

Despite the extremely long work days—rarely less than 16 hours—and the hardships of travel, Lewis and Clark diligently collected not only flowers, but shrubs, ferns and grasses. These were often drawn and described in minute detail. Careful notes were made about trees and fruits. They also collected birds, mammals, insects and shellfish. Not to be missed were notes on soil, rocks and every facet of Native American life they encountered.

THE EXPEDITION

The expedition started up the Missouri River from St. Louis on May 14, 1804. They traveled in several cumbersome boats built especially for them. Basic supplies included gunpowder and shot, pork, flour, salt and biscuits. The theory was that with hunters out almost

William Clark

every day they would be able to supplement their supplies with wild game and fish. In favorable big-game hunting areas they hunted almost every day.

They also carried red, white and blue beads in large numbers for the purpose of trading. They discovered that blue beads were most favored. With almost daily perils, they continued north on the river until they reached an area almost in the center of present-day North Dakota. There they built a small fort, Fort Mandan, and wintered with the Sioux.

Before continuing next spring, they employed a French-Canadian interpreter who brought his Native American wife, Sacajawea. She proved very helpful as an interpreter and in winning the friendship of other Native Americans. Despite her endurance and help in various endeavors, neither Lewis nor Clark ever refers to her by name in their journals; she is always "the squar," probably a corruption of "squaw."

From Fort Mandan, the course for the travelers was westward to Montana, where in "Big Country" they were able to buy or trade for horses. Despite continual hazards, they managed to cross the Rockies—the Continental Divide—a major feat of exploration in itself. Food was a major concern, especially when the various edible roots were unavailable and deer and bear were in the high mountains.

Fort Clatsop

Provisions all out, which compells us to kill one of our horses to eate (and make suep for the sick men).
—Clark, October 2, 1805

Cap. Lewis & myself eat a supper of roots boiled, which filled us so full of wind, that we were scarcely able to Breathe all night.
—Clark, October 15, 1805

When they came to the headwaters of the Clearwater River and further down it found giant trees (western redcedar), they built boats. Despite the hazards of canyons, rapids and whirlpools in the Snake River, and the inhospitable, near-desert country, they reached the Columbia River near today's town of Pasco.

Traveling down the Columbia River with its periodic series of chutes and falls posed one dangerous challenge after another, but not a man was lost. They reached tidal waters on the Columbia, November 15, 1805. There they built a small fort, Fort Clatsop, near present-day Astoria, and they wintered under miserable conditions, plagued by fleas, continual rain and a shortage of food.

[The Pacific's] waters are foaming and perpetually break with immense waves on the sands and rocky coasts, tempestuous and horrible.

—Lewis, November, 1805

We are all wet, our bedding and stores are also wet. This wind and rain continued with short intervals all the latter part of the night. O! how disagreeable is our Situation during this dreadfull weather.

—Clark, November 28, 1805

This evening we had what I call an excellent supper it consisted of a marrowbone a piece and brisket of boiled Elk that had the appearance of a little fat on it. This for Fort Clatsop is living in high style.

—Lewis, February 7, 1806

There was a constant search for food for the 32 people at camp. Twenty deer and 181 elk were killed in a four-month period. Wapato was the most sought after root. It grew abundantly in ponds along the lower Columbia River and was the most prized item of trade.

Wappatoe... [is] the principal article of traffic....The natives of the seacoast will dispose of their most valuable articles too obtain this root.

—Lewis, March, 1806

They began the return trip the following March, much too early for crossing the Continental Divide, which was still buried in winter snow. But after the hardships and discomfort of a long winter, any course of action seemed preferable.

We loaded our canoes at 1 pm, left Ft. Clatsop, on our homeward bound journey, at this place we have wintered and remained since the 7th of Dec. 1805 to this day....We were never one day without 3 meals of some kind either pore Elk or roots.

—Clark, March 23, 1806

The explorers crossed the southerly part of the state using the same general route as Highway 12 of today. At Clarkston and Lewistown they transferred to the Clearwater River and followed this eastward to the Rockies. They were forced to camp in the lee of the Rockies and wait for better conditions.

Even now I shudder with the expectations of great difficulties in passing these mountains—that wretched portion of our journey—where hunger and cold in their most rigorous forms await to assail the wearied traveller.

—Clark, April, 1806

In a perilous march, they crossed the divide and were able to pick a less difficult route eastward, further south than their original route westward. Using the Marias and Yellowstone rivers, they reached the Missouri River. Then it was a comparatively easy trip downstream to St. Louis, where they made shore with much excitement on September 23, 1806.

Lewis and Clark discovered 178 plants then unknown to Europeans. Two-thirds of these plants were found west of the Rocky Mountains. The wide range of knowledge they brought back, the maps and charts, and the publicity of this expedition put great value in substantiating the United States' claim to the territory.

Lewis and Clark's collections were examined by Frederick Pursh, a European botanist who was living in Philadelphia while he worked on a flora of North America. He was the person who gave many of the scientific names to their plants.

THE JOURNALS

The detailed journals of these explorers provide a vivid picture of their travels, perils and hardships, interwoven with their amazingly perceptive and detailed notes on natural history. The following few pages attempt to provide some of the botanical information related to their return trip across Washington in early spring, 1806. There is a great deal of variance in spelling from account to account; the original notes were written in a hurry and under difficulties, and they were later rewritten. The original has been retained here in most cases.

Lewis and Clark's return route was eastward through the scenic, and now historic, Columbia Gorge, and then stayed with the Columbia River to Wallula. There they left the Columbia and followed a route that quite closely parallels State Highway 12 to Clarkston and Lewiston. Today's travelers on State Highway 14 in Washington, or Highway 30 across the Columbia River in Oregon, can easily relate to the comments and travels as they also follow the river towards The Dalles. Beacon Rock, for example, is a landmark today, and there is a popular campsite not far away.

It is only in the fall of the year when the river is low that the tides are perceptible as high as the beacon rock. This remarkable rock rises to a height of seven hundred feet...and is visible for 20 miles [32 km] below on the river.

—Lewis, April 6, 1806

We passed several beautiful cascades which fell from a great height over the stupendous rocks which close the river on both sides nearly....The most remarkable of these cascades [Multnomah] falls about 300 feet [91 m] perpendicularily over a solid rock into a narrow bottom.

—Lewis, April 9, 1806

Today this general area carries an abundance of poison-ivy and poison-oak. However, no mention is made of these plants or any afflictions that might have arisen from contact. The leaves would have dropped, but berries should have been clearly visible.

The mountains through which the river passes...are high, broken, rocky, partially covered with fir [Douglas-fir], white cedar [western redcedar], and in many places exhibit very romantic scenes....I observed...the long leafed pine [ponderosa pine], this pine increases in quantity as you ascend the river ...and where the lower country commences [near Bingen] it supersedes the fir altogether.

—Lewis, April 14, 1806

Lewis and Clark were very aware of the change when they entered the start of the extensive sagebrush ecosystem.

Our present station [about 16 km (10 miles) west of The Dalles] is the last point at which there isn't a single stick of timber on the river for a great distance and is the commencement of the open plains which extend nearly to the base of the rocky Mt.

—Lewis, April 16, 1806

There are no deer, antelope or elk which we could depend for substence.

—Clark, April 16, 1806

Even at this place [The Dalles]...the climate seems to have changed the air feels dryer and more pure the plain is covered with a rich verdure of grass and herbs....[It is] a beautiful seen.

—Lewis, April 17, 1806

At this point, Lewis and Clark made a partial change in travel. They cut up two of the large canoes for firewood, and they dickered for horses, but they also continued up the river with five small canoes. Again and again they refer to the problem of getting firewood. "Southern wood" (sagebrush) was used as a substitute, but apparently it wasn't too plentiful.

I entered the largest house....They made a light of straw, they having no wood to burn.

—Clark, April 18, 1806

There is no timber in this country, we are obliged to purchase our fuel of the natives, who bring it from a great distance, we can only afford one fire, and are obliged to lie about without shelter.

—Lewis, April 22, 1806

On April 30, 1806, they left the Columbia River near present day Wallula—a name that was in use even in their time. They continued eastward and took an overland route that approximates that of State Highway 12 all the way to Clarkson. You will see references to their names many times along this highway.

This plain is covered with arromatic shrubs [possibly sagebrush and antelope brush], herbatious plants and a short grass. Many of these plants produce those esculent roots which form a principal part of the subsistance of the natives. ...One produces a root somewhat like the sweet pittaitoe [probably large-fruited desert-parsley].

—Lewis, April 30, 1806

The expedition would have had even more serious food problems if it hadn't been for their extensive use of roots—wapato, large-fruited parsley, cous and camas. The cous bulb was collected as soon as the snow disappeared, until camas root became available in late spring.

> [Members of the party] *returned from the village with about 6 bushels of the root the natives call cowse* [cous] *and some bread of the same root.*
> —Lewis, May 19, 1806

> *The cows* [cous] *is a knobby root of an irregular rounded form not unlike the ginsang in form and consistance, this root they collect, rub off a thick black rhind...and pounding it exposes it in cakes to the sun....They either eat this bread alone or boil it and make a thick muscilage.*
> —Clark, May 28, 1806

When a collection of plants became bulky, especially on the westward journey, it was wrapped and buried in the ground in some key place for a later pick-up.

> *Had the cash* [cache] *opened and found my bear skins entirely destroyed by the water, the river having risen so high that the water had pinitrated all my specimens of plants also lost.*
> —Lewis, July, 1806

David Douglas • 1824 to 1827, 1833 to 1834

David Douglas

This adventurous young Scotsman (1799-1834) roamed a vast wilderness encompassing much of present-day Oregon, Washington and British Columbia. He recorded many new plant species and introduced no less than 254 plants to Great Britain. The wide-ranging Douglas-fir tree was named after him. His journals provide an intriguing glimpse of his thoughts about the flora and conditions relating to his travels.

Douglas, as a child, developed a strong interest in natural history. His father apprenticed him to the head gardener at Scone Palace in Scotland when Douglas was only 11 years old. He started a botanical collection and learned quickly. His enthusiasm brought rapid advancement and he came to the attention of William James Hooker, who had a world-wide reputation in botany. Hooker recommended Douglas to the Royal Horticultural Society as a potential collector.

When the Royal Horticultural Society and the Hudson's Bay Company organized an expedition to explore an area of north Pacific wilderness (now Oregon, Washington and British Columbia), Douglas was proposed for the project. He studied for 18 hours a day to prepare for the expedition, which set out on a sailing ship on July 26, 1824. It was April 17, 1825 when he landed near the mouth of the Columbia River after "a long and tedious voyage of 8 months and 14 days."

Douglas was immediately on the go, marveling at everything he saw. Eleven days after landing he was sitting around a fire with Native Americans, enjoying barbecued sturgeon. Douglas was 26 years old and the product of the intellectual society of Great Britain. He quickly "turned native" and learned the crafts of the woods and water travel, and how to deal with the Native American people. He avidly identified plants and collected seeds and samples. Birds and mammals were also a matter of high interest to him. He carried some bird skins and even a live eagle for many hundreds of miles.

Fort Vancouver– Bakery

He was a persistent explorer and collector who often made hazardous trips in late fall and early winter when most plants had long faded. He would go back to some area he had noted in the summer for the purpose of collecting seeds. One might wonder how he could find his way to some local area he had noticed a month or so before.

His equipment was meager indeed. Many times he was grateful for a few roots the Native Americans shared with him. His daily routine was to rise before or at first light, travel for three to four hours before breakfast, then carry on through a jungle of vegetation, fording or swimming chilling rivers, and finally stopping just before dark. With persistence and discipline, despite the fatigue of 16-hour days, he prepared his plant specimens and then carefully recorded, at some length, the details of the collecting and a travel summary. It was common for him to write that he "had gained" 40 miles (64 km) or more that day.

By the end of 1825, he estimated he had covered 3389 km (2105 miles). During the winter of 1825-26 he stayed, very uncomfortably, at Fort Vancouver on the Columbia River. The fever of collecting was in his blood and he wanted to stay another year: "Most cheerfully will I labour without remuneration, if I get only wherewith to purchase a little clothing." And travel he did: during 1826 he estimated covering a distance of nearly 6500 km (4000 miles).

Fort Vancouver – Store

My store of clothes is very low, nearly reduced to what I have on my back—one pair of shoes, no stockings, two shirts, two handkerchiefs, my blanket and cloak; thus I adapt my costume to that of the country. I am now here, and God knows where I may be in the next, in all probability consigned to the tomb, I can be satisfied with myself. I never have given cause for remonstrance or pain to an individual on earth. I am in my twenty-seventh year.

When my people in England are made acquainted with my travels, they may perhaps think I have told them nothing but my miseries. This may be very correct but I know that such objects I am in quest of are not obtained without a share of labour, anxiety of mind, and sometimes risk of personal safety.

David Douglas did, indeed, suffer many miseries, and at times they were such that he himself became unsure of his course.

All hungry and no means of cooking a little of our stock; travelled 33 miles, drenched and bleached with rain and sleet, chilled with a piercing north wind, and then to finish the day experiencing the cooling, comfortless consolation of lying down without supper or fire. On such occasions I am liable to become fretfull.

—Douglas, November 11, 1826

In early 1827, he sorted, packed and sent a great collection of specimens back from the Columbia River to England on one of the Hudson's Bay Company ships. Then, in an unbelievable journey, he took the fur trade route north up the Columbia River, crossed the Rockies far to the north in British Columbia, and traveled over a thousand miles to a fort on Hudson's Bay, from where he sailed to England.

The cases of plants and seeds that Douglas had collected from 1825–27 (and shipped back to England) were studied by the great botanist Sir William Hooker, and, by late 1829, Douglas' findings were printed in *Flora Boreali-Americana*.

I cannot tell you how pleased I am…to take it with me to America. The map is good…the plates are truly beautiful.

—Douglas, October 27, 1829

Douglas returned to Fort Vancouver in 1833 and was eager to start a dream he had long in mind: to go back to America and then cross from Alaska to Russia and then travel back to Britain via the southerly route through Russia near China.

Douglas made a start by water and land, covering over 1900 km (1200 miles) to reach remote Fort St. James in northern British Columbia. Despite the immensity of travel to and through the wilderness of British Columbia, he was keen to continue on to Alaska, but he could not find a guide, and the Native Americans he met were unfriendly. Despondent, he back-tracked to the Fraser River at Prince George and launched a canoe, only to be upset in the nearby rapids and nearly drowned—a serious blow in that he lost his specimens and precious journal. Somehow it seemed only a matter of course to cover about 1450 km (900 miles) of wilderness travel back to Fort Vancouver.

Shortly after, he had a chance to sail to the Sandwich (Hawaiian) Islands. While on The Big Island (Hawaii), he climbed Mauna Loa (4169 m [13,674']). On July 12, 1834, he fell into a pit to trap wild cattle, and he was gored to death by a trapped bull.

Douglas was only 35 years old when he died, but in that short lifetime he made a major contribution to the world's knowledge of Northwest flora. His carefully collected seeds are now reflected in large areas of forest in Great Britain and in specimen trees in major arboretums.

Douglas' diary recounts almost daily hardships, probably assessed as adventures by him, and a remarkable understanding and appreciation of the Native American culture. It was the world's misfortune that David Douglas, in the prime of life, lost it in one careless moment. Could he not be classed as the world's most enthusiastic botanist?

THE ECOSYSTEMS

FOR ORIENTATION, remember that the ecosystem listing is running from west to east. Traveling from the ocean up and to the summit of the Cascade Mountains, over the bordering alpine terrain and down through the subalpine brings a person to the mountain forest classification on the eastern slopes of the Cascades. Below that are the ponderosa pine, the bunchgrass and the sagebrush ecosystems.

San Juan Islands

SAN JUAN ISLANDS: The San Juan Islands lie between the southern tip of Vancouver Island and mainland Washington. South-facing lands with grassy slopes feature arbutus and Garry oak. In protected areas, a rich mixture of deciduous and evergreen trees adds more variety and color. These islands are world-famous for their mild climate and low precipitation. The average annual rainfall is 75 cm (29.5"), and snow is unusual, which result from being in the rain shadow of the Olympic Mountains.

Coast Forest

COAST FOREST: This term is used in the broadest sense to cover forests on the Pacific side of the Cascades up to subalpine elevations. A more complex classification would see a division at around 1200 m (3940'), where lowland coastal species are replaced by mountain hemlock, amabilis fir, alpine fir and yellow-cedar. Coastal rainfall (Seattle) averages 85 cm (33") a year. Winters are mild, but at higher elevations there is considerably more snow and colder temperatures.

Subalpine

SUBALPINE: Above the dense coastal forests, this region of green glades, picturesque trees and expansive, multi-colored flower meadows is backed by magnificent mountain scenery. It draws millions of visitors each year to the Olympics, Mt. Baker and Mt. Rainier. Hikers reach less well-known areas, such as Mt. Shuksan and Mt. St. Helens. The Blue Mountains have high ridges in the subalpine. Winters are long and severe, and snow accumulates to great depths. Open terrain and deep snow create ideal conditions for ski resorts.

Here is a quick and generalized introduction to the flower spectacle: the red flowers are paintbrush, the spikes of blue flowers are lupines, the pink-purple daisies are mountain daisies, the large yellow flowers are arnicas, and the white heads of small flowers are either mountain valerian or bistort.

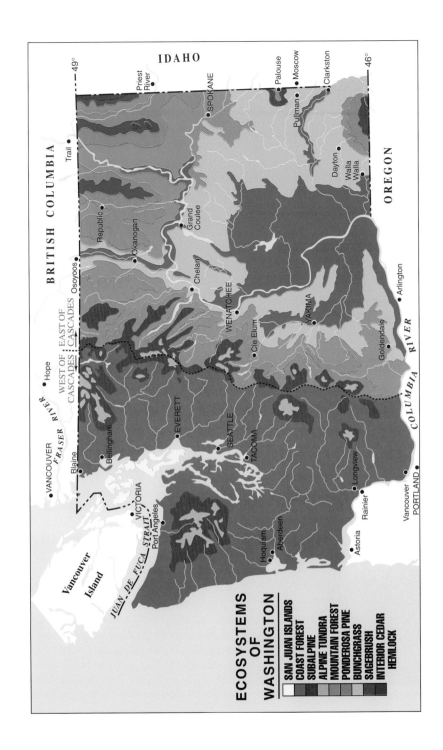

ECOSYSTEMS OF WASHINGTON

- SAN JUAN ISLANDS
- COAST FOREST
- SUBALPINE
- ALPINE TUNDRA
- MOUNTAIN FOREST
- PONDEROSA PINE
- BUNCHGRASS
- SAGEBRUSH
- INTERIOR CEDAR HEMLOCK

IDAHO

Priest River
SPOKANE
Palouse
Moscow
Pullman
Clarkston

BRITISH COLUMBIA

Trail

Hope

VANCOUVER
FRASER RIVER
Vancouver
Island

Blaine
Bellingham

VICTORIA
Port Angeles

JUAN DE FUCA STRAIT

Osoyoos

Republic
Okanogan

Grand Coulee

Chelan

WENATCHEE

Cle Elum

YAKIMA

Goldendale

COLUMBIA RIVER

Arlington

Dayton
Walla Walla

OREGON

EVERETT
SEATTLE
TACOMA

Longview

Rainier

Vancouver
PORTLAND

Astoria

Hoquiam
Aberdeen

WEST OF CASCADES | EAST OF CASCADES

49°

46°

Alpine Tundra

ALPINE TUNDRA: The name "alpine tundra" is replacing the more common term "alpine." But where is the division between the subalpine and the alpine tundra? The matter is more simple than in the case of timberline, for stunted trees creep high up some mountains. The boundry where the rich growth of grasses and flowers gives way to near barren rocky slopes and ridges is more discernible. There the rockery plants take over: the heathers, campanulas, moss campions and saxifrages.

This change-over occurs at about 1350 m (4430') on southern coastal mountains and at about 1800 m (5900') east of the Cascades. Weather conditions are severe, with long winters and short summers. With mountain roads and helicopter access, the alpine tundra is a spectacular setting for winter sports.

Mountain Forest

MOUNTAIN FOREST: Like the Coast Forest, this ecosystem also has several arbitrary divisions. As you enter it from the subalpine, it consists almost entirely of white spruce, Engelmann spruce and alpine fir; as you move lower there is a transition to lodgepole pine, larch, cottonwood and birch. Engelmann spruce continues into these lower elevations. The bulk of this ecosystem lies on the eastern slopes of the Cascades, but other areas are found at higher elevations in northeastern Washington, within the Okanogan and Colville National Forests, and on the northern slopes of the Blue Mountains.

Ponderosa Pine

PONDEROSA PINE: This ecosystem is easily identified by the presence of these beautiful trees, growing either in pure, open stands or mixed with Douglas-fir up to an elevation of 900 m (2950'), where it is replaced by the mountain forest ecosystem. A strip of ponderosa pine ecosystem extends northward from about the midpoint of the Columbia Gorge, through Klickitat, Kittitas and Chelan counties to the hillsides of the Okanogan Valley. It is common both north and south of Spokane. The climate is extremely arid, with hot summer days and freezing winter temperatures. Annual rainfall is 25–50 cm (10–19 1/2").

BUNCHGRASS: This ecosystem classification takes in the terrain between the lower edge of the ponderosa pine and the upper border of the sagebrush ecosystem. Before the advent of large-scale land clearing and irrigation, the bunchgrass zone would have covered a large portion of the state. Now, looking at the fields tightly locked together for many miles on end, one needs a good deal of imagination to visualize this as bunchgrass prairies, once home to Native Americans and a wealth of wild animals. The greed for land left no significant part as a representative sample of the vast ecosystem.

The boundaries of the bunchgrass can be described as flanking the sagebrush zone of Douglas, Yakima, Franklin and Walla Walla counties, with the Columbia and Spokane rivers as a northern boundary. Elevation boundaries are between 450 m (1480') and 720 m (2360'). Extremely hot summers contrast with cold winters. Snow to a depth of 30–60 cm (11 1/2–23 1/2") covers the ground for several months.

Bunchgrass

SAGEBRUSH: This ecosystem is synonymous with the most arid regions of the state. Its boundaries are often quite obvious. Although there are usually several other shrubs than sagebrush, nearly all have a "sagebrushy" color and form. This ecosystem covers a large part of the Columbia Plateau, and a wide arm branches along the Yakima River toward Cle Elum. Another strip borders the Columbia River from Pasco westward to The Dalles, and there is a bordering strip along the Snake River. Stream courses, ponds, marshes and coulees are part of this landscape, and their small but special habitats make a wide variety of flora possible. The summer heat is intense, winters see freezing temperatures, and the annual rainfall is less than 25 cm (10").

Sagebrush

INTERIOR CEDAR-HEMLOCK: This ecosystem is difficult to define because it is greatly influenced by river courses and adjoining mountain slopes. It tends to form north and south strips and pockets largely at 600–1500 m (1970'–4920') in elevation. These are a southward projection from fairly extensive forests in British Columbia.

Interior Cedar-Hemlock

The yellow-green fronds of the redcedar provide the easiest identification. Western hemlock is quite scarce. There is an easy melding with larch, spruce, lodgepole pine, white pine, Douglas-fir, aspen, birch and cottonwoods.

The Pend Oreille River and its tributaries north of Tiger contain the bulk of this ecosystem. A stand of giant redcedar once stood at Sullivan Lake before it was flooded. Highway 31 is flanked by redcedar for 16 km (10 miles) south of the British Columbia border. The rather heavy precipitation of 50–100 cm (19 1/2–39") is caused by rain falling on the windward side of high mountain systems.

FLORAL AREAS

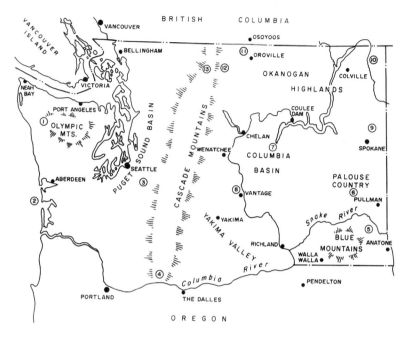

ALTHOUGH THE MAIN highway system may get applause for its design and construction, if you are in search of Nature's wonders, you will do best by getting off it. Buy a *Washington Atlas and Gazeteer* and *Exploring Washington's Past* (Kirk and Alexander 1990) and you are set for added knowledge and adventure on the back roads. Beside the alternate routes for getting from here to there is the system of Forest Service roads that branch up lesser valleys and drainage systems.

My vote for the best road sign of all is the one that says "Primitive Road. No Warning Signs."

The following is a guide to my favorite areas:

1. OLYMPIC NATIONAL PARK: From ocean side to subalpine meadows. Hoh Valley and Hurricane Ridge.

2. COASTAL BEACHES: From Ruby Beach in the north to Long Beach in the south. Shore plants and adjacent slopes.

3. MT. RAINIER: Roads leading to Paradise and Sunrise areas traverse fine mountain forests. Trails pass through colorful subalpine flora to alpine tundra.

4. COLUMBIA GORGE: Wide floral variety both sides of the river for 160 km (100 miles). Superb scenery, many parks. Seasonal display from March to July.

5. SNAKE RIVER AND BLUE MOUNTAINS: The southeast corner of the state. The Snake River Road takes you southward through scenic drylands. Best from April to July. For the Blue Mountains and its colorful flora, take State Highway 129 from Clarkston to Anatone; gravel roads lead eastward through forests and along high ridges. May to August.

6. STEPTOE AND KAMIAK BUTTES: Both in Whitman County and north of Pullman. Isolated buttes among the farm country of the Palouse. Good variety of flora from April to July.

7. GRAND COULEE SOUTH: State Highway 155 offers fine scenery as it follows Banks Lake. The Dry Falls area and the nearby Sun Lakes area are rich in plants of the sagebrush ecosystem, with a touch of ponderosa pine thrown in. Spring to early summer.

8. VANTAGE REGION: A dead end road follows the Columbia River southward for about 10 km (6 miles). Good desert flora in spring to early summer. Same for the Vantage Highway to Ellensburg.

9. MT. SPOKANE STATE PARK: Paved road to summit at 1792 m (5878'). A good sampling of plants with the changes in elevation.

10. PEND OREILLE RIVER: A wide variety of flora northward to the Canadian border.

11. NORTH OKANOGAN: Sagebrush and ponderosa pine ecosystems. Roads branching east and west from Interstate Highway 97 take you into backcountry and a wealth of spring and early summer wildflowers. Yours to explore!

12. HARTS PASS ROAD: A steep gravel road from Mazama (west of Winthrop) to subalpine terrain. Hiking trails.

13. NORTH CASCADES HIGHWAY 20: A scenic cross-over in northern Washington. Numerous branch trails. A transition from interior to coastal flora.

HOW TO IDENTIFY A WILDFLOWER

Is It a Wildflower?

WILDFLOWERS typically have soft stems that die each year, though some species remain green throughout the winter. Perennials have a root or bulb that survives winter, producing new growth each spring. Annuals always grow anew from seed each year, since they only live one year. Biennials live for two years, usually producing flowers and seed in the second year.

Shrubs (and small trees), on the other hand, have tough, woody stems with a bark cover, and they live for many years.

Quick Flower Identification

NO ATTEMPT HAS been made in this book to group flowers by their botanical familes, an arrangement that is understood only by fairly competent botanists. Instead, I have emphasized simple and positive means of identification: flowers are first divided by color, and then by easily observed characteristics, such as the number of petals or the flower shape (tubular, pea-shaped, etc.). Within each category the species are arranged roughly in order of increasing size, with similar-looking species close together. Remember that flower colors can vary considerably, so check several color possibilities. Additional key facts, such as height, types of leaves and stems, habitat, blooming season and range, should furnish all the clues necessary. Closely related and similar-looking plants are cross-referenced.

It was not practical to include photographs and full descriptions for all species, so minor species have generally been grouped with more important plants to which they are related, even though their flowers may be of different colors.

Make Sure You Have a Typical Example

YOUNG SHOOTS AND stems of some flowers have unnaturally large or misshapen leaves. So look around for a typical specimen. If a flower has gone to seed, look nearby in a cooler, shadier place for one that is still in bloom. A flower's color may change with age, so compare several. Blues and purples are confusing colors to pin down. Check both if in doubt.

WHAT'S IN A NAME?

Scientific (or Latin or botanical) names are known throughout the world, while common names are often a matter of local usage. The scientific name is usually in two parts, like a person's. The following chart shows how a comparison might be made between human and plant names:

Anglo-Saxon (a clan of people)　　　　　*Ericaceae* (a "clan" of plants)

Jones, Smith (families in the clan)　　　　*Vaccinium, Rhododendron* ("families" in the clan)

Jones, William (a certain person)　　　　*Vaccinium ovalifolium* (a certain blueberry)

In the above example, *Vaccinium* is the genus (plural is "genera"), while *ovalifolium* identifies the particular species.

The following abbreviations are also used in scientific names:

spp. 　　**species:** Used with a genus name (e.g., *Penstemon* spp.) to indicate several (or all) species of that genus.

ssp. 　　**subspecies:** Used after a species name (e.g., *Populus balsamifera* ssp. *trichocarpa*) to indicate a finer division of the species, often corresponding to different geographical ranges.

var. 　　**variety:** Similar to **ssp.** (e.g., *Penstemon fruticosa* var. *scouleri*), but typically used to distinguish between plants with a common range, but with slightly different characteristics (e.g., in leaf or flower).

KEY TO THE FLOWERS

In general, each section (for a given color and number of petals) goes from short to tall. Plants are also grouped according to related species or look alikes. As well, some secondary species have flower colors that are different than those they are listed under.

COLOR: Decide on the basic color of your plant's flowers: white, yellow, orange, red, purple, blue, brown or green. A cream-colored flower would be a variation of white or yellow, while mauve may resolve into either blue or purple on nearby plants. If your first choice doesn't work out, try a promising alternative.

NUMBER OF PETALS: If your flower has distinct petals, count them. Some plants have bracts or sepals that look like petals. If they look like petals, count them as petals. Some petals are deeply divided, so make sure you are counting whole ones. Now look in the appropriate section of the book for color and number of petals. If the design of the flower does not lend itself to an easy petal count, then match the flower to one of the following designs. The examples are listed in order of color as they appear in the book, starting with white. Species with several color possibilities are listed only once, so be sure to cross-reference if necessary.

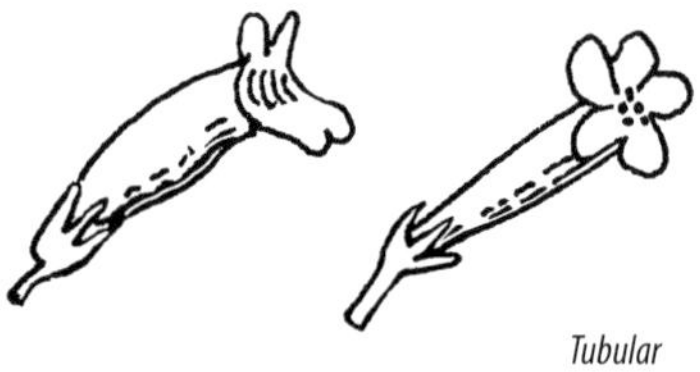

Tubular

TUBULAR: Tubular shape is the overriding key. Petals and/or sepals are united or fused. Many tubular flowers also have a confusing petal design. Examples: *campion, valerian, monkey-flower, musk-flower, touch-me-not, toadflax, butter-and-eggs, foxglove, butterwort, hedge nettle, penstemon, blue-eyed Mary, gentian, bluebell, mertensia*

PEA: Typical "sweet pea" flower. Some are very small and may be grouped into heads; check "clustered" as an alternative. Examples: *lovage, locoweed, milk-vetch, lupine, sweet-clover, trefoil, clover, peavine, vetch*

CLUSTERED: Clusters, spikes, plumes or heads of flowers. Individual flowers are usually too small to see structure with the naked eye. Examples: *false lily-of-the-valley, plectritis, partridgefoot, pussytoes, saxifrage, cotton-grass, vanilla-leaf, death-camas, pathfinder, coltsfoot, yarrow, pearly everlasting, paintbrush, bistort, baneberry, beargrass, owl-clover, sand-verbena, lousewort, fiddleneck, skunk cabbage, sanicle, tansy, goldenrod, clover, water smartweed, sea blush, thrift, elephant's head, sorrel, dogbane, teasel, burdock, self-heal, waterleaf, kittentails, dock, pineapple weed, bur-weed, sarsaparilla, stinging nettle*

UMBEL: "Umbrella" design, whether single or compound, overrides possible petal count in very small flowers. Flower stems branch from a common point. Individual flowers are usually small. Examples: *buckwheat, desert-parsley, water-parsnip, water-hemlock, poison hemlock, wild carrot, yampah, cow parsnip, spring gold, desert parsley (yellow), buckwheat (yellow)*

DANDELION: Flowerhead of similar, narrow ray flowers (look like petals). Usually yellow. Seed heads usually a white ball. Examples: *luina, cat's-ear, agoseris, silvercrown, salsify, hawkweed, hawksbeard, sow-thistle, knapweed, thistle*

DAISY: Flowers to 5 cm (2") across, with ray flowers (look like petals) and button centers. Usually yellow, white or purple. Examples: *daisy, fleabane, aster, chamomile, groundsel, butterweed, goldenweed, haplopappus, woolly sunflower, Oregon sunshine, brown-eyed Susan, black-eyed Susan*

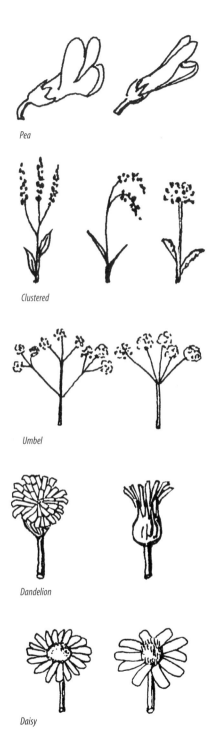

Pea

Clustered

Umbel

Dandelion

Daisy

Sunflower   Orchid

SUNFLOWER: Usually a yellow flower more than 5 cm (2") across. Wide, showy petals often pleated or notched. Contrasting button center of tiny disk flowers. Examples: *balsamroot, mule's-ears, Cusick's sunflower, helianthella, common sunflower*

ORCHID: Most people recognize the attractive design of an orchid. Some flowers will be very small and require a close look. The leaves have parallel veins. Examples: *rattlesnake-plantain, ladyslipper, phantom orchid, rein-orchid, ladies' tresses, coralroot, fairy-slipper, bog-orchid, twayblade*

UNUSUAL: Plants with unique floral designs. Examples: *bleeding heart, steer's head, columbine, meadowrue, sickletop lousewort*

Unusual

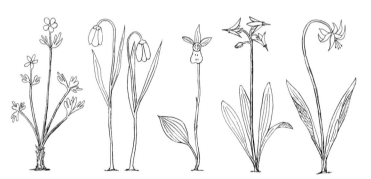

Spring flowers

Summer flowers

THE FLOWERS

Elegant mariposa lily • *Calochortus elegans*

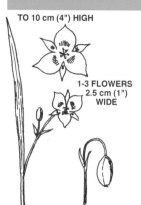

TO 10 cm (4") HIGH

1-3 FLOWERS
2.5 cm (1")
WIDE

FORM: Flower 10 cm (4") tall. Leaf to 30 cm (12").

BLOOMS: May through June.

FLOWERS: 1–3 flowers, to 2.5 cm (1") across, on the single stem. Note **3 broad petals and 3 shorter, narrower sepals.** Each petal has a **dark purple "horseshoe" ring near its base.** Each greenish sepal has a purple spot.

LEAVES: Single, grass-like leaf, about twice height of flower, stays green during blooming period.

RANGE: Grasslands and ponderosa pine ecosystem of eastern Washington. Pullman. Skyline Drive just over into Idaho.

NOTES: *Calochortus* is a Greek word meaning "beautiful grass"; the lovely flowers of this plant are dominant.

Big-pod mariposa lily • *Calochortus eurycarpus*

FORM: 10–50 cm (4–19 1/2") tall.

BLOOMS: June to July.

FLOWERS: Usually several blooms (or buds) on a stem. Flowers are creamy white to pale lavender, with a red-purplish blotch that shows through center of each petal. Purple hairs on lower inside of each petal.

FRUITS: Seed pods larger than most.

LEAVES: 1 ribbed leaf from base of plant, **reaching about one-third or more up stem.** Much smaller leaf higher up.

RANGE: Columbia Plateau, eastern Washington. Also in open forests of ponderosa pine and Douglas-fir. To 1200 m (3940') in Blue Mountains.

NOTES: Douglas recorded this species in 1827 at Celilo Falls on the Columbia River.

THREE-SPOT MARIPOSA LILY (*C. apiculatus*) grows to 10–30 cm (4–12") tall and has **1 leaf (usually shorter than the flower stem).** It blooms in June. The flowers are to 5 cm (2") across. **Each petal has finely hairy base with a dark, oval mark** that shows through petal and gives this species its common name. It is found in dry places and ponderosa pine areas of northeastern Washington.

Lyall's mariposa lily • *Calochortus lyallii*

FORM: 10–50 cm (4–19 1/2") tall. Single, erect stem.

BLOOMS: May into June.

FLOWERS: Most striking of the white mariposa lilies. Flowers generally white, but sometimes lavender-tinged. **Petals sharp-pointed and fringed with hairs. Purple crescent** on each petal above the nectar gland.

LEAVES: 1 main leaf; usually shorter than flower stem.

RANGE: East of Cascades to 900 m (2950') in ponderosa pine and Douglas-fir forests.

Sessile trillium • *Trillium chloropetalum*

FORM: 10–30 cm (4–12") tall. Short, erect stem.

BLOOMS: April into May.

FLOWERS: Erect cluster of 3 purple to greenish-white petals and 3 shorter sepals. Flowers rise directly from the leaves' juncture and are stemless.

LEAVES: Conspicuous, large, **oval, purple-mottled leaves.**

RANGE: Moist, shady, lowland forests west of the Cascades. Tacoma south through Pierce County.

Western trillium • white trillium, wake robin • *Trillium ovatum*

FORM: 15–60 cm (6–23 1/2") tall. Stout stem, mostly erect.

BLOOMS: April to late May. Cherished springtime flower.

FLOWERS: Short-stemmed flower with **3 petals,** to 2.5–5 cm (1–2") long, and **6 yellow, fuzzy stamens** in the center. **Flowers turn pink or purple with age.** 3 green sepals.

LEAVES: 3 large, veined leaves **form a whorl high on the stem—** a fitting frame for the single flower. Note the sharp "drip-tip" to each leaf.

RANGE: Shady forest borders with moist conditions. Most abundant at lower coastal elevations, but will range into high mountains. Widespread in suitable habitats.

Wapato • arrowhead, duck potato • *Sagittaria latifolia*

FORM: Leafless flower stem may rise several feet above water, with leaves about half as tall.

BLOOMS: June to August.

FLOWERS: Whorls of 3 small, white, waxy flowers.

LEAVES: Distinctive, **arrow-shaped,** long-stemmed leaves are to 25 cm (10") long. Narrow, submerged leaves go unnoticed.

RANGE: West of Cascades, in ponds and lakes at low elevations.

NOTES: The name "wapato" is from the Chinook word for this tuberous plant. A valuable food, the tubers were dug out of the mud in water to 90 cm (3') deep and boiled or roasted. Lewis and Clark made repeated references to buying this food from Native Americans, as did David Douglas. It was probably the most valuable vegetable food they could obtain.

The wappetoe...grows in great abundance in the marshey grounds. This bulb forms a principal article of traffic.
　—Lewis, January 22, 1806
Great numbers of both the large and small swans, geese and ducks seen today...in the ponds where the wappatoe is found, they feed much on this bulb.
　—Lewis, March 29, 1806

Spring whitlow-grass • vernal whitlow-grass • *Draba verna*

FORM: Often tiny—perhaps not 2.5 cm (1") tall—but to 25 cm (10") under ideal conditions. 1 to several stems from a basal leaf clump.

BLOOMS: Early spring.

FLOWERS: Each of the **4 petals is so deeply divided** that it looks like there are 8 petals.

FRUITS: Flat, gauze-like pod, about 6 mm (1/4") long. Note that **pods are alternate** on stem.

LEAVES: A basal clump of oval glandular leaves to 2.5 cm (1") long.

RANGE: Southern Washington east of the Cascades. Common on dry ground at lower elevations. East Columbia Gorge.

NOTES: There are many drabas in Washington; spring whitlow-grass is **the only one with split petals**. It blooms in early spring, along with **gold stars** (p. 87), **satin-flowers** (p. 123) and **woodland stars** (p. 39).

Pepperpod • scale pod • *Idahoa scapigera*

FORM: 2.5–15 cm (1–6") tall. Thin, erect or leaning stems.

BLOOMS: March to April.

FLOWERS: Tiny—only 3 mm (1/8") long

FRUITS: Circular, flat pods, seen in late April to May. Pods are 2 thin, papery films marked with small, purplish-brown blotches of the enclosed seeds.

LEAVES: Small basal leaves, 0.6–2.5 cm (1/4–1") long; some entire, some lobed.

RANGE: Dry places, sagebrush, bunchgrass and ponderosa pine ecosystems east of the Cascades. Valley bottoms to higher plateaus.

NOTES: David Douglas recorded this species in the eastern (dryland) section of the Columbia Gorge. He spent a good deal of time along the Columbia River because it was the principal artery of travel.

Drummond's rockcress • *Arabis drummondii*

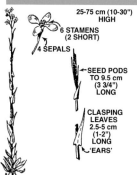

25-75 cm (10-30") HIGH
6 STAMENS (2 SHORT)
4 SEPALS
SEED PODS TO 9.5 cm (3 3/4") LONG
CLASPING LEAVES 2.5-5 cm (1-2") LONG
'EARS'

FORM: 25–75 cm (10–30") tall. Single, erect stem.

BLOOMS: Late spring to summer.

FLOWERS: Cross design of 4 petals, with 4 sepals and 6 stamens, of which 2 are short.

FRUITS: Seeds are in long, narrow, flat pods.

LEAVES: Basal clump of narrow leaves. Higher leaves clasping, 2.5–5 cm (1–2") long, **short "ears" at their bases**.

RANGE: Common throughout Washington on dry mountain slopes above the sagebrush ecosystem.

NOTES: There are too many species and varieties of rockcress to list them all. All rockcresses have basically the same type of flowers and fruits, however, as described here.

Bunchberry • dwarf dogwood • *Cornus canadensis*

FORM: 7.5–20 cm (3–8") tall. Often a low, colorful carpet.
BLOOMS: May to June, depending on altitude. Sometimes blooms again in late summer.
FLOWERS: Large, **white bracts** around a **central cluster of tiny, greenish flowers**. Flower cluster is about 2.5 cm (1") across.
FRUITS: Bright red berries, in a cluster, in August to September.
LEAVES: Terminal whorl **of 4–7 evergreen leaves** with parallel, curved veins.
RANGE: Throughout Washington, in moist, open forests, road edges and glades from valleys to subalpine elevations.
NOTES: The berries are edible raw or cooked, but they are mealy and insipid, so they are not sought after by berry pickers.

Pale evening-primrose • pallid evening-primrose • *Oenothera pallida*

FORM: 15–40 cm (6–15 1/2") tall. **A gnarled, branched plant**.
BLOOMS: April to early summer.
FLOWERS: Flowers are a dingy white and about 2.5 cm (1") across. **Buds are pinkish**. The long sepals generally **twist together at their tips**.
LEAVES: Alternate, very narrow. Grow thickly along stem.
RANGE: Sandy plains and banks at lower elevations east of the Cascades. Wanapum Road south of Vantage. Eastern section of Columbia Gorge (where Douglas noted it). Snake River.
NOTES: There is a **yellow evening-primrose** on p. 77.

Desert evening-primrose • *Oenothera cespitosa*

FORM: To 25 cm (10") tall. Short-stemmed, leafy, with several flower stems.
BLOOMS: April to July.
FLOWERS: Large white "tissue paper" flowers, to 7.5 cm (3") wide, turning pinkish with age. **4 long, curved sepals arch downward**.
LEAVES: Many long, narrow leaves notched and toothed.
RANGE: Dry hills, canyons and desert terrain of eastern Washington.

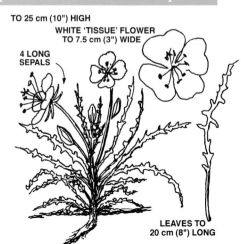

TO 25 cm (10") HIGH
WHITE 'TISSUE' FLOWER TO 7.5 cm (3") WIDE
4 LONG SEPALS
LEAVES TO 20 cm (8") LONG

Northern bedstraw • *Galium boreale*

FORM: 20–40 cm (8–15 1/2") tall. Often rather bushy from several short branching stems. Note that plant stems are square in cross-section.

BLOOMS: June to September, depending on elevation.

FLOWERS: Broad, plume-like masses of **tiny flowers, to 6 mm (1/4")** **across. 4 petals. No sepals.** Very fragrant.

LEAVES: In whorls of 4 at stem joints. Leaves 3-veined.

RANGE: Often a roadside plant seen from a car. Moist forest edges and more open slopes at higher elevations. Mountain forest to subalpine ecosystems. Olympics. Ferry and Stevens counties. Columbia Gorge.

NOTES: The name "bedstraw" relates to the time of Christ's birth: according to legend, it was one of the plants used for bedding in the manger.

Common watercress • *Nasturtium officinale* • *Rorippa nasturtium-aquaticum*

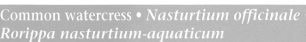

FORM: An **aquatic plant** raising leafy stems to 40 cm (15 1/2") above the water.

BLOOMS: Spring to mid-summer.

FLOWERS: Small clusters of tiny, **4-petalled flowers**.

FRUITS: Thin, curved seed pods.

LEAVES: Individual leaves have 3–9 leaflets.

RANGE: Widespread at lower elevations in clean waters, irrigation ditches, springs and small streams. Sagebrush to mountain forest ecosystems.

NOTES: This was a tangy salad plant introduced to North America by Europeans and welcomed by early miners and settlers.

Field pennycress • *Thlaspi arvense*

FORM: Usually a compact mass of plants, 15–60 cm (6–23 1/2") tall. May form **an extensive bed**.

BLOOMS: May to July.

FLOWERS: Tiny 4-petalled flowers in massed heads, soon replaced by fruits.

FRUITS: Spikes of silvery "penny" seeds, each with **notch at tip**.

LEAVES: Alternate, large, coarse and clasping.

RANGE: Widespread. Roadsides in semi-cultivated areas.

NOTES: This introduced weed is typically "mustard" in design.

Desert thelypody • thick-leaf thelypody • *Thelypodium laciniatum*

FORM: 30 cm–2.1 m (1–7') tall. Great range in height and form depends on growing conditions. Usually a bushy shape, owing to many ascending branches. Plant skeletons may remain until following spring.
BLOOMS: May to June.
FLOWERS: Dense **columnar spikes of very small, dull white or pale purple flowers. Projecting black styles.**
LEAVES: Basal rosette of deeply lobed leaves to 30 cm (12") long.
RANGE: On volcanic cliffs, rock slides, sometimes sandy soil. Central and eastern Washington. Yakima Canyon. Walla Walla. Columbia Gorge (where Douglas recorded it).

SAXIFRAGES • *Saxifraga* spp.

WITH ABOUT 24 species on record, it is difficult to choose which saxifrages to feature, and to keep track of the common and botanical names of recent nomenclature. The names used here are from *The Vascular Plants of British Columbia* (Douglas et al. 1991).

SAXIFRAGE DESIGN
5 PETALS—FREE TO BASE
5 SEPALS—GREEN
2 HORN-LIKE STYLES
5 OR 10 STAMENS

Saxifrages, although seldom 30 cm (1') tall, are so widespread, so attractive in their daintiness and so pleasantly ensconced in their particular habitat— a rocky niche in alpine terrain or beside a shady forest stream—that they immediately capture your attention.

Most saxifrages have small white flowers, and all have **5 petals (free to the base), 5 green sepals, 5 or 10 stamens and 2 horn-like styles** in the exact center. Variations in the color of the petals and sepals, the number of stamens and the leaf shape will help you make a fairly speedy identification.

Another **white-flowered saxifrage** is on p. 58. **Sandworts** (p. 177) are rather similar to saxifrages, but sandworts have several pairs of small, thin leaves on the stem.

ALASKA SAXIFRAGE (*S. ferruginea*) flowers have **2 kinds of petals: 3 broad ones**—each with **2 orange-yellow spots**—and **2 narrow ones without markings.** Note **the rust-colored sepals**, which justify the scientific name *ferruginea*. The distinctive **leaves taper and end in coarse teeth.** It is found in moist places on rocks and streambanks, from valley bottoms to the alpine, in the Cascade Mountains, on Mt. Adams and in Palouse County.

TUFTED SAXIFRAGE (*S. cespitosa*) can be identified quickly by the **narrow leaves with 3–5 prongs.** Some of the petals may be notched. The anthers are longer than the often-purplish sepals. It is found in rocky places, from lowlands to the alpine. It is widespread and most abundant in the Cascades and Olympics.

MERTENS' SAXIFRAGE (*S. mertensiana*) has **large, round leaves that are distinctive.** Note the uniform lobes, each with 3 teeth. The hairy leaf stems are 1–3 times as long as the blades. Some of the white flowers are replaced by pink bulblets. It is found in moist, rocky places, from lowlands to the subalpine, in the Cascades and along the coastal strip in Washington.

Tolmie's saxifrage • *Saxifraga tolmiei*

FORM: 5–10 cm (2–4") tall. Slender, reddish stems arising from a leafy mat.

BLOOMS: Summer. Dependent on snow melt and weather conditions at higher elevations.

FLOWERS: White "star" flowers, 6 mm (1/4") across. **Usually 3 to a stem.** Each of the **5 narrow, petal-like rods between the real petals supports a pair of stamens.**

LEAVES: Thick evergreen leaves, to 6 mm (1/4") long; tend to curl over along the edges.

RANGE: Stream and snowfield edges at high elevations in the Cascades and Olympics.

Spotted saxifrage • *Saxifraga bronchialis*

FORM: 5–10 cm (2–4") tall. **Branching, reddish stems** rise from **a mat of spiny leaves.**

BLOOMS: May to August, depending on elevations.

FLOWERS: Always a joy to find! **Tiny white petals** are **speckled with maroon and yellow dots**—positive identification.

LEAVES: Persistent and some withering. Spiny, to 1.3 cm (1/2") long, with white hairs along the edge.

RANGE: Widespread in rocky, open places, medium to alpine elevations. Cascades, Olympics and Blue Mountains.

Western saxifrage • *Saxifraga occidentalis*

FORM: 7.5–40 cm (3–15 1/2") tall. Stems rise from a basal grouping of leaves and branch near top.

BLOOMS: April to August, depending on location.

FLOWERS: Branching stems carry white flowers, marked by **10 orange stamens.** Flowers may age to cream or greenish.

FRUITS: Reddish-brown seeds.

LEAVES: Leathery, egg-shaped, with coarse teeth. 2.5–7.5 cm (1–3") long. Broad leaf stems. Leaves and leaf stems may be finely reddish-hairy.

RANGE: Moist areas, mostly east of the Cascades, at medium to subalpine elevations. Chelan County south. Kittitas County.

LYALL'S SAXIFRAGE (*S. lyallii*) often forms a mat of interlocking leaves along damp, subalpine meadows and streambanks. The stems are red to purple. The leaves are fan-shaped and coarsely toothed. The petals have several pale yellow dots on them. It is common in the northern Cascades and northeastern Washington.

Grassland saxifrage • *Saxifraga integrifolia*

FORM: 10–20 cm (4–8") tall. Single, stout, red-hairy stem from a group of basal leaves.
BLOOMS: March to April.
FLOWERS: In branch-top, **conical clusters**.
LEAVES: Thick; **many are reddish beneath**; variable shape.
RANGE: Dry, grassy areas. Lowlands to middle elevations. Coastal Washington and San Juan Islands. Cascades and south to Columbia Gorge.
NOTES: Grassland saxifrage blooms with **shootingstars** (pp. 116–117), **satin-flower** (p. 123) and **spring gold** (p. 95).

Thread-leaved sandwort • *Arenaria capillaris*

FORM: 7.5–15 cm (3–6") tall.
BLOOMS: June to August, depending on elevation.
FLOWERS: 5 petals, **10 stamens** and **3 styles. Purplish sepals are about one-half petal length**.
LEAVES: A tufted base of **needle-like leaves**. 2–5 opposite pairs on the stem.
RANGE: East side of the Cascades, usually in moist woods, but also on exposed banks. Up to near subalpine elevations.
NOTES: The many sandworts look like **saxifrages** (pp. 31–33), but sandworts have **several pairs of small, narrow leaves on the stem**.

Hood's phlox • grey phlox • *Phlox hoodii*

FORM: A mat **15 cm (6") tall** and 40 cm (15 1/2") wide.
BLOOMS: April to May.
FLOWERS: The spiny mat is covered with a mass of buds and flowers. While usually white, they **can tint blue or pink**. The flower, about 1.3 cm (1/2") across, has a yellow center.
LEAVES: **Stiff, spine-tipped leaves** about 6 mm (1/4") long tend to be in tufts.
RANGE: On hard, dry ground from sagebrush ecosystem to the foothills.
NOTES: Hood's phlox blooms with **death-camas** (p. 61) and **balsamroots** (pp. 108–110). All phloxes—there are more than a dozen in Washington—have **symmetrical flowers with long tubes and 5 spreading petals**. The definitely **pink phloxes** are on p. 120.

Prickly phlox • *Leptodactylon pungens*

FORM: 30–60 cm (1–2′) tall. Stout, erect, with short leafy branches.
BLOOMS: May to July, but **only at night.**
FLOWERS: A single, typical "phlox" flower is carried at each branch tip. Slightly aromatic.
LEAVES: Whorls of thin, prickly leaves.
RANGE: Dry places in sagebrush and ponderosa pine regions. East of Cascades.
NOTES: Prickly phlox blooms only at night, and it is pollinated by nocturnal moths.

TUFTED PHLOX (*P. cespitosa*) resembles prickly phlox, but tufted phlox is only one-third as tall. The white flowers can tint to pink, lavender or purple, and they **bloom by day.** The **whorls of spiny leaves are close together.** Its range is as for prickly phlox, but tufted phlox has some preference for shade.

WHITE SHOWY PHLOX (*P. speciosa*): A **white** color phase of the usually pink showy phlox is described on p. 120.

Dwarf hesperochiron • *Hesperochiron pumilus*

FORM: 5–10 cm (2–4″) tall. Short flower stems.
BLOOMS: April to June.
FLOWERS: 1–5 white flowers with a yellow center. **Petals lie wide open**, not bell-shaped as in California hesperchiron.
LEAVES: Basal clump of narrow, oblong leaves.
RANGE: Sagebrush and ponderosa pine. East of Cascades.

CALIFORNIA HESPEROCHIRON (*H. californicus*) has lavender or purple-tinged petals that **curl to make a bell-shaped flower.** The flower's center is not yellow. It is found in wet, alkaline bottomlands and foothills of eastern Washington.

Yerba buena • *Satureja douglasii*

FORM: Creeping vine with square stems, to 1.2 m (4′) long, with short, upright branches.
BLOOMS: June to July.
FLOWERS: Tiny, white or purple tinged. Single flower on a slender stalk, but **usually "twins" from the same leaf axil.** Sepals fused into a tube, while the 5 petals are united at their base, but flower has 2 short, upper lips and 3 longer, lower ones, hence its classification under "5 petals."
LEAVES: Paired, **bright green, oval-shaped, evergreen.** 1.3–3 cm (1/2–1 1/4″) long, irregular margins.
RANGE: Open coniferous and Garry oak forests at low to middle elevations west of Cascades. San Juan Islands. Columbia Gorge.
NOTES: "Yerba buena" means "good herb," and it was given to this plant by early Spanish priests in California. Native Americans and early settlers made a tea from the aromatic, dried leaves.

Field chickweed • meadow chickweed • *Cerastium arvense*

FORM: 7.5–50 cm (3–20") tall. Stems erect or sometimes bent or trailing. Usually a clump of flowers.

BLOOMS: April to July.

FLOWERS: To 1.3 cm (1/2") across, the **5 petals deeply cleft** and 2–3 times as long as the sepals. (There are several other native chickweeds not described here.)

LEAVES: Hairy stems carry sharp-pointed, narrow, opposite leaves which often appear in a tangled clump.

RANGE: A native chickweed found worldwide. Open ground, low to middle elevations.

NOTES: Catchflies (p. 55) also have divided petals.

Round-leaved sundew • round-leaved drosera • *Drosera rotundifolia*

FORM: 5–15 cm (2–6") tall. 1 or several stems from a rosette of leaves.

BLOOMS: Late spring to late summer.

FLOWERS: Small, white, 5-petalled. Several flowers on 1 side of stem. Flowers **open fully only in strong sunlight**.

LEAVES: A basal rosette of round, prostrate or erect leaves, terminating in a disk-like blade that bristles with long, reddish, sticky hairs.

RANGE: **Sphagnum bogs** and lake margins to middle elevations.

LONG-LEAVED SUNDEW (*D. anglica*) is similar to round-leaved sundew, but long-leaved sundew has long, narrow leaf blades. It is found in boggy soils.

One-sided wintergreen • side bells • *Orthilia secunda*

FORM: To 20 cm (8") tall. Single, leafless stem is upright, or curved near top.

BLOOMS: July to August.

FLOWERS: White to pale green; **hang like bells from inside curve at top of stem. A long style projects** beyond the flower.

LEAVES: Mostly basal, but a few on lower stem. **Shiny**, **evergreen** and **toothed**.

RANGE: In forests with moist soil. Lowlands to the lower edge of the subalpine.

NOTES: This wintergreen blooms along with **single delight** (p. 36) and **pipsissiwa** (p. 121).

Single delight • one-flowered pyrola • *Moneses uniflora*

FORM: 5–10 cm (2–4") tall. A single, short, erect flower stem.

BLOOMS: June to August.

FLOWERS: Nodding, **saucer-shaped, waxy** and fragrant, and sometimes greenish. About 2.5 cm (1") across. **5 spreading petals. 10 golden stamens** in 5 paired sets. **Long, protruding style and stigma.**

LEAVES: Evergreen, mostly basal, but sometimes a few on the stem.

RANGE: Moist coniferous forests with heavy humus or moss. Sea level to middle mountain heights. Both slopes of the Cascades. Olympics. Columbia Gorge.

White-veined wintergreen • white-vein pyrola • *Pyrola picta*

FORM: 10–20 cm (4–8") tall. Single, erect stem.

BLOOMS: July to August.

FLOWERS: Small, waxy flowers, white to greenish, **single along stem, in drooping position.** Clearly 5 petals. Large numbers of anthers. **Protruding, curved style.**

LEAVES: A basal rosette of several distinctive leaves. Leaves are **thick** and **dark green**, with **the vein system being clearly outlined in white.**

RANGE: Shady, coniferous forests. Low to medium elevations. Abundant west of the Cascades.

NOTES: Rattlesnake-plantain (p. 73) also has marked leaves.

LESSER WINTERGREEN (*P. minor*) is similar to white-veined wintergreen, but the flowers of lesser wintergreen are white to pink and do **not** have a long style, and the **leaves are clear green and rounded.** It is widespread and found in moist, mossy forests.

Heart-leaved springbeauty • *Claytonia cordifolia* • *Montia cordifolia*

FORM: To 15 cm (6") tall. 1 to several stems.

BLOOMS: May to June.

FLOWERS: White, often with pink or red lines. About 1.3 cm (1/2") across. 2 sepals, 5 petals, 5 stamens and 1 pistil.

LEAVES: Basal leaves are slightly heart-shaped. Another pair of leaves about half-way up the stem.

RANGE: Wet places. Low to medium elevations. Both sides of the Cascades.

NOTES: There are **pink claytonias** on p. 119.

Western springbeauty • Indian potato • *Claytonia lanceolata*

FORM: To 15 cm (6") tall. Usually several erect, bending, even reclining, stems from a corm—a round bulb that is marble-sized or larger.
BLOOMS: Late March to May. **Among the earliest spring blooms.**
FLOWERS: Generally **white or light pink, with darker lines.** Petal tips slightly notched.
LEAVES: Basal leaves withered by blooming time. **Narrow stem leaves just below the flowers.**
RANGE: Abundant across Washington, from sagebrush valleys to high mountains. Ponderosa pine ecosystem. Cle Elum. Columbia Gorge.
NOTES: The name "Indian potato" reflects the past importance of these small bulbs as a food. They were dug after the plant had flowered and eaten fresh or steamed. They could be dried in a cake form and preserved for months.

Miner's lettuce • *Claytonia perfoliata* • *Montia perfoliata*

FORM: 10–35 cm (4–14") tall. Succulent, upright.
BLOOMS: Late March to May.
FLOWERS: Very small, 5-petalled, **white to pinkish** flowers. **Several in a cluster above the leaf disk.**
LEAVES: Basal leaves are numerous, long-stemmed and variable in shape and color. **High on the stem, 2 opposite leaves fuse to form a "saucer"** around the stem.
RANGE: Widespread at lower elevations in moist areas.
NOTES: Early settlers and miners discovered that the leaves make a good salad green.

Siberian miner's lettuce • Siberian springbeauty • *Claytonia sibirica* • *Montia sibirica*

FORM: 12.5–30 cm (5–12") tall. **Succulent**; erect to spreading.
BLOOMS: April to July.
FLOWERS: White, **often** with **pink lines.** Flowers in small, open clusters. **Petals** noticeably **notched.**
LEAVES: Lower leaves are long-stemmed. **Pair of leaves high on the stem are separate and short-stemmed,** not the disk of miner's lettuce. Leaves make salad greens, but had some medicinal uses among Native Americans.
RANGE: Moist rich soils of shady ditches or meadows at lower elevations. Both sides of the Cascades, but most abundant on west side.
NOTES: This species was first discovered in Siberia.

Wild strawberry • blue-leaved strawberry • *Fragaria virginiana*

FORM: To 15 cm (6") tall, **from rooting runners.**

BLOOMS: April to August, depending on elevations. **Among the earliest of spring flowers.**

FLOWERS: 5 white petals. Yellow center.

FRUITS: Small, sweet strawberry.

LEAVES: Typical strawberry leaves with 3 toothed leaflets. **Bluish-tinged;** on a short stem. **Leaflets also have short stems.**

RANGE: Common in open places to middle mountain elevations, except in arid regions.

WOODLAND STRAWBERRY (*F. vesca*) has **petals that are often pinkish.** It blooms in April to June. **The leaves have a yellow tinge.** The leaflets are stemless, which distinguishes it from wild strawberry. The berries

are reddish and sweet. It ranges from the Olympics through the Cascades, in moist areas.

COASTAL STRAWBERRY (*F. chiloensis*) is distinguished by its **coastal habitat.** It is found from sandy places to rocky bluffs in sight of the sea. It blooms from April to June. **The waxy, green leaves,** which have **silvery undersides,** are coarsely toothed. The runners, which are sometimes bright red, run from one plant to another. The berries are sweet and small. It is found near many beaches. Long Beach.

Five-leaved bramble • *Rubus pedatus*

FORM: An unarmed creeper that roots at the nodes. Low leaves. Flower stems less than 15 cm (6") tall.

BLOOMS: May to August, depending on elevation.

FLOWERS: About 1–2 cm (3/8–3/4") across. The **5 pure white petals lie flat.**

FRUITS: A small cluster of tiny, jewel-like, red berries (druplets). Juicy and tasty during September.

LEAVES: About 2.5 cm (1") across, with **3 rounded leaflets,** 2 of which are so deeply lobed that there seem to be 5 leaflets.

RANGE: Shady places in mid-altitude to subalpine coastal forests. Olympics. Cascades.

Small-flowered woodland star • fringecup, prairie star • *Lithophragma parviflorum*

FORM: To 25 cm (10") tall. Erect, slim stems.

BLOOMS: March to June.

FLOWERS: In **white to pinkish** clusters. **5 petals, each 3-fingered.** Several buds on upper stem.

LEAVES: The **basal group of small leaves arise from ground level**, not a short distance up the stem (as in slender woodland star [below]). Several small stem leaves.

RANGE: Widespread below mountain forest levels in ponderosa pine ecosystem. Gulf and San Juan Islands. Columbia Gorge.

NOTES: Small-flowered woodland star often blooms with **gold stars** (p. 87), **shootingstars** (pp. 116–117), **yellow bells** (p. 86), **white plectritis** (p. 58) and **vernal whitlow-grass** (p. 28). • There is a **pinkish woodland star** on p. 119.

BULBLET WOODLAND STAR (*L. bulbiferum*) is a typical springtime woodland star. The flowers are white to pinkish, with 3–5 thin fingers. **There are tiny red bulblets in the axils of the upper stem leaves.** It is abundant on dry, open ground east of the Cascades.

Slender woodland star • *Lithophragma tenellum*

FORM: To 25 cm (10") tall. Slender, upright stem.

BLOOMS: From March to June.

FLOWERS: White, 5-petalled. **Each petal divided into 5 thin to broad "fingers."** Single flowers are spaced on top one-third of stem.

LEAVES: Unlike the ground-level basal arrangement of leaves in small-flowered woodland star (above), **the bottom cluster of small, deeply lobed leaves is about 2 cm (3/4") above the ground** in this species.

RANGE: Most abundant in ponderosa pine ecosystem, but ranges below and above. East of the Cascades. Okanogan, Chelan, Yakima and Spokane counties. Columbia Gorge.

Elmera • *Elmera racemosa*

FORM: To 30 cm (12") tall. A number of erect stems arising from a thick clump of basal leaves. Stems and leaves are hairy.

BLOOMS: June to September, depending on location.

FLOWERS: Creamy white, bell-shaped and alternating along top half of stem. Note the fringes on the 5 (3–7) tiny petals.

LEAVES: The **dark green**, attractive leaves are wide rather than long; **roundish, with scalloped edges**.

RANGE: High rocky slopes. Olympics. Cascades.

Fringecup • *Tellima grandiflora*

FORM: 30–90 cm (1–3′) tall. A number of flowering, hairy stems from a rich growth of basal leaves.

BLOOMS: April to July.

FLOWERS: Flowers may change color as they age: to greenish, pinkish or brown. **Petals frilly. 10 stamens.**

LEAVES: Basal leaves long-stalked, roughly heart-shaped and toothed. A few smaller stem leaves.

RANGE: Moist forests and openings at low to middle elevations. Generally coastal, but also in eastern forests.

NOTES: This is the only *Tellima* species in Washington. Don't confuse it with elmera (p. 39) or with an **alumroot** (pp. 45–46). Fringe-cup is distinguished by its **fringed petals**, best seen on the highest flower. Mitreworts (p. 178) **also have fringed flowers**, but they have **5 stamens rather than 10.**

Foamflower • *Tiarella* spp.

FORM: To 50 cm (20″) tall.

BLOOMS: May to July.

FLOWERS: Tiny white flowers on short, thin stems. 5 petals. 10 stamens.

LEAVES: Only 1 leaf on each stem. A group of long-stemmed leaves at base. Leaf shapes are key to identifying species.

THREE-LEAVED FOAMFLOWER (*T. trifoliata*) is widely distributed across Washington. Each leaf is divided into **3 short-stemmed leaflets.**

ONE-LEAVED FOAMFLOWER (*T. unifoliata*) is found east of the Cascades up to middle forest elevations. Each leaf has **3–5 shallow lobes**.

CUT-LEAVED FOAMFLOWER (*T. laciniata*) is found in the San Juan Islands and coastal areas. Each leaf is divided into **3 leaflets. Each leaflet is deeply cut into several lobes.**

Indian pipe • *Monotropa uniflora*

FORM: 10–25 cm (4–10″) tall. **Fleshy, waxy, white** stems bend over at top.

BLOOMS: Late spring to August.

FLOWERS: With some imagination, you might deduce that there are 5 petals forming a nodding flower. **Plants turn black with age.**

LEAVES: Thick, colorless and **scale-like**; press closely to the stem.

RANGE: Shady coniferous forests at low to middle elevations. Most common west of the Cascades. Columbia Gorge.

NOTES: Indian pipe is an odd plant that feeds on the roots of nearby coniferous trees.

Canada violet • *Viola canadensis*

FORM: To 30 cm (12") tall. Often rooting at the nodes of creeping stems, with leaves rising directly from the nodes.

BLOOMS: May to June.

FLOWERS: White. Back of petal has a bluish tinge, which may spread enough to suggest a light blue flower. **Dark veins on lower 3 petals** are guides to the yellow petal bases and the spur that holds the nectar.

LEAVES: Leafy stems with long-stemmed, heart-shaped leaves. Smaller leaves on upper stems.

RANGE: Moist forests with rich soils. Wetlands from valley to mid-mountain elevations.

NOTES: The leaves and flowers of violets are quite edible raw.

Oregon oxalis • redwood sorrel • *Oxalis oregana*

FORM: 5–18 cm (2–7") tall, arising from shallow, scaly roots.

BLOOMS: April and May are the best times.

FLOWERS: A single white or pinkish flower, to 2.5 cm (1") across, carried on a stem shorter than the leaves.

LEAVES: Clover-like when not folded. To 4 cm (1 1/2") across. Very adaptable to variations in weather conditions by expansion of folding leaves.

RANGE: Damp, shady woods west of Cascades. Columbia Gorge.

NOTES: There is a **yellow** oxalis on p. 79.

GREAT OXALIS (*O. trilliifolia*) grows to 25 cm (10") tall, with **clusters of several white flowers** per stalk. It blooms in June to July. The petals are notched. It is found at low to high elevations on the west slopes of the Cascades.

Globeflower • *Trollius laxus*

FORM: 10–50 cm (4–19 1/2") tall. 1 or several flower stems, each with a **single flower**.

BLOOMS: May to August, as snow recedes.

FLOWERS: Showy white flower, to 4 cm (1 1/2") across. **5–6 sepals (look like petals)** surround a **golden center—a circlet of 7–15 tiny petals**.

LEAVES: Long-stemmed basal leaves palmately divided into 5 sections. Each section coarsely lobed or toothed. Stem leaves become smaller and shorter stemmed up the stem.

RANGE: Edge of melting snow and cold meadows of subalpine and alpine ecosystems. Usually east of the Cascades.

ANEMONES • *Anemone* spp.

THERE ARE about 8 anemones with a variety of colors in Washington. They are sometimes known as "windflowers"—they supposedly open for spring breezes. The flowers **lack petals**; the large, shiny sepals, which are generally blue-tinged on the outside, are a substitute. There is a **whorl of leaves high on the stem**. The seeds are in the form of a cottony tuft.

Northern anemone • *Anemone parviflora*

FORM: 7.5–25 cm (3–10″) tall. Single erect stem from a low basal cluster of leaves.

BLOOMS: April to June, depending on elevation.

FLOWERS: A single white bloom, to 2 cm (3/4″) across. 5 (sometimes 6) **petal-like** sepals, **usually blue-tinged on the outside**.

FRUITS: Cottony, tufted seed head.

LEAVES: Basal leaves are so deeply lobed that it looks like there are 3 leaflets, and these are also lobed. 1 **small leaf cluster high on stem**.

RANGE: Moist meadows and shady forests. From valleys to the subalpine in northern Cascades.

LYALL'S ANEMONE (*A. lyallii*) grows to 30 cm (12″) tall, with small, **white to pale blue** flowers. There are no basal leaves, but there are **3 leaves high on the stem**. Each leaf is trifoliate—it has 3 coarsely toothed leaflets. It is found up into the subalpine in the Olympics and Cascades, and in the Blue Mountains in eastern Washington.

Three-leaved anemone • western white anemone • *Anemone deltoida*

FORM: 15–35 cm (6–14″) tall. Stem more or less erect.

BLOOMS: April to June, depending on elevations.

FLOWERS: Large, white, single flowers, to 4 cm (1 1/2″) across. Asymmetrical, only sepals. A bright green raised center holds numerous white stamens.

LEAVES: 3 coarsely toothed leaves, in **whorled arrangement** typical of anemones. Leaves not trifoliate like in Lyall's anemone (above).

RANGE: Not in Olympics, but on west slope of Cascades from State Highway 2 south. Columbia Gorge.

POPCORN FLOWERS • *Plagiobothrys* spp.

THE 3 SPECIES described here are the most common popcorn flowers in the state. Several others may barely intrude from the east and south. **All are under 45 cm (17 1/2") tall and carry tiny, 5-petalled, white flowers the same size and shape as well-known forget-me-not flowers.** The "popcorn" part of the name comes from the appearance of the several **tightly clustered flowers** and **adjoining coil of buds**, which are reminiscent of kernels of popcorn. Popcorn flowers grow abundantly, and they tend to form a mass of bloom—a valued addition to other spring wildflowers.

Scouler's popcorn flower • *Plagiobothrys scouleri*

FORM: To 30 cm (12") tall. Branching into thin stems from the base, erect or sometimes prostrate. The top becomes slightly coiled.

BLOOMS: Late spring (May) to early summer.

FLOWERS: Tiny, 5-petalled flowers with **5 hairy sepals**. Flowers in clusters with adjoining buds on a slightly coiled stem.

LEAVES: Unusual! Narrow leaves on lower stem are opposite, those higher alternate.

RANGE: Moist areas, wet meadows, stream and pond edges. Lower elevations, widespread across Washington. Eastern section of Columbia Gorge.

SLENDER POPCORN FLOWER (*P. tenellus*) is usually under 20 cm (8") tall, but it is so abundant in some areas that it **creates a massed bloom**. During April and May, it may be found with **white plectritis** (p. 58), and **woodland stars** (p. 39). Note the **small basal rosette of small leaves**. The stem leaves are all alternate. It ranges widely across Washington, on dry, open ground at lower elevations. It is found on the San Juan Islands and in the eastern section of the Columbia Gorge and eastward.

FRAGRANT POPCORN FLOWER (*P. figuratus*) is the **tallest** of the 3 popcorn flowers, growing to **45 cm (17 1/2") tall**. It is a slender plant with several long, branching stems; it often grows massed. Its flower is the largest of the three, being 1.3 cm (1/2") across. Note the yellow eye and the fragrance. It blooms from May to June and is found mostly west of the Cascades in open areas that are damp in spring and dry in summer. It occurs through the Columbia Gorge to Klickitat County.

Slender popcorn flower

Buckbean • bog bean • *Meyanthes trifoliata*

FORM: An aquatic plant rooted in mud, but raising leaves and flowers to 30 cm (12") tall.

BLOOMS: May to September, depending on elevation.

FLOWERS: Most unusual! 5 white petals, perhaps light purplish tinged, are covered with long white hairs. Few to several flowers in a cluster at stem tip. A rank smell attracts certain insects.

LEAVES: Branching alternately from root stalk. Long leaf stems each hold 3 short-stemmed, oval leaflets.

RANGE: Bogs, marshes and shallow ponds. To the subalpine. Mostly west of Cascades.

White water buttercup • *Ranunculus aquatilis*

FORM: A floating water plant, with flowers just above water.

BLOOMS: Late May to mid-August, depending on altitude.

FLOWERS: Small, white flowers, about 1.3 cm (1/2") across, with bright yellow centers. Base of petal lacks small scale found in other buttercups.

LEAVES: 2 leaf types: conspicuous, small, deeply lobed, floating leaves and submerged tangle of thin, green filaments.

RANGE: Ponds, backwaters and sluggish streams. Lowlands to middle mountain heights.

Fringed grass-of-Parnassus • *Parnassia fimbriata*

FORM: 15–30 cm (6–12") tall. 1 or several stems from a basal leaf clump. In no way grass-like, despite common name.

BLOOMS: July to September.

FLOWERS: Particularly attractive because of hair-like fringing along base of each petal. 5 fertile stamens alternate with 5 broad sterile stamens. Petals twice as long as sepals.

LEAVES: Glossy, evergreen, kidney-shaped leaves. Small clasping leaf about half-way up stem.

RANGE: Wet places, bogs, small streams. Middle mountain to alpine elevations.

NOTES: Fringed grass-of-Parnassus is often in bloom after most subalpine flowers have finished.

KOTZEBUE'S GRASS-OF-PARNASSUS (*P. kotzebuei*), also called "alpine grass-of-Parnassus," is the only other grass-of-Parnassus in Washington. Its petals and sepals are the same length, and its petals are not fringed. It is found mostly east of the Cascades, and it ranges south from British Columbia to the Cascades in Okanogan County.

Newberry's knotweed • fleeceflower • *Polygonum newberryi*

FORM: A **sprawling, succulent plant** from a thick, fleshy root. Sometimes to 30 cm (12") tall.

BLOOMS: Since it grows at subalpine heights, blooming depends on how long the snow lasts. **August is an average time**.

FLOWERS: Tiny, **5-petalled** flowers, less than 6 mm (1/4") across. **Barely noticeable** in small clusters in upper leaf axils.

LEAVES: Many oval leaves, 2–5 cm (3/4–2") long, in a loose mat to a couple meters (several feet) across. Leaves are **pink to reddish when they first develop**, then **turn green**, to be followed by an eye-catching **pinkish-purple by early September** as they start to wither.

RANGE: Generally above 1800 m (6000') in the subalpine ecosystem. Wenatchee Mountains and Seven Lakes Basin in the Olympics. Higher roadsides and dry slopes around Sunrise at Mt. Rainier.

NOTES: This species is named after John Newberry, a surgeon-naturalist on a U.S. Army exploring party in 1858. The alternate name "fleeceflower" refers to the fine fuzz, or fleece, that covers the plant. (This feature escapes the author's eye.)

ALUMROOTS • *Heuchera* spp.

ALUMROOTS GET their name from their **astringent roots**. Generally, they have **leafless stems**, their **petals aren't divided**, and their small flowers are white to cream to greenish. They have a **basal group of long-stemmed leaves**. There are 5 alumroot species in Washington. Remember that **fringecup** (p. 40) has fringed petals. The similar **mitreworts** (p. 178) have **greenish** flowers.

Small-flowered alumroot • *Heuchera micrantha*

FORM: 30–45 cm (12–17 1/2") tall. Often a spray of brown-hairy flower stems with hundreds of tiny flowers.

BLOOMS: May to August.

FLOWERS: White, very small flowers in loose clusters.

LEAVES: Long-stemmed leaves, with rounded lobes and heart-shaped base. Hairy leaf stems and undersides.

RANGE: Rocky, shady streambanks, rock slides. Low to subalpine elevations. Widespread. Columbia Gorge. Blue Mountains.

SMOOTH ALUMROOT (*H. glabra*) is very similar to small-flowered alumroot, but smooth alumroot's leaf blade is as broad as it is long, and it is almost hairless beneath. There are 1 or 2 small leaves on the stem. The flowers are in open sprays. It is found in moist, rocky places from sea level to the subalpine. It is widespread in the Olympics, Cascades, Wenatchee Mountains and Columbia Gorge.

Round-leaved alumroot • oval-leaf alumroot • *Heuchera cylindrica*

FORM: 30–50 cm (12–19 1/2") tall. A number of tall, erect stems.

BLOOMS: May to July.

FLOWERS: Close clusters on topmost section of stem. **Small, white to creamy flowers point upward. Tiny, distinct petals.**

LEAVES: A basal rosette of broadly lobed, round to oval, long-stemmed leaves.

RANGE: Open rocky areas, bluffs, slides. From east slope of Cascades eastward.

NOTES: Douglas found this species "on the declivities of low hills and on the steep banks of streams on the west side of the Rocky Mountains." MEADOW ALUMROOT (*H. chlorantha*) is a tall alumroot, to 40–80 cm (15 1/2–32"), with a tightly packed head of **greenish flowers pointing upward**. It blooms from May to August and is found on moist bluffs and riverbanks up to middle mountain forest elevations, being most common west of the Cascades, in the western section of the Columbia Gorge.

Silverleaf phacelia • white-leaved phacelia • *Phacelia hastata*

FORM: 25–40 cm (10–15 1/2") tall. Sturdy, curving stems.

BLOOMS: Late spring into summer.

FLOWERS: Small, white to lavender flowers. 5 petals of uniform size. **5 narrow, fringed sepals and 5 protruding stamens** create a **fuzzy appearance.** Flowers and buds clustered in a tight coil.

LEAVES: As the common names suggest, the leaves look **silver or white**, from the fine white hairs. Broadly lance-like, but some may be "eared."

RANGE: Open places. To the subalpine. East of Cascades.

NARROW-SEPALLED PHACELIA (*P. leptosepala*) **has a more or less prostrate form and dull olive-green leaves**, which separate it from silverleaf phacelia. It is common on roadsides, mostly east of the Cascades, in ponderosa pine and Douglas-fir regions.

Varileaf phacelia • *Phacelia heterophylla*

FORM: To 40 cm (15 1/2") tall. **A large, bushy, tousled plant.**

BLOOMS: Middle to late summer.

FLOWERS: Usually white, but may be a light purplish blue. In small clusters on upper stems.

LEAVES: In a low, dense cluster. **Deeply veined**, hairy leaves, to 15 cm (6") long and with **2 "ears" or thin lobes**.

RANGE: Dry, open areas, exposed banks and foothills of sagebrush ecosystem. Mostly east of Cascades. Vantage.

Fendler's waterleaf • *Hydrophyllum fendleri*

FORM: To 60 cm (2') tall. A large thick clump of leaves to 90 cm (3') across.

BLOOMS: July to August.

FLOWERS: Rather inconspicuous. White, bell-shaped, to 8 mm (1/3") across. **Long, protruding stamens.** Many **long, hairy sepals.** Flowers in clusters in upper leaf axils.

LEAVES: Large and deeply divided into sharply toothed segments.

RANGE: Moist meadows, from middle to subalpine elevations. Abundant in northern Cascades. Pasayten Wilderness, Cascades to Columbia Gorge, Olympic and Blue Mountains.

NOTES: Pacific waterleaf (p.153) closely resembles Fendler's waterleaf, and it can sometimes have white or greenish, instead of purplish-tinged, flowers, but the leaves of Pacific waterleaf are generally less segmented.

Bigroot • manroot, wild cucumber • *Marah oreganus*

FORM: A vigorous, vine-like plant that climbs over rocks, fences or simply makes a large patch of green on a hillside.

BLOOMS: April to June. New flowers appear as plant sends out long runners.

FLOWERS: White male flowers, 1.3 cm (1/2") across, lack symmetry. Female flowers, small and inconspicuous.

FRUITS: A smooth or bristly melon, 2.5–7.5 cm (1–3") across. Not edible.

LEAVES: Usually less than 7.5 cm (3") across (small for such a large plant).

RANGE: Moist lowlands. West slope of Cascades. Columbia Gorge.

Black nightshade • *Solanum americanum*

FORM: To 60 cm (2') tall. A bushy erect shrub.

BLOOMS: Summer.

FLOWERS: Small, white flowers in **drooping clusters of 3–8.**

FRUITS: Clusters of **glossy black berries.** May be poisonous!

LEAVES: To 10 cm (4") long and half as wide. Irregular, shallow teeth along edge.

RANGE: An introduced species now widely distributed in dry places east of the Cascades.

NOTES: There is a **purple**-flowered nightshade on p. 143.

CUT-LEAVED NIGHTSHADE (*S. triflorum*) is a sprawling, weed-like plant with deeply lobed leaves, clusters of 2–3 white flowers and green, inedible berries. It is found in waste places, mostly east of Cascades.

Field bindweed • orchard morning-glory • *Convolvulus arvensis*

FORM: Grows in a **blanket** that **crawls over fences** and other vegetation.

FLOWERS: To 4 cm (1 1/2") across, **often pinkish**. Petals are fused to create a wavy saucer-shape.

LEAVES: Arrowhead-shaped, 2–6 cm (3/4–2 1/4") long.

RANGE: Field borders, roadsides, waste places. Lower elevations. Common in Whitman County.

NOTES: These 2 European imports are variously regarded as quite beautiful or as darned pests.

HEDGE BINDWEED (*C. sepium*), also called "wild morning-glory," is a twining, climbing vine with **large, white to pink flowers to 7.5 cm (3") across**. It is found in moist soils of the Pacific coast and around Puget Sound.

Blue Mountains onion • *Allium fibrillum*

FORM: 5–15 cm (2–6") tall. A short, erect stem from an elongated bulb that is 5 cm (2") underground. Bulbs divide and may **first produce 2 leaves before a flower stem**.

BLOOMS: May to June, depending on altitude and exposure.

FLOWERS: A tightly packed, **terminal cluster of flowers**, each about 6 mm (1/4") long.

LEAVES: 2, thin, grass-like leaves that are longer than the flower stem. **Green at time of flowering, but quickly withering.**

RANGE: Most abundant above 1200 m (3940') on open bare ground. Blue Mountains of Washington and Oregon.

NOTES: The common name of this species is not recorded elsewhere, but seems appropriate; this species is limited in general range, but it is **abundant in the Blue Mountains**, where David Douglas discovered it—he was the first white man to explore there. • There are some **pink-flowered onions** on p.124.

Rock onion • *Allium macrum*

FORM: To 30 cm (12") tall. Reddish, erect stem.

BLOOMS: May to June.

FLOWERS: In a loose cluster. Each **white to pinkish-tinged flower** is on a stem almost twice as long as the flower. **Petals taper to a sharp point**, have a greenish midrib.

LEAVES: 2 deeply grooved leaves appear before flowers; longer than flower stem; quickly wither.

RANGE: Spotty. On poor, dry soils at lower elevations. South from Kittitas and Douglas counties. West of Yakima with prickly-pear cactus. Toppenish area.

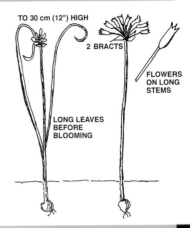

TO 30 cm (12") HIGH

2 BRACTS

FLOWERS ON LONG STEMS

LONG LEAVES BEFORE BLOOMING

White fawn lily • Easter lily • *Erythronium oregonum*

FORM: 15–30 cm (6–12") tall.

BLOOMS: April.

FLOWERS: White, curved-back petals with yellow-orange base. Flowers usually single and nodding. Faint perfume.

LEAVES: Distinctive, with paired basal leaves being a **glossy green mottled with paler green and dark brown**.

RANGE: A low-elevation lily. San Juan Islands south. Puget Sound. West end of Columbia Gorge.

NOTES: There is an *Erythronium* with **yellow** flowers on p. 86.

AVALANCHE LILY (*E. montanum*), also called "white glacier lily," is 15–35 cm (6–14") tall. **It blooms in July**. The flowers are very similar to those of white fawn lily. It is found in **subalpine meadows** in the Olympics and the Cascades (Mt. Rainier to Mt. Hood).

PINK FAWN LILY (*E. revolutum*) is a beautiful lily with pink flowers. It is otherwise like white fawn lily. It blooms in April. It has a scattered distribution in coastal Washington.

White fawn lily

Pink fawn lily

Avalanche lily

Queen's cup • blue-bead lily • *Clintonia uniflora*

FORM: 10–20 cm (4–8") tall.
BLOOMS: May to July.
FLOWERS: 1 pure white flower, about 2.5 cm (1") across. **Center is of golden stamens.**
FRUITS: A distinctive, unpalatable berry. **Deep china blue** in color.
LEAVES: 2–3 shiny green basal leaves to 15 cm (6") long.
RANGE: Shade tolerant at low to middle mountain elevations. Often abundant in moist forest openings. Widespread. Pend Oreille County. Blue Mountains. Olympics.

Western anemone • tow-headed baby, western pasqueflower • *Anemone occidentalis*

FORM: Plant springs up as snow leaves; eventually grows to 50 cm (19 1/2") tall in seed.
BLOOMS: June to July, before leaves open.
FLOWERS: Large, bowl-like to 6 cm (2 1/4") across, solitary (usually), blue-tinged on outside. Fuzzy center of stamens and pistils.

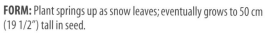

FRUITS: Up-ended "dust mop" seeds.
LEAVES: Basal leaves long-stemmed and fern-like. **Note typical cluster well up on stem.**
RANGE: Abundant in subalpine ecosystem. Cascades. Olympics.
NOTES: For general information on anemones, see p. 42.

Drummond's anemone • alpine anemone • *Anemone drummondii*

FORM: 5–20 cm (2–8") tall. May be dwarfed and smaller.
BLOOMS: July to August.
FLOWERS: To 2.5 cm (1") across, with many protruding stamens. 6–9 sepals, which lie flat and have blue tint on backs.
LEAVES: Basal leaves are long-stemmed and divide into leaflets, which divide again. **Whorl of leaves high on stem.**
RANGE: Rocky dry places in **subalpine and alpine zones** of Cascades and Olympics.
NOTES: For general information on anemones, see p. 42.
PIPER'S ANEMONE (*A. piperi*), also called "western wood anemone," is **slightly larger** than Drummond's anemone. Its white flowers are often tinged with purple. It has 1 to several long-stemmed basal leaves that are divided into leaflets. There is a whorl of leaves high on the stem. It is found in **moist mountain forests** in eastern Washington.

Fool's onion • harvest lily, white hyacinth • *Triteleia hyacinthina* • *Brodiaea hyacinthina*

FORM: To 60 cm (2') tall. A single slender stem.

BLOOMS: May to July, depending on elevation.

FLOWERS: An umbel (umbrella) design of flower stems, each with a trim white flower, forming a tightly packed cluster. Each petal has a green line down it. Stamens are about one-half the length of the petals. Resembles an onion, but no smell.

LEAVES: Thin, grass-like and longer than flower stem. Disappear at flowering time or shortly thereafter.

RANGE: West of Cascades. San Juan Islands and south. Also east of Cascades, in sagebrush areas south from Chelan County.

NOTES: Douglas was keen to introduce new plants to England, since, in part, it would justify his employment as a botanical collector for the Royal Horticultural Society. Seeds had to be properly matured at the time of picking, however, and he made many small notes to himself to check on this and that plant. Once obtained, seeds had to be carefully dried and packed to withstand the trials of time and distance back to England.

The remainder of this month was devoted to packing up my gleanings of dried plants, ...a large chest of seeds, one of birds and quadrupeds, and one of various articles of dress.
—Douglas, September, 1825

Howell's tritelia • bicolored cluster lily • *Triteleia howellii*

FORM: To 50 cm (19 1/2") tall, placing it above most spring wildflowers.

BLOOMS: Very abundant and **showy** from **April to May**.

FLOWERS: Up to 12 buds and flowers in cluster. Flowers **often have a blue tinge**, with a darker blue line down each petal.

LEAVES: 2 grass-like leaves almost as long as flower stem. Still green at flowering.

RANGE: Through the San Juan Islands, Puget Sound and south. Mid-section of Columbia Gorge. Wenatchee Valley southwards and westwards. High plateaus in Klickitat County.

NOTES: The bulbs of Howell's tritelia were a food item. **Its flowers are often light blue**, and it is noted again on p. 165. It is similar to fool's onion (above), but that species blooms in mid-June. The closely related **purple brodiaeas** are on p. 144.

Hooker's fairybells • Oregon fairybells • *Disporum hookeri*

FORM: 30–75 cm (1–2 1/2') tall. Usually arching stems. Several short branches.

BLOOMS: May to June.

FLOWERS: Usually **2 creamy white**, **paired** flowers, 1.3 cm (1/2") long, **hanging** from branch tip.

FRUITS: Smooth, **egg-shaped berry** that changes **from yellow to orange** with age. Not palatable.

LEAVES: Waxy, **green**, to 12 cm (4 3/4") long, **with distinct veins**. Drip tip to aid rain run-off. **Hairy margins.**

RANGE: Widespread in moist lowland forest both sides of Cascades.

ROUGH-FRUITED FAIRYBELLS (*D. trachycarpum*) has larger, greener flowers than Hooker's fairybells. **The leaf edges are not hairy.** The rounded berry is rich red. It is found at lower forest elevations east of the Cascades, in Okanogan County and eastern Washington south to the Blue Mountains.

Clasping twistedstalk • *Streptopus amplexifolius*

FORM: 30–90 cm (1–3') tall. Usually arching and branching.

BLOOMS: May to July.

FLOWERS: Distinctive, white to cream flowers, **usually single, hang down with a sharp twist to the stem.** Petals (sepals) flare downward and upward.

FRUITS: Bright red berries. Not palatable.

LEAVES: Leaves are alternate, prominently veined and clasping.

RANGE: Moist areas in forests of low to middle elevations. Widespread across Washington.

False Solomon's-seal • *Smilacina racemosa*

FORM: 30–60 cm (1–2') tall. Arching stem.

BLOOMS: May to June.

FLOWERS: Pyramids of creamy, star-like flowers, sweet-scented.

FRUITS: Clusters of **mottled, greenish berries** that **age to an unusual red.** Edible but tasteless.

LEAVES: Very attractive! Stout, unbranched, arched stems carry **2 rows of glossy green, clasping, ribbed leaves** that are to 15 cm (6") long.

RANGE: Widespread in damp, shady habitats. Low to subalpine elevations across Washington.

NOTES: Although the tiny flowers might well fit the "clustered" category, they do have 6 petals, and this species is grouped here with other look-alikes.

Star-flowered false Solomon's-seal • *Smilacina stellata*

FORM: 30–60 cm (1–2') tall. Arching, unbranched stem.
BLOOMS: April to July.
FLOWERS: Terminal cluster of 5–10 star-like blooms.
FRUITS: Round, greenish-yellow berries, later turning dark.
LEAVES: Alternate, with prominent, parallel veins, and forming 2 upward-pointing rows.
RANGE: Moist woods, shady areas. Low to middle elevations.

MANY PETALS   **WHITE**

White mountain-avens • white dryas • *Dryas octopetala*

FORM: 7.5–20 cm (3–8") tall. Slender stems with single flower.
BLOOMS: June to August, depending on location.
FLOWERS: Usually 8 petals, but variable. White to cream in color.
FRUITS: Fluffy seed heads.
LEAVES: Often forming **evergreen mats** that slowly expand. About 1.3 cm (1/2") long, thick, **coarsely toothed**. Dark green.
RANGE: Subalpine to alpine elevations. North Cascades.

White marsh-marigold • elkslip marsh-marigold • *Caltha leptosepala*

FORM: 5–15 cm (2–6") tall. Slender, short stems from a mat of basal leaves.
BLOOMS: Late May to July.
FLOWERS: 1–2. **Usually 8 petals forming a flower** to 4 cm (1 1/2") across. Petals may have a greenish and bluish tinge. **Large, pale gold center**.
LEAVES: Succulent, waxy green leaves, sometimes with reddish stems. To 10 cm (4") long. Often convoluted.
RANGE: Widespread in wet marshy places (even ice water). Subalpine and alpine elevations.
NOTES: See **globeflower** (p. 41) for a similar plant.

TWO-FLOWERED WHITE MARSH-MARIGOLD (*C. leptosepala* var. *biflora*) has 2 flowers or a flower and a bud on each stem. The leaves are similar to those of white marsh-marigold. It is found in Cascade passes at about 1200 m (3940'). It is most common in high, wet places west of the Cascades' crest.

Fragrant waterlily • *Nymphaea odorata*

FORM: Showy leaves, flowers raised on short stems.

BLOOMS: July to October.

FLOWERS: White to pinkish, to 20 cm (8") across. Fragrant flower opens in morning, closes in afternoon.

LEAVES: Circular leaves to 25 cm (10") across.

RANGE: Sporadic in ponds and lakes. Both sides of Cascades.

NOTES: There are showy **yellow** waterlilies on p. 87.

White false hellebore • California corn lily, white veratrum • *Veratrum californicum*

FORM: To 2.1 m (7') tall. A stout, erect, unbranched stem.

BLOOMS: June to August, depending on area.

FLOWERS: Flower head may be **30–60 cm (1–2') tall, compact or freely branching**. Small, dull white, symmetrical flowers cover the branches. There is a Y-shaped, green gland near the petal base.

LEAVES: Many **large leaves** to 30 cm (12") long, **not whorled**, sheathing at base.

RANGE: 2 varieties give this species a wide range: *V. californicum* var. *caudatum* is infrequent west of the Cascades; *V. californicum* var. *californicum* ranges east of the Cascades. Abundant in low Douglas-fir and ponderosa pine forests near Cle Elum southward and eastward. Steptoe Butte.

NOTES: White false hellebore can be confused with 2 other tall plants with large leaves: **clustered frasera** (p. 161) has **blue** flowers, and **giant frasera** (p. 177) has **yellowish-green** flowers.

JOHN DAVIES, author of *Douglas of the Forests*, and a professional forester, now lives in Dumfriesshire, Scotland. While close by in July 1997, I phoned him and found he was no stranger to the rigors of wilderness travel. He has covered much of David Douglas' routes, even crossing the Rockies on the same hazardous trail. His kindness in allowing me to use information from his book adds a new aspect to this floral guide.

CATCHFLIES AND CAMPIONS • *Silene* spp.

THE GENUS *Silene* is a confusing group of plants for the amateur, with about a dozen species in Washington. Most have opposite, narrow leaves. The sepals are united for at least half their length into a **tube that is inflated to some degree** to form a veined bulb. The petals may be lobed, divided or fringed, and each petal has **a fragile scale of varying shape at its base**—a main identifying feature. Some *Silene* species go by the name of "catchfly," a reference to their sticky hairs, which trap insects. The 2 campions described here are good representatives of the genus.

Bladder campion • *Silene vulgaris* • *Silene cucubalus*

FORM: To 90 cm (3') tall. Several plants with branching stems usually bunched together.

BLOOMS: May to July.

FLOWERS: Main feature is **a large, hairy, translucent, veined calyx**, about 2 cm (3/4") long and 1.3 cm (1/2") wide. The 5 white petals are very deeply lobed. The flower is 2 cm (3/4") across.

LEAVES: Narrow, paired leaves, with clasping base.

RANGE: Widely distributed. Waste places.

SCOULER'S CAMPION (*S. scouleri*) is a native species that grows to 30–70 cm (12–28") tall. It is an erect plant with white flowers that may be tinged with green or pink. It blooms from May to July. **The petals are divided into 4 lobes**, the **central 2 being much wider and longer**. The basal leaves are gray and velvety. With 2 subspecies, it has both coastal and interior distributions at lower elevations.

Sitka valerian • mountain heliotrope, mountain valerian, dirty socks • *Valeriana sitchensis*

FORM: 40–100 cm (16–40") tall. An erect or leaning stem.

BLOOMS: June into August.

FLOWERS: A rounded head of tiny, white to pinkish flowers with long protruding stamens. **Sweet smell** attracts tiny insects and hikers.

LEAVES: Usually 3–5 pairs of opposite coarsely toothed leaves.

RANGE: Common, higher mountain forests and subalpine.

NOTES: Sitka valerian is a treasured plant among subalpine wildflowers. The alternate name "dirty socks" comes from the smell of the roots, which contain the drug valerian. • **Gray's lovage** (p.56) is similar in appearance.

YELLOW PENSTEMON (*Penstemon confertus*) appears white-flowered at first glance. It grows to 30 cm (2') tall, and its erect stems carry several distinct flower clusters in whorls. Each flower is less than 1.3 cm (1/2") long. It is widespread and abundant in open ponderosa pine and sagebrush areas.

Gray's lovage • *Ligusticum grayi*

FORM: 25–60 cm (10–23 1/2") tall. A number of single, erect stems, usually branched once, from a basal clump of "carroty" leaves.

BLOOMS: July to August.

FLOWERS: Typically not pea flowers, but its closeness in shape and habitat to Sitka valerian suggests placing it here. A **compound umbel head** formed by small clusters of tiny flowers. **No fragrance**.

LEAVES: Mostly basal. **A tangle of "carroty" leaves**.

RANGE: Locally common on dry, open slopes bordered by clumps of subalpine fir. Grows with lupines, daisies, bistort and magenta paintbrush. Middle to subalpine elevations in Cascades. Mt. Rainier. Columbia Gorge. Blue Mountains.

NOTES: Compare this species with **Sitka valerian** (p. 55).

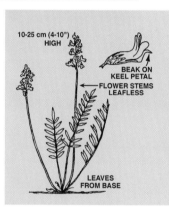

10-25 cm (4-10") HIGH

BEAK ON KEEL PETAL

FLOWER STEMS LEAFLESS

LEAVES FROM BASE

LOCOWEEDS • *Oxytropis* spp.

THERE ARE OVER a dozen locoweeds in Washington, nearly all east of the Cascades. Locoweed **flowers have a small beak in the keel**. The **flower stems are leafless**; the leaves are in a loose basal clump. Some locoweeds are poisonous, causing violent (loco) behavior. Several species are differentiated by the number of leaflets on a leaf—up to 17 or more.

Locoweeds closely resemble **milk-vetches** (*Astragalus* spp., below and p. 127).

Longleaf milk-vetch • *Astragalus reventus*

FORM: To 40 cm (15 1/2") tall. Usually several flower stems.

BLOOMS: April to June.

FLOWERS: Pea-like, to 2 cm (3/4") long, in a loose arrangement near stem top.

LEAVES: Long fronds branching from low on the stem; about 25 cm (10") long; carrying a **ladder of tiny leaflets**, these about 1.3 cm (1/2") long.

RANGE: Scablands (the flood-scoured area between Moses Lake and Spokane), sagebrush and ponderosa pine regions. East of the Cascades. Yakima Canyon. Goldendale to Toppenish. East section of Columbia Gorge.

NOTES: White-flowered lupines (p. 57) look similar. There is a **pink** milk-vetch on p. 127. Unlike in locoweeds, milk-vetch flowers don't have a beak, and the leaves aren't in a basal clump. There could be as many as 50 species of these confusing plants in Washington.

Velvet lupine • *Lupinus leucophyllus*

FORM: To 90 cm (3') tall. Bushy, with many hairy flowering stems. Plant a soft green color.

BLOOMS: May to July.

FLOWERS: Many small **flowers about 6 mm (1/4") long** and crowded in a long flowering spike.

LEAVES: 7 leaflets; velvety due to many very small hairs.

RANGE: Sagebrush ecosysytem and into ponderosa pine. Eastern Washington. Coulee Dam south to Pasco. Ephrata.

NOTES: Velvet lupine and Blue Mountains lupine are the **only white-flowering lupines in Washington.** For general information on lupines and for **blue** lupines, see pp. 170–173; **yellow** lupines are on p. 91.

BLUE MOUNTAINS WHITE LUPINE (*L. sericeus* var. *asotinensis*) is typically "lupine" in every respect. It grows to 60 cm (2') tall, with several flower stems. The stem leaves are divided into 7 large leaflets. It is very showy and blooms in May to June. It is locally abundant in open forests from 1200 m (3940') upwards, in the Blue Mountains, Asotin County and Whitman County.
• Common name supplied by author.

Blue Mountains white lupine

White sweet-clover • *Melilotus alba*

FORM: To 2.1 m (7') tall. Usually about 1 m (3 1/4') tall. **A large, sparse, loose-branching plant**.

BLOOMS: June to September.

FLOWERS: **Tiny pea flowers** crowded into spike-like clusters near the tops of stiff stems. **Sweet smelling** and attractive to bees.

LEAVES: Tiny, 3-leaflet leaves, scarcely noticeable.

RANGE: Could rate with **oxeye daisy** (p. 72) as the most widespread roadside flower. Most abundant east of Cascades.

YELLOW SWEET-CLOVER (*M. officinalis*) closely resembles white sweet-clover in everything but color. Its range is similar.

False lily-of-the-valley • beadruby, two-leaved Solomon's-seal • *Maianthemum dilatatum*

FORM: 10–25 cm (4–10") tall.

BLOOMS: May.

FLOWERS: Spike of **tiny, white, clustered flowers with flower parts in 4s.** Protruding anthers. Delicate fragrance.

FRUITS: A string of **green and brown berries changing into ruby beads**, hence the alternate name "beadruby."

LEAVES: Heart-shaped, glossy green and deeply veined; often the only distinguishing feature when the flowers are absent.

RANGE: Moist, shady, low-elevation forests, streamsides, under coastal Sitka spruce. West of Cascades.

NOTES: The berries were once considered edible in times of need. The roots, leaves and berries had many medicinal uses.

White plectritis • *Plectritis macrocera*

FORM: 5–15 cm (2–6") tall. Erect, single stems.

BLOOMS: April. White plectritis blooms with other early white blooms, such as **woodland stars** (p. 39) and **slender popcorn flower** (p. 43).

FLOWERS: Clusters of tiny, 5-petalled flowers, often forming rings, quickly yellowing.

LEAVES: Basal rosettes of tiny, oval leaves to 1.3 cm (1/2") long. Quickly yellowing. 1 to several opposite pairs of clasping stem leaves.

RANGE: Moist areas from Puget Sound region south. Meadows and around Garry oak and ponderosa pine forests in Columbia Gorge.

NOTES: There is a common **pink** *Plectritis* species on p. 130.

Partridgefoot • meadow spirea • *Luetkea pectinata*

FORM: 5–10 cm (2–4") tall. Erect stems from **leaf clump or carpet.**

BLOOMS: June to August, as snow recedes.

FLOWERS: Small, **white to cream flowers** in a **dense, terminal cluster.**

LEAVES: Small, **finely fringed**, their shape a fanciful resemblance to the shape of a partridge's foot or its imprint in snow. **Evergreen, bright green leaves** often form an extensive carpet.

RANGE: Widespread in subalpine and alpine ecosystems of the Cascades. Alaska to California.

NOTES: The genus name *Luetkea* honors Count F. P. Luetka, a 19th-century Russian sea captain and explorer.

PUSSYTOES • *Antennaria* spp.

THERE ARE a dozen or more pussytoes in Washington. All are relatively short, single-stemmed, erect plants. They have a basal tuft of small leaves, which often forms a mat. There are usually only a few small stem leaves, but several pussytoes have relatively leafy stems. The most noticeable feature is the soft, rounded flowerhead, whether smooth or lumpy, which gives this genus the name "pussytoes." The basic flower design is a central, soft tuft of disk flowers (tiny tubular flowers, as in the center of a daisy). This is surrounded by a row of bracts, which, if colored, impart the tones to rosy pussytoes and umber pussytoes.

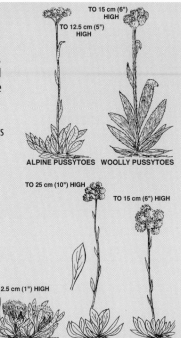

Umber pussytoes is included here, but wholly **pink** pussytoes are on p. 130. **Pearly everlasting** (p. 62) is a rather similar, but much taller, plant.

ALPINE PUSSYTOES (*A. alpina*) is **5–10 cm (2–4")** **tall**. Its basal, spoon-shaped, mat-forming **leaves**, to 2.5 cm (1") long, are **white-woolly on** **both sides**. There are a few narrow stem leaves. The flowerhead is a tight, papery, white to yellow tuft held by **thin bracts** that are **dark-colored at** **top**. It is widespread in the subalpine and alpine.

UMBER PUSSYTOES (*A. umbrinella*) is similar to alpine pussytoes, but umber pussytoes' **bracts have brownish tips**. It blooms from June to July. It is found at middle mountain to sub-alpine elevations.

WOOLLY PUSSYTOES (*A. lanata*) is about 15 cm (6") tall. Its leafy stems arise from a tuft of lance-shaped, basal leaves with 3 or more veins. It has **whitish, woolly stems and leaves**. The flowerhead is a compact **cluster of flower "balls"** that are whitish on top but dark beneath, because of the greenish to black bracts. It is a characteristic high-mountain plant with its **woolly hair covering** to give it protection from cold temperatures and the extremes of sun rays on hot days. It is abundant in damp places in and above the subalpine in the Olympics.

RACEMOSE PUSSYTOES (*A. racemosa*) is **quickly identified by the** **open spacing of short-stemmed flowers on the top one-third of** **the plant**—not in tight, ball-like clusters. It is common in the Cascades and eastern mountains, at low to subalpine elevations.

FIELD PUSSYTOES (*A. neglecta*) grows to 25 cm (10") tall. It is the **only species with a faint greenish-white bloom**. The small **stem** **leaves** are smooth and **green above**, and **white-woolly beneath**. It is widespread in open, dry forests at low to medium elevations.

Field pussytoes

LOW PUSSYTOES (*A. dimorpha*) its tiny size—**barely 2.5 cm** **(1") tall**—gives instant recognition. The woolly, white flower sits on a mat of tiny, sharp-pointed **leaves**. It blooms in early spring on dry ground at low elevations in eastern Washington.

Leatherleaf saxifrage • *Leptarrhena pyrolifolia*

FORM: 15–20 cm (6–8") tall. Often a number of stems in a small area. **Very showy**, with attractive, **reddish stems**.

BLOOMS: May to June, soon after snow leaves.

FLOWERS: White, very small flowers in **clusters at stem tips**.

FRUITS: Attractive, **purplish-red seed clusters** in July and August.

LEAVES: Mostly **basal, leathery, glossy green**, lighter green beneath, deeply veined.

RANGE: Damp meadows, streambanks. Subalpine and lower elevations. Cascades. Olympics.

NOTES: There are more **white-flowering saxifrages** on pp. 31–33.

Cotton-grass • *Eriophorum chamissonis*

FORM: 25–60 cm (10–23 1/2") tall. Single stems.

BLOOMS: Spring to summer, depending on elevation.

FLOWERS: Tiny, normally go unnoticed.

FRUITS: Eye-catching, fluffy seed heads, sometimes so abundantly displayed that there is **a field of cotton** over an entire wet meadow.

LEAVES: A few near the base; short and grass-like.

RANGE: Sedgy, wet meadows. Low to high elevations. Widespread, but spotty, occurrence.

NOTES: If the fluffy seed heads have a brownish center (from a darkening at the lower end of the bristle) then the species is *E. chamissonis*; if the seed heads are pure white, then it is *E. augustifolium*.

Vanilla-leaf • May leaves, sweet-after-death • *Achlys triphylla*

FORM: 25–40 cm (10–15 1/2") tall. Thin, wiry stems.

BLOOMS: April to May.

FLOWERS: Unusual, in that they have **neither sepals or petals, only long, white stamens.** The tiny blooms are clustered in an elongated spike of flowers at the tip of a thin stem.

LEAVES: A **single, large leaf**, divided into 3 wavy-edged segments.

RANGE: Low to middle elevations, on both slopes of the Cascades, but most abundant along coast in shady moist forests. Columbia Gorge.

NOTES: This species' common names reflect a faint vanilla odor from the dried leaves, which are also said to repel flies.

Meadow death-camas • *Zygadenus venenosus*

FORM: 25–40 cm (10–15 1/2") tall. Erect single stem from an onion-shaped bulb.

BLOOMS: April to June.

FLOWERS: Small, creamy flowers in a tightly packed cluster at stem top. **6 petals.**

LEAVES: Thin, grooved basal leaves, shorter than flower stem.

RANGE: **Showy in its abundance** on meadows and dry lands at lower elevations. San Juan Islands. Both sides of Cascades. Common in eastern Columbia Gorge.

NOTES: The bulbs and leaves of meadow death-camas are very poisonous.

Pathfinder • silver green, trail plant • *Adenocaulon bicolor*

FORM: 25–60 cm (10–24") tall. A single, erect, leafy stalk.

BLOOMS: July to August.

FLOWERS: Inconspicuous. Tufts of very small flowers on upper branching stem.

FRUITS: Seeds catch on anything that passes.

LEAVES: Large, long-stemmed, broadly triangular basal leaves. Common names reflect the contrast between **green upper side** and **stark silvery underside** of leaves; when disturbed, they leave a very visible clue to a trail for a pathfinder.

RANGE: Shady forests—often Douglas-fir— at low to medium elevations. Mostly west of Cascades.

Palmate coltsfoot • *Petasites palmatus*

FORM: 30–60 cm (1–2') tall. Stout stems precede basal leaves.

BLOOMS: From March onwards. **Among earliest of blooms**.

FLOWERS: White to pink to purple flower clusters (small balls) form a wide flowerhead.

FRUITS: Stem extends as flowers go to seed in white heads.

LEAVES: To 30 cm (12") across. **Palmate** (spread-like fingers), with **5–7 toothed lobes**. Green above, but **white-woolly beneath**.

RANGE: Moist, shady ground, seeps and ditches; seen along wet roadside banks. Low to middle elevations. Cascades. Greatest abundance in coastal areas.

Yarrow • *Achillea millefolium*

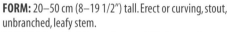

FORM: 20–50 cm (8–19 1/2") tall. Erect or curving, stout, unbranched, leafy stem.

BLOOMS: Late April (in south-central Washington) to September (at high elevations).

FLOWERS: Slightly rounded flowerhead, 5–10 cm (2–4") across, is composed of many **small, scaly "flowers"**: white to pink ray flowers and often creamy disk flowers.

LEAVES: Dull, alternate leaves, **finely divided into fringes**, arch from the stout stem. **Pungent smell when crushed**.

RANGE: Drier sites. Into the subalpine. Throughout Washington.

NOTES: The genus *Achillea* commemorates the famous Greek warrior, Achilles, who used yarrow in treating the wounded. Native Americans employed it to treat many illnesses.

Pearly everlasting • *Anaphalis margaritacea*

FORM: 30–60 cm (1–2') tall. Stems erect, unbranched, **leafy** and **white-woolly. Often in masses**.

BLOOMS: July to September, after spring flowers have finished.

FLOWERS: Flat-topped masses of small flower clusters, each with a packed yellow center of disk flowers surrounded by dry, glistening white bracts. Flowers retain their shape and color for many months, hence the name everlasting.

LEAVES: Alternate, dull green above, white-woolly beneath.

RANGE: Widespread. Low elevations into subalpine.

American bistort • *Polygonum bistortoides*

FORM: 25–75 cm (10–30") tall. Erect, unbranched stems, with **plants dotted over a wide expanse.**

BLOOMS: June to August, depending on elevation.

FLOWERS: White, **elongated clusters** of tiny, white to pink flowers with **fuzz of projecting stamens.**

LEAVES: Basal leaves are long-stemmed. Higher leaves are smaller and stemless.

RANGE: Meadowlands, open slopes. Subalpine and alpine elevations in Cascades and Olympics. Subalpine elevations in eastern mountains.

NOTES: American bistort is easily recognized by its flowers and its high mountain habitat.

White small-flowered paintbrush • *Castilleja parviflora* var. *albida*

FORM: 5–25 cm (2–10") tall. So small and bland that it is difficult to think of it as a paintbrush.

BLOOMS: June to August.

FLOWERS: White to pinkish bracts.

LEAVES: Alternate, lobed.

RANGE: Open dry ground of the subalpine. From British Columbia border south through Cascades to Mt. Rainier.

Baneberry • *Actaea rubra*

FORM: 30–90 cm (1–3') tall. Stems erect to arching.

BLOOMS: April to June.

FLOWERS: In loose, rounded **clusters of small, white flowers, fuzzy** from many **protruding stamens.**

FRUITS: Handsome scarlet, sometimes white, **berries** appearing in August.

RANGE: Moist shady places at low elevations across Washington.

NOTES: All parts of the plant are generally regarded as poisonous, as the common name reflects.

Beargrass • squaw-grass • *Xerophyllum tenax*

FORM: Usually to 90 cm (3') tall. A stout, single stem, but plants often in a close cluster.

BLOOMS: June to August. Blooms irregularly, but usually enough plants in bloom to create an eye-catching sight.

FLOWERS: A very large, **rocket-shaped ball** of **tiny, white to creamy, fragrant flowers**.

LEAVES: Large basal clumps of **long, wiry, evergreen leaves**. Finely toothed. Stem leaves becoming shorter as they climb the stem.

RANGE: Mostly at medium and subalpine elevations. Spotty distribution in Cascades. Mt. Rainier in the Paradise area. Mountains north of midsection of Columbia River. Willard region. At high elevations on Mt. Spokane.

NOTES: The alternate name "squaw-grass" refers to the Native Americans' use of these wiry leaves for weaving, which was considered woman's work ("squaw" being a term, no longer in favor, for a Native American woman).

Many of the natives...wear hats of a conic figure....These hats are made of the bark of Cedar and beargrass wrought with the fingers so closely that it casts the rain most effectively.

—Clark, January 29, 1806

Their baskets were formed of cedar bark and beargrass so closely interwoven with their fingers that they were water-tight without the use of gum or resin.

—David Douglas

BUCKWHEATS • *Eriogonum* spp.

THERE ARE MORE than 24 buckwheats in Washington. Some are annuals, some are perennials, some are shrubby (with twisted stems), some carry as many as 3 colors, and many have leaves that are so tiny as to beggar description, but all buckwheats provide such a widespread mass of bright color that you feel you must know. The **umbel flowerhead** is common to all buckwheats. The **flower stems are generally unbranched**, and the **tiny flowers have 9 stamens**. Buckwheats are plants of open, dry ground, whether at low elevations with sagebrush or high on rocky slopes in subalpine terrain. Some of the most common and easily identified buckwheats are included in this book.

Yellow buckwheats are on pp. 97–98; **pink** on p. 132.

Creamy buckwheat • *Eriogonum heracleoides*

FORM: 10–50 cm (4–19 1/2") tall. Single, erect stem.
BLOOMS: May to August. **Often the most abundant flower.**
FLOWERS: White to cream to yellow. Bracts whorled beneath flowerhead.
LEAVES: Important: **Basal leaves of 2 designs,** 1 type narrow and paddle-like, the other a tuft at the end of leaf stem. **A whorl of leaves near stem center.**
RANGE: Probably the most widespread of the buckwheats. Sagebrush to ponderosa pine ecosystems. East of Cascades. Tonasket east and south to Blue Mountains.

Strict buckwheat • *Eriogonum strictum*

FORM: To 30 cm (12") tall. Single stem.
BLOOMS: June to July.
FLOWERS: White, cream, yellow, pink, or white-and-rose. Often in a mass and very eye-catching. **Note flower in crotch.**
LEAVES: Basal, long-stemmed, dull green.
RANGE: East of Cascades. Okanogan County south. Yakima Canyon. Spokane. Blue Mountains.

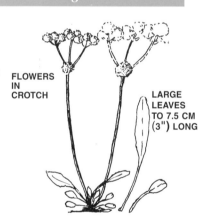

FLOWERS
IN
CROTCH

LARGE
LEAVES
TO 7.5 CM
(3") LONG

Alpine buckwheat • *Eriogonum pyrolifolium*

FORM: To 15 cm (6") tall.
BLOOMS: July to August.
FLOWERS: White head with purple stamens. Bad odor!
LEAVES: Basal, broadly paddle-shaped, to 5 cm (2") long. Mealy.
RANGE: Dry, rocky, slopes. Higher mountains of Cascades. Harts Pass.

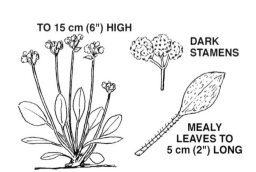

TO 15 cm (6") HIGH

DARK
STAMENS

MEALY
LEAVES TO
5 cm (2") LONG

DESERT-PARSLEYS • *Lomatium* spp.

DESERT-PARSLEYS are another group of plants with more than enough problems for the amateur. They are often referred to as "lomatiums," and with at least 30 different types (including varieties), 2-color flowers, indescribable fern-like leaves and many identified by the structure of their seeds, which you likely will never see, they are a challenge!

Many desert-parsleys were prized by Native Americans for their large, woody taproots. Although they can be eaten raw, they were usually pounded into flour, boiled, steamed or roasted. When dried they could be stored for many months. The large seed heads were gathered as a spice for drinks and food.

Yellow desert-parsleys are on pp. 95–97; **purple** on p. 154.

Large-fruited desert-parsley • Indian carrot, biscuit-root • *Lomatium macrocarpum*

FORM: To 30 cm (12") tall. **Usually sprawling.**

BLOOMS: April to May. **An early bloomer.**

FLOWERS: Dirty white to yellow to purple. **Flowerheads may be lying on the ground.**

FRUITS: Flattened seeds to 2.5 cm (1") long.

LEAVES: Dissected like a carrot's; grayish.

RANGE: Rocky, open places at lower elevations. Sagebrush and ponderosa pine. East of Cascades.

Salt-and-pepper • *Lomatium gormanii*

TO 15 cm (6") HIGH

PURPLE ANTHERS ON WHITE PETALS

FORM: To 15 cm (6") tall.

BLOOMS: April to May. **Among earliest flowers.**

FLOWERS: White flowers (salt) sprinkled with **purple anthers** (pepper). **Flowers stems in umbel are of varying lengths.**

LEAVES: Sparse, easily overlooked.

RANGE: Usually associated with sagebrush. East of Cascades at lower elevations. Lincoln and Kittitas counties. Ellensburg. Yakima Canyon. Pullman.

NOTES: The size of salt-and-pepper helps in its identification.

Hemlock water-parsnip • *Sium suave*

FORM: 60–120 cm (2–4') tall. Erect or arching stems.

BLOOMS: July to August.

FLOWERS: White, flattish heads (umbels) of tiny flowers less than 3 mm (1/8") across.

LEAVES: Long-stemmed leaves, once-divided into **7-15 narrow leaflets**.

RANGE: Ditches, ponds, shorelines. Lower elevations. Across Washington.

NOTES: Avoid any use of this plant because of possible confusion with Douglas' water-hemlock (below).

Douglas' water-hemlock • Oregon water-hemlock • *Cicuta douglasii*

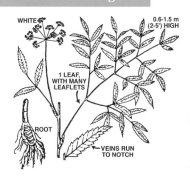

FORM: 60–150 cm (2–5') tall. Usually arching, purplish stems.

BLOOMS: July and August.

FLOWERS: White to greenish. Small clusters of tiny flowers forming a large, **rounded ball**.

LEAVES: Twice divided into 3–5 leaflets. **Leaflet veins run toward the bottom of the teeth notches** rather than to the points.

RANGE: Wet swamps, meadows, ditches, lake margins. Wide range, low to middle elevations.

NOTES: Douglas' water-hemlock is sometimes rated as the most poisonous plant in North America. Its leaves differ from those of hemlock water-parsnip (above), which has once-divided leaves, and poison hemlock (below), which has fringed leaflets.

Poison hemlock • *Conium maculatum*

FORM: 50 cm–2 m (1 1/2–7') tall. Erect. **Stem blotched with purple**.

BLOOMS: June to August.

FLOWERS: White, very small; **forming small, umbel clusters in a large, open head** (compound umbels).

FRUITS: Very small, egg-shaped seeds, with raised ribs.

RANGE: Adaptable to drier ground, so in wastelands, roadsides and moister soils. Mostly west of Cascades at lower elevations.

NOTES: This species is the very poisonous plant that ancient Greeks used to put to death condemned prisoners. Socrates killed himself with it in 399 BC. Native Americans may have used it as a poison on arrows.

> *We would make the men collect these roots them-selves but there are several species of hemlock which are so much like the cows [cous]...we are afraid they might poison themselves.*
> —Lewis, May 21, 1806

Wild carrot • Queen Anne's lace • *Daucus carota*

FORM: 30–120 cm (1–4') tall. Single, erect stem.

BLOOMS: July to September.

FLOWERS: Tiny, 4-petalled, white to creamy flowers in small clusters in a **flat to slightly rounded head. Central flower is often pink-purple.** With aging, flowerhead often forms a **bird's nest-shape.** Each individual cluster contains 20 or more flowers.

LEAVES: Finely dissected, like a carrot's leaf.

RANGE: Along with **oxeye daisy** (p. 72), a very common and widespread roadside flower. Fields, meadows at low elevations.

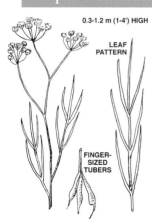

NOTES: This long-naturalized plant is the ancestor of the common carrot. It is said that Queen Anne of England wore its tiny flowers in preference to lace.

AMERICAN WILD CARROT (*D. pusillus*), a native plant, differs from wild carrot in that it is smaller, its leaves are fewer and smaller, it has only **5–12 flowers in each tiny cluster**, and it blooms later in summer. It is found west of the Cascades.

Yampah • Gairnder's yampah • *Perideridia gairdneri*

0.3-1.2 m (1-4') HIGH

LEAF PATTERN

FINGER-SIZED TUBERS

FORM: 30–120 cm (1–4') tall. Erect, with branching stems.

BLOOMS: August to September.

FLOWERS: Small, white to pinkish, grouped in compact heads separated by branching stems.

LEAVES: Along the stem, divided into very thin fingers.

RANGE: Low to medium elevations. Both sides of Cascades. San Juan Islands and adjacent mainland south.

NOTES: Yampah has a thickened root that was prized by Native Americans as a food. Lewis and Clark found the roots "very palatable, either fresh, roasted or dried." • They have a definite carrot flavor and rate highly for their nourishment and taste. • Meredith Gairdner was a surgeon in the employ of the Hudson's Bay Company and also a botanist. He was active at about the same time as Douglas.

Cow parsnip • *Heracleum lanatum*

FORM: To 1.8 m (6') tall at low elevations. Thick, stout, hollow stems.

BLOOMS: May to September, depending on location.

FLOWERS: Massive, rounded flowerhead, 10–25 cm (4–10") across, of small white flowers.

FRUITS: Flattened oval seeds without ribs.

LEAVES: Very large leaves, divided into 3 coarsely toothed leaflets.

RANGE: Widespread in moist, rich soils to subalpine.

NOTES: Cow parsnip is another plant that was eaten by Native Americans.

> *I observed them eat the inner part of the young and succulent stem of a large coarse plant with alternate leaf. I tasted of this plant and found it agreeable and ate heartily of it without feeling any inconvenience.*
> —Lewis, May 2, 1806

Silverback luina • *Luina hypoleuca*

FORM: 15–30 cm (6–12") tall. Many leafy, woolly stems spreading from a leafy base.

BLOOMS: June to September, depending on location.

FLOWERS: Whitish or yellowish: rayless, white flowers may be overshadowed by yellow stamens and styles. **Tall, narrow bracts** surround the small, soft flowerhead.

LEAVES: Distinctive; in a rather formalized pattern of **stiff alternate leaves** all the way up the stem to the head. Leaves are **green on upper surface**, with a very **contrasting "silverback."**

RANGE: Dry, rocky ground. From 1200 m (3940') to the subalpine. Generally occurs from Cascades westward. Probably on both sides of northern Cascades. Olympics.

On Hurricane Ridge Highway, Olympics

FLEABANES and ASTERS • *Erigeron* spp. and *Aster* spp.

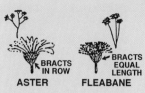

BRACTS
IN ROW
ASTER

BRACTS
EQUAL
LENGTH
FLEABANE

THE BROAD "daisy" classification is for "flowers" with ray flower "petals" and a button center, and that are less than 5 cm (2") across. Larger than that they are grouped as "sunflowers." Daisy flowers may be white, yellow, pink, red, purple or blue. All have ray flowers (strap-like flowers that look like petals) and disk flowers (tiny flowers compressed into a button center).

A quick, but not always precise, rule to separate fleabanes from asters is that most fleabanes bloom in spring to mid-summer, and asters bloom after that. There are other distinguishing characteristics as well.

Fleabanes, also called "daisies," have green, smooth bracts that are usually in 1 or 2 rows and are of equal length. The ray flowers are numerous and very narrow.

Asters have bracts that are pale at the base and green at the tip and are usually in 3 or more shingled rows. The ray flowers are less numerous and wider. The buds are often nodding.

There are many species of fleabane and aster that have not been included in this book.

The difficulty of identifying fleabanes is shown by the 3 species included here and on the following page. While their ray flowers are often white, they might be pink or blue.

Cut-leaved daisy • dwarf mountain fleabane • *Erigeron compositus*

FORM: 5–25 cm (2–10") tall.

BLOOMS: May to August.

FLOWERS: Many white or pink, narrow ray flowers; greenish center. About 2 cm (3/4") across.

LEAVES: Distinctive. In basal tufts. Long-stemmed before dividing into very narrow segments, which then divide again to form tufts. Leaves hairy, olive-green.

RANGE: Widespread in open areas at low to medium elevations.

NOTES: The leaves are the best identifying feature of cut-leaved daisy. Lewis recorded this species "on the banks of the Kooskoosky [near Lewiston]."

Tufted fleabane • *Erigeron caespitosus*

FORM: 15–30 cm (6–12") tall. **Stem curved at base**, then branching. Stem and leaves **dull green** from fine hair.

BLOOMS: May to July (typical for a fleabane).

FLOWERS: White to pinkish, 2–2.5 cm (3/4–1") across, many **narrow ray flowers** on branching stems. Yellow-green button center.

LEAVES: Basal leaves **long-stemmed, paddle-shaped**. Stem leaves are stalkless, and decrease in size higher on stem.

RANGE: Dry, rocky places. East of Cascades. Ellensburg. Cle Elum and southward.

Shaggy fleabane • *Erigeron pumilus*

FORM: To 40 cm (15 1/2") tall. Several erect, leafy, finely hairy stems.
BLOOMS: April to July.
FLOWERS: White, pink or blue; varies with age. **50–100 thin ray petals. Bracts in 1 row, finely hairy.**
LEAVES: Olive-green leaves, to 5 cm (2") long, cover all the stem.
RANGE: Sagebrush valleys to the foothills.
NOTES: Douglas recorded this species "in the valleys of the Blue Mts., and of the Spokane R."

Olympic mountain aster • *Aster paucicapitatus*

FORM: Less than 40 cm (15 1/2") tall. Bushy, many-stemmed.
BLOOMS: July to September.
FLOWERS: 1 or 2 typical "daisy" blooms to a stalk. **About 12 rather ragged ray flowers,** some overlapping. Prominent yellow center.
LEAVES: Many narrow, stemless leaves the length of the stem —key identifying feature.
RANGE: Open slopes, roadsides in subalpine. Olympics. Hurricane Ridge. Obstruction Point.
NOTES: Piper, a botanist, first collected Olympic Mountain aster in the Olympics in September 1890. There are **purple** asters on pp. 155–157.

Engelmann's aster • *Aster engelmannii*

FORM: To **1.5 m (5') tall** (a good clue in itself).
BLOOMS: July to September (after most fleabanes).
FLOWERS: Attractive. Rather tousled, to 6 cm (2 1/4") across. **11–17 white to pink ray flowers.** Yellow button center.
LEAVES: Important: **Lower leaves usually small and scale-like;** those higher on the stem (all are alternate) are longer and wider than in most asters. Stem leaves 5–10 cm (2–4") long and 1.3–4 cm (1/2–1 1/2") wide; stemless and entire (no teeth).
RANGE: Open forests and slopes. Medium to subalpine elevations. Eastern slopes of Cascades.
NOTES: This species is the **only white-blooming, tall, large-leaved aster** in Washington.

Corn chamomile • dog fennel, mayweed • *Anthemis arvensis*

FORM: 25–50 cm (10–19 1/2") tall. Often **tousled in form**; much branched.

BLOOMS: April to September; year-round on the coast.

FLOWERS: Typical "daisy" flowers, but small—only to 2.5 cm (1") across. **Many in bloom at same time**.

LEAVES: Finely dissected, like a carrot's leaves. Not bad smelling (unlike stinking chamomile).

RANGE: Naturalized weed. Waste places, fields, roadsides. Lower elevations. Coastal strip. San Juan Islands.

NOTES: Oxeye daisy (below) is similar, but it has long, erect stems.

STINKING CHAMOMILE (*A. cotula*), also called "dog fennel", is much like corn chamomile except for the **unpleasant smell of the crushed leaves**. The upper stems are much branched, so there are many flowers. It is found along roadsides and fields **east of the Cascades**, especially in Whitman County.

Stinking chamomile

Oxeye daisy • *Leucenthemum vulgare*

FORM: 20–60 cm (8–23 1/2") tall. Sometimes a single, erect stem. Usually a mass of plants—a long-lasting contribution to roadside beauty.

BLOOMS: May through August, depending on elevation.

FLOWERS: A good example of a daisy. **To 5 cm (2") wide** with a yellow center. **Single at the stem top**.

LEAVES: Loose cluster of basal leaves. Leaves are alternate, narrowly spoon-shaped, margins toothed and lobed.

RANGE: Non-native plant. Wide-ranging below 1200 m (3940') along roadsides, meadows.

NOTES: Oxeye daisy is regarded as a weed by farmers. The lower leaves are edible as a salad green. The name "daisy" is from an English flower that closed at night and opened at dawn—the "day's eye."

Rattlesnake-plantain • *Goodyera oblongifolia*

FORM: 15–35 cm (8–14") tall. Single, erect stem.

BLOOMS: July to September.

FLOWERS: Small, greenish-white flowers, hooded like an orchid, in a scattered spike along 1 side of the stem.

LEAVES: Dramatic coloration! **Basal leaves**, usually **flat on the ground, are dark green**, but vaguely striped **with a dull white along the vein pattern**, creating a mottled effect.

RANGE: Shady, rich humus in forests of low to medium elevations. Widespread, but most abundant in San Juan Islands and coastal strip.

NOTES: White-veined wintergreen (p. 36) is similar, but its leaves are more clearly marked. • Early woodsmen and pioneers were wont to attribute any peculiar marking or shapes of plants to a nature sign. Thus the snake skin markings were taken as indicative that the leaves might be a remedy for snake bite.

Mountain ladyslipper • *Cypripedium montanum*

FORM: To 60 cm (2') tall. Single, erect stem.

BLOOMS: May to June.

FLOWERS: A floral jewel! 1–3 flowers (usually 2) ranked 1 above the other, each **set off by a large, green, leaf-like bract.** The wide, **pure white "slipper" with purple veins** is just 1 petal. **2 long sepals twist like coppery ribbons.** Exquisite perfume, too. Plants require protection.

RANGE: Open woods, often in moist glades. Low to middle elevations. East of Cascades. Stevens and Spokane counties. Blue Mountains. Likely in mountains of Okanogan County.

Phantom orchid

PHANTOM ORCHID (*Cephalanthera austinae*) is unmistakable. **The entire plant is whitish to greenish**; it is a saprophyte, so it needs no leaves. It has **typical, small orchid flowers.** It is quite rare and is found in damp, mossy to dry soils under conifers in the Olympics and Cascades.

Mountain ladyslipper

White rein-orchid • white bog-orchid • *Platanthera dilatata*

FORM: 25–50 cm (10–19 1/2") tall. Single, stout, hollow stem.

BLOOMS: June to August.

FLOWERS: White to greenish-tinged flowers with **delicate perfume. 5–30** flowers clustered along **upper one-third of stem.** Upper sepals and 2 petals curve to form a hood. Pick a flower to see the **slender spur,** which is **longer than the lip.**

LEAVES: Fleshy, **sheathing leaves cover lower part of stem.** Leaves quickly decrease in size upward.

RANGE: Seeps, wet meadows, moist forest edges. Middle to subalpine elevations. Wide distribution. **Usually abundant** in a favorable habitat.

NOTES: White rein-orchid is the most abundant of the many rein-orchids in Washington, and dozens of these white "candles" lend their fragrance to the surrounding glades. • **Green-flowered** rein-orchids are on p. 181.

Round-leaved rein-orchid • *Platanthera orbiculata*

FORM: 25–60 cm (10–23 1/2") tall. A stout, erect stem.

BLOOMS: June to August.

FLOWERS: 5–25 greenish-white to pale cream flowers spaced **alternately along top one-third of stem. Long, narrow tip petal; spur considerably longer.**

LEAVES: Easiest identification is by **2 large, oval leaves at stem base,** usually lying on ground.

RANGE: Widely distributed (but scarcer than white rein-orchid) across Washington in moist, mossy forests.

LADIES' TRESSES (*Spiranthes romanzoffiana*) superficially resembles a rein-orchid. It grows to 50 cm (19 1/2") tall and has **narrow, grass-like leaves.** The white, creamy or greenish-white flowers are **in several vertical rows, with a definite spiral pattern.** The flowers have a sweet perfume. Blooming in July to August, it is widespread in marshes, bogs and wet meadows at low to medium elevations.

Ladies' tresses

Columbia bladder pod • *Lesquerella douglasii*

FORM: 20–40 cm (8–15 1/2") tall. Many loosely arching, silvery-hairy stems.

BLOOMS: April through May.

FLOWERS: Typically "mustard" design of 4 "cross" petals. Yellow-orange flowers, **about 6 mm (1/4") across**, 1 above the other on stem.

FRUITS: Oval to round seeds, each with a fine projection.

LEAVES: Basal rosette of small, oval, long-stemmed leaves. Stem leaves alternate, smaller, very narrow. All leaves silvery-hairy

RANGE: Usually on dry sandy banks. Sagebrush and ponderosa pine ecosystems. East of Cascades. Okanogan County and southward. Columbia Gorge and plains east of The Dalles.

Rough wallflower • prairie rocket, western wallflower • *Erysimum asperum*

FORM: 15–60 cm (6–24") tall. 1 to several stems from root base.

BLOOMS: June to August.

FLOWERS: Showy, dome-shaped, golden flowerhead. 4 petals in "mustard" design.

FRUITS: Upright seed pods to 5 cm (2") long.

LEAVES: Grayish due to fine hairs (**a distinguishing feature**); alternate; narrow; rough to the touch.

RANGE: Widespread, but spotty range. Low to medium elevations. Locally abundant in dry, sandy areas. Cascades. Western Columbia Gorge.

NOTES: There are several wallflowers in Washington that have not been included in this book.

SAND-DWELLING WALLFLOWER (*E. arenicola*) is a close copy of rough wallflower, but sand-dwelling wallflower has **greenish, rather than gray, leaves** with **lemon-yellow flowers**. Its fruits (siliques) are flattened, rather than partially rounded. Blooming in July to August, it ranges up to the subalpine and higher in the Cascades and Olympics. It is found on Hurricane Ridge.

SMALL WALLFLOWER (*E. inconspicuum*) and rough wallflower are the most abundant wallflowers in Washington. The name "small" gives the best distinguishing clue to this species. On a plant, usually not branched, that is 15–45 cm (6–17 1/2") tall, **the pale yellow flowers** are just 1.3 cm (1/2") across—**half the size of other wallflowers**. The seed pods angle upward. It is found east of the Cascades in dry, open areas at lower elevations.

PALE WALLFLOWER (*E. occidentale*) is a bushy plant that grows to 35 cm (14") tall. The flowers are pale yellow. The leaves are gray-green. Blooming in April to May, it is found in sandy soils and sagebrush areas east of the Cascades.

Field mustard • rape • *Brassia campestris*

FORM: To 1.2 m (4') tall. A bushy, many branched plant.

BLOOMS: April to September. **Among the earliest flowers.**

FLOWERS: 12 or more **pale yellow** flowers in clusters at branch tips. 4 petals (mustard family).

LEAVES: Lower leaves are alternate, have **a clasping base** and are deeply lobed into irregular sections. Higher leaves have a clasping base and a regular, narrow leaf blade.

RANGE: Very common and with abundant bloom. Waste places, fields, roadsides. Lower elevations.

NOTES: This European import, or its close relative *B. nigra,* may be seen in solid blocks of yellow in cultivated fields. They are grown for canola oil. Turnip, rutabaga, broccoli and cauliflower are all close relatives.

Pinesap • *Hypopitys monotropa*

FORM: 10–30 cm (4–12") tall. Stout, fleshy, tawny to pinkish-white stems, with drooping tips, may be in a cluster. Entire plant **turns black** with age.

BLOOMS: May through July.

FLOWERS: 3–10 large, 4-petalled flowers hang from curving stem. Flowers range from dull yellow to pinkish.

LEAVES: Scale-like leaves cover the stem.

RANGE: Rich humus soil of coniferous forests. Low to medium elevations. Widespread across Washington.

NOTES: Pinesap is the **only plant of this color and design**. There are several other saprophytes in Washington: Indian pipe (p. 40) is **white**; candystick (p. 136) and pinedrops (p. 136) are **reddish**.

Yellow willowherb • *Epilobium luteum*

FORM: 15–60 cm (6–23 1/2") tall. Vary from upright to a sprawling, bushy clump.

BLOOMS: Early to late summer. Late August at Mt. Rainier.

FLOWERS: Single flowers to 2 cm (3/4") long, on slender stems. Large, wavy-edged petals **overlap**, so that **flower looks partly closed**. Look closely to see the floral design, which is typical of *Epilobium* species: **4 sepals**, **4 petals** and **8 stamens**.

LEAVES: A very leafy plant. Leaves opposite, finely toothed, to 7.5 cm (3") long.

RANGE: Moist meadows and streamsides. Middle to alpine elevations. Mt. Rainier. Olympics and southward through Cascades. West end of Columbia Gorge.

NOTES: The flowers sometimes appear **more white than yellow**. The name "willowherb" relates to the similarity of the leaves' shape to those of a willow.

Yellow evening-primrose • *Oenethera villosa*

FORM: To 1.2 m (4') tall. Very stout, usually unbranched stem. Coarse appearance.

BLOOMS: June to August.

FLOWERS: Satin-like, soft yellow flowers, about 2.5 cm (1") across. **Sepals are green and down-curving. Flower stem is swollen at base** (where ovary is enclosed). Flowers open in the evening—hence the common name—and also in early morning or on cloudy days.

LEAVES: Many leaves, to 20 cm (8") long.

RANGE: Rich, moist soils, ditches, meadows. Low to middle elevations. Mostly east of Cascades.

NOTES: Flowers are pollinated by several species of moths. This flower is the source of evening primrose-oil.

BUTTERCUPS • *Ranunculus* spp.

BUTTERCUPS ARE seemingly so easy to spot, but putting a name to them is something else: there are more than 24 species in Washington. They are found floating in ponds and in the mud of shorelines, wet and dry meadows, forest glades, sagebrush flats and edging the snow in the subalpine. Wherever they grow, these "little frogs" (a literal translation of *Ranunculus*) are a cherished part of the landscape.

Buttercups have **shiny, pale yellow to golden petals, with a scale at the base of each.** They have 5 greenish sepals, which feature in some identifications. The tiny conical seed heads that develop after the plant blooms are usually missed. They contain several dozen rounded seeds, **many with a tiny beak.** The shape of this beak is a key identifying feature in some species.

Meadows of western buttercups and common camas under Gary oaks

The buttercups included in this book were chosen based on relative abundance, and also on the presence of an understandable identifying feature.

Don't confuse buttercups with **cinquefoils** (pp. 82–83).

Sagebrush buttercup • *Ranunculus glaberrimus*

FORM: 5–15 cm (2–6") tall.

BLOOMS: April to May. May be the first spring bloom.

FLOWERS: Typical, bright, "varnished" yellow flowers. Each petal has a small scale (the nectary) at the base.

LEAVES: 2 different shapes: 1 broad and shallowly lobed, the other divided into 3 distinct fingers.

RANGE: Associated with sagebrush lowlands, but also into foothills with ponderosa pine and Douglas-fir.

NOTES: The shape of the leaves is the best identification feature.

Western buttercup • *Ranunculus occidentalis*

FORM: 30–75 cm (1–2 1/2') tall. Erect, branching, hairy stems.

BLOOMS: March to May.

FLOWERS: 1.3–2.5 cm (1/2–1") across. **Flowers are well separated** at the end of long stalks. Sometimes with 6 or 7 petals. The **5 sepals twist downward** on young flowers, but **drop off as flower ages.**

FRUITS: Seeds are packed in a **domed cluster.** The hooked beak (seen on some buttercups) is so minute here that it escapes notice.

LEAVES: A difficult feature, because many species appear almost the same. Long-stemmed, lower leaves are 3-parted into wedge-shaped sections that are coarsely lobed and toothed.

RANGE: Common. Very **abundant.** Grows with Garry oak in meadows, forest edges. Foothills west of Cascades.

NOTES: The reflexed sepals fall at the time of blooming, and this is the best identification feature.

Straight-beaked buttercup • *Ranunculus orthorhynchus*

FORM: To 60 cm (2') tall. Twice-branched stems.

BLOOMS: April to June.

FLOWERS: Pale yellow flowers are larger than most buttercups. **Petals are narrow—twice as long as broad—which creates a wide space between them.**

FRUITS: Seeds have a **long straight beak.**

LEAVES: Leaves are very hairy. Basal leaves have 3–7 leaflets.

RANGE: Moist areas, meadows, streamsides, lakeshores. Widespread (in 2 varieties) at lower elevations.

NOTES: Straight-beaked buttercup has distinctive flowers and seeds. It blooms at the same time as, and often with, **camas** (p. 166). Douglas recorded that this species was "not infrequent on the lower points of land near rivers in North West America."

Subalpine buttercup • *Ranunculus eschscholtzii*

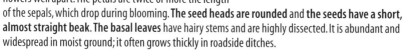

FORM: 5–15 cm (2–6") tall.

BLOOMS: May to July, as snow recedes.

FLOWERS: 1–3 large, golden yellow flowers on a stem top.

FRUITS: Seeds with a short, straight, or curved beak.

LEAVES: Lower leaves are long-stemmed and 3-lobed. Lobes are lobed again.

RANGE: Edges of snowbanks, streams, wet meadows. Subalpine. **High mountains of Washington**.

NOTES: The collar of leaves on the stem, and the subalpine habitat are distinguishing features.

MEADOW BUTTERCUP (*R. acris*) is an erect plant that grows to 90 cm (3') tall. It is freely branching, which spreads the flowers well apart. The petals are twice or more the length of the sepals, which drop during blooming. **The seed heads are rounded** and **the seeds have a short, almost straight beak**. **The basal leaves** have hairy stems and are highly dissected. It is abundant and widespread in moist ground; it often grows thickly in roadside ditches.

CREEPING BUTTERCUP (*R. repens*) is very much like meadow buttercup in form and habitat. It is **a creeping plant** that **roots at the nodes**. It forms **extensive masses** because of its runners. It blooms in late spring to summer. The flowers are showy. The sepals are hairy. The seeds usually have **a stout, curved beak**. It is an introduced species that is now widespread in ditches and meadows.

SMALL YELLOW WATER-BUTTERCUP (*R. gmelinii*) is a **small, yellow-flowered, floating buttercup** that is attached to a loose mat of floating stems. It is found in ponds, slow-flowing waters and creeping on to wet ground at lower elevations across Washington.

SHORE BUTTERCUP (*R. cymbalaria*) has 2 main identifying features: the **wet habitat** of lakeshores, muddy ponds and saline meadows, and **the distinct, conical seed mass** at the center of the flower in seed. It is found in Grant and Whitman counties.

Western yellow oxalis • *Oxalis suksdorfii*

FORM: To 15 cm (6") tall. Leaves and flowers periodically rise from a slender, non-rooted, trailing stem.

BLOOMS: Spring to summer.

FLOWERS: Single, yellow to pale pinkish flowers, 2 cm (3/4") across, rise on stems to just clear the leaves.

LEAVES: Clover-like leaves, but the 3 heart-shaped leaflets are broader. Leaves unfold, turn and close as they adjust to changes in sunlight.

RANGE: Moist, coastal forests of southern Washington west of the Cascades.

NOTES: The leaves contain oxalic acid, which gives them a sharp, bitter taste. Young, fresh leaves were eaten by some Native Americans, and the juice was used medicinally.

STONECROPS • *Sedum* spp.

THIS IS A group of low plants, perhaps 7–8 species in the state that, from a cursory glance, look much the same. Leaves are fleshy and succulent. However, getting each species down to a specific name is rather difficult. Dry, rocky soils and rocky exposures are common to all. Most have a wide state and elevation range. Another, spreading stonecrop, below, is unique on the basis of having most of its leaves opposite rather than alternate. The leaves of all stonecrops are edible and had various medicinal uses among Native Americans.

Spreading stonecrop • *Sedum divergens*

FORM: 5–15 cm (2–6″) tall. **Stout, fleshy stems**, some sterile, others with flower clusters.

BLOOMS: July.

FLOWERS: In stem-top clusters. 5 narrow petals. 10 stamens, slightly shorter than petals.

LEAVES: Important: The only stonecrop with **mostly opposite stem leaves**. Leaves are stubby, almost oval lengthwise and in cross-section. In exposed areas, **some leaves may be bright red. Basal leaves are mat-forming** (and diverging) since roots follow any crevice.

RANGE: Low to high elevations. Cascades. Olympics. Wenatchee Mountains.

Lance-leaved stonecrop • *Sedum lanceolatum*

FORM: 5–15 cm (2–6″) tall. Usually a cluster of stout, reddish stems, but **may lie flat on the ground**.

BLOOMS: May to July.

FLOWERS: Dense, flat-topped clusters of flowers. Narrow petals are longer than the stamens.

LEAVES: Alternate, lance-like stem leaves **may wither and die**, leaving a series of dry scales on a nearly naked stem. Often a basal cluster of round, stubby leaves.

RANGE: Widespread on dry soils, rocky places. Medium to subalpine elevations. Mt. Spokane.

NOTES: All stonecrops have edible leaves, a fact well-known to Native Americans. Spreading stonecrop was favored because of the succulent leaves. Medicinal values were attributed to leaves prepared in various ways.

WORM-LEAVED STONECROP (*S. stenopetalum*) has alternate stem leaves that look like a **series of sharp-pointed tufts. The largest leaf is boat-like**, with a keel on the lower side. It blooms in June to July. It is found east of the Cascades in Chelan County, on Mt. Spokane and on Steptoe Butte.

5-15 cm (2-6") HIGH

SPREADING

WORM-LEAVED

Broad-leaved stonecrop • *Sedum spathulifolium*

FORM: 5–15 cm (2–6") tall. Erect, fleshy, leafy stem. Forms extensive growth on rocky slopes.

BLOOMS: May to June.

FLOWERS: Bright yellow flowers in flat-topped clusters. **Pointed petals.**

LEAVES: Stem leaves well-spaced, **alternate, thick, oval. Basal leaves form attractive rosettes of sage-green**, often mixed with reds.

RANGE: Rocky bluffs, dry open slopes. West of Cascades. San Juan Islands and south. Columbia Gorge. Olympics.

NOTES: Broad-leaved stonecrop is a beautiful element of the spring landscape.

VIOLETS • *Viola* spp.

VIOLET FLOWERS are pansy-like and have 5 showy petals: 2 upper ones, 2 side ones and 1 larger lip petal. The lip and side petals may be streaked. There are 5 sepals and 5 stamens. There are perhaps a dozen yellow violets in Washington; only a few of the common ones are described here.

White violets are on p. 41; **purple** on p. 141; **blue** on p. 161.

Round-leaved violet • *Viola orbiculata*

FORM: 2.5–5 cm (1–2") tall. **Flowers just higher than leaves.** Note that **flower and leaf stems come out of the ground individually**, rather than branching from a main stem.

BLOOMS: June to August.

FLOWERS: Bright yellow. **3 lower petals with brown lines.**

LEAVES: Distinctive—almost perfectly round. Leaves may remain green over winter.

RANGE: Moist areas. Middle mountain elevations into the subalpine. Both sides of Cascades. Olympics. Mt. Rainier.

STREAM VIOLET (*V. glabella*) closely resembles round-leaved violet, but stream violet is taller—to 30 cm (12") tall. **The leaves are broad, long-stemmed and heart-shaped with a pointed tip.** There are **2 leaves high on an otherwise leafless stem.** Perhaps the **most common** violet, it is found in damp places, wet meadows and stream edges and is widespread at low to high elevations.

YELLOW SAGEBRUSH VIOLET (*V. vallicola*) grows in **sagebrush and ponderosa pine country.** It is only 5–10 cm (2–4") tall. It has several long-stemmed, egg-shaped leaves that may hide the flowers. **The upper 2 petals usually have brown backs; the lower petals have 3 dark lines.** It is found in Okanogan and Spokane counties and southward.

Yellow sagebrush violet

CINQUEFOILS • *Potentilla* spp.

THERE ARE about 24 cinquefoils in Washington, but only the most abundant and eye-catching are described here. Cinquefoils generally have small, **non-waxy,"buttercup"** flowers. The **petals lie flat** or are slightly dished. **Many cinquefoils have notched petals**, while buttercups never do. The calyx (holding the flower) has 10 parts: 5 bracts alternating with 5 green sepals that just show their tips. Although "cinquefoil" means "5 leaves," the name also applies to plants having from 3–7 leaves.

A **red-purple** cinquefoil is on p. 143.

Silverweed • *Potentilla anserina*

FORM: 15–40 cm (6–15 1/2") tall. Thin runners root at nodes, sending up a spray of leaves with many leaflets and usually shorter flower stems.

BLOOMS: May to September.

FLOWERS: Single, on leafless stems, about 2.5 cm (1") across and often mixed with the leaves.

LEAVES: Often create a thick, widespread, flattened growth. Long leaves carry a number of opposite, coarsely toothed leaflets of varying sizes. Leaflets **are bright silvery beneath**—the most visible identifying feature for this plant.

RANGE: Edges of marshes, mudflats, ponds. Lower elevations. Mostly east of Cascades.

NOTES: Silverweed and Pacific silverweed have fleshy roots, and they were important foods for Native Americans. The roots were dried or stored fresh. The bitter flavor was removed by steaming or cooking them.

PACIFIC SILVERWEED (*P. anserina* ssp. *pacifica*) differs from silverweed in that its **leaves are pale whitish-green beneath**. It is usually found in damp areas near the ocean.

Fan-leaved cinquefoil • *Potentilla flabellifolia*

FORM: 7.5–30 cm (3–12") tall. In **early growth, the clump of leaves presses close to the earth**; it gradually heightens as flowers appear. Usually a large leafy mass by summer.

BLOOMS: June to July.

FLOWERS: Looks like a robust buttercup, but notice the **notched petals** and **many yellow stamens**. Flower is 1.3–2 cm (1/2–3/4") across.

LEAVES: 3 broad leaflets, these crinkled and coarsely toothed.

RANGE: Moist meadows, tree borders of subalpine. Cascades. Olympics. Blue Mountains.

NOTES: Don't confuse this cinquefoil with **subalpine buttercup** (p.79). Fan-leaved cinquefoil is one of the **first flowers to bloom in subalpine meadows**. It often appears with western anemone and diverse-leaved cinquefoil. Douglas noted fan-leaved cinquefoil at the "summit of Mt. Rainier." It was obviously a lesser ridge; the summit is ice-clad all year.

DIVERSE-LEAVED CINQUEFOIL (*P. diversifolia*) has the same general form and habitat as fan-leaved cinquefoil, but diverse-leaved cinquefoil has larger, longer-stemmed leaves with 5–7 deeply toothed leaflets, all radiating from the same point. It is widespread in the subalpine.

Sticky cinquefoil • *Potentilla glandulosa*

FORM: 40–60 cm (15 1/2–23 1/2") tall. Sometimes taller. Erect, branching, finely hairy stem.

BLOOMS: May to August.

FLOWERS: Pale to deep yellow flowers, 1.3 cm (1/2") across, in fairly tight clusters at stem tips. Petals are nearly the same length as the massed stamens.

LEAVES: Stalked, basal leaves **usually have 7 coarsely toothed leaflets—3 opposite pairs and 1 at tip.** Stem leaves are much smaller and are in tight clusters.

RANGE: Meadows, open forests. Very widespread, mostly east of Cascades. Okanogan County south to Klickitat County. Western section of Columbia Gorge.

GRACEFUL CINQUEFOIL (*P. gracilis*) is much like sticky cinquefoil in form and color; the important difference is in the shape of the leaves. While sticky cinquefoil has opposite pairs of leaflets, the main leaf of graceful cinquefoil has 5 leaflets originating from the same point. The leaflets are coarsely toothed. Several varieties of graceful cinquefoil cover a wide range. It is found in the Columbia Gorge, on Steptoe Butte and in the Blue Mountains. Douglas collected it on the banks of the Columbia River. The seed he sent to England was soon producing plants.

SULPHUR CINQUEFOIL (*P. recta*) has distinctive, **pale sulphur yellow flowers** above dull green leaves. It grows to 70 cm (27 1/2") tall. It blooms in early summer. The leaves are divided into 7–9 finger-like, toothed segments. A weed in farm fields at times, it is found east of the Cascades.

Graceful cinquefoil

WHITE CINQUEFOIL (*P. arguta*) is grouped with other similar cinquefoils despite its color. It grows **to 1 m (40") tall. Its white flowers** rate it as the **only white cinquefoil** in Washington. The flowers can shade to weak yellow. It is found in meadows on lower mountain slopes east of the Cascades. It is also on the lower slopes Steptoe Butte, where the flower color is pure white.

Lemonweed • *Lithospernum ruderale*

FORM: Typically 30–60 cm (1–2') tall. A cluster of rough, hairy stems.

BLOOMS: May to July.

FLOWERS: Small, pale yellow, funnel-like flowers in small clusters almost hidden in stem-top leaves.

LEAVES: Thick growth of leaves on stems. Alternate, narrow, bunching together at flower cluster.

RANGE: Widespread at lower elevations in drier areas. Often with sagebrush and rabbit-brush, but will range higher.

Large-leaved avens • *Geum macrophyllum*

FORM: 30–90 cm (1–3′) tall. Stout, erect stem with flower cluster at top.

BLOOMS: April to July.

FLOWERS: Bright yellow "buttercups," but without varnished look and not bowl-shaped. 5 green sepals and 5 bractlets—resembles a cinquefoil. Flowers grow singly or in a small cluster at stem tips.

LEAVES: Large, coarse basal leaves to 30 cm (12″) long have a ragged **scattering of mismatched, lobed leaflets** and a **large terminal leaflet.**

RANGE: Widespread in moist, shady woodlands, stream edges. Not in sagebrush and ponderosa pine ecosystems.

NOTES: The large basal leaves are the best distinguishing feature of large-leaved avens.

Blazing-star • *Mentzelia laevicaulis*

FORM: To 90 cm (3′) tall. Usually much branched.

BLOOMS: Late spring into summer, **in bright sunshine!**

FLOWERS: May be 12 on a plant, unique in their design. 5 sharp-pointed petals have a shorter, thin bract between them. **Petals lie flat** and the bowl is enclosed in a **delicate mass of slender stamens.**

LEAVES: Basal leaves, to 10 cm (4″) long, are dull green, rough and coarsely toothed.

RANGE: Sand or gravelly banks. Lower elevations. East of Cascades.

NOTES: Douglas found blazing-star "on the gravelly islands and rocky shores of the Columbia, near the Great Falls." That area, a mile down river from Wishram, Celilo Falls, is now flooded.

Wall lettuce • *Lactuca muralis*

FORM: To 1.2 m (4′) tall. **Tall, weedy-looking plant** with branching stems.

BLOOMS: June to July.

FLOWERS: Very unusual! Looks like a tiny, 5-petalled flower about 6 mm (1/4″) across. **Each "petal" is actually a distinct flower** with a toothed margin and 1 stamen. Possibly 100 or more of these yellow gems are held on the wire-thin branches.

LEAVES: Each leaf is an unusual design with irregular indentations and lopsided lobes. Lower leaves are to 20 cm (8″) long, with clasping bases. Leaves get rapidly smaller higher up the stem.

RANGE: Gardens, open forests, roadsides. Widespread west of Cascades at lower elevations.

NOTES: Wall lettuce was introduced from Europe, where it apparently grew on walls. Its common name is a direct translation of the scientific name. It is in the same genus as garden lettuce.

Common St. John's-wort • *Hypericum perforatum*

FORM: 30–90 cm (1–3') tall. Stout, erect, branching stem. Plant dies back to a ragged head of brown husks visible all winter.

BLOOMS: June to September.

FLOWERS: Showy, bright yellow flowers to 2.5 cm (1") across. Important: Center is **a mass of protruding yellow stamens** that are held in clusters. Petals may be faintly black-dotted. Note mass of flowers and **top-heavy look** of plant—a distinctive feature visible from a passing car.

LEAVES: Opposite, to 2.5 cm (1") long with black-dotted margins.

RANGE: South of Tacoma, but most abundant east of the Cascades from low to high elevations. Ferry and Spokane counties. To summit of Mt. Spokane at 1763 m (5878').

NOTES: This is a European weed pest with poisoning properties for grazing animals. This plant often lines roadsides for miles, and it can be the most abundant and visible yellow flower during the summer months. The name "St. John's-wort" relates to St. John the Baptist's Day (June 24), when the plant was said to bloom. In Europe, it has been used medicinally since ancient times. It is achieving similar importance in the Pacific Northwest.

BOG ST. JOHN'S-WORT (*H. anagalloides*) has **yellow-orange flowers** above a creeping mat of leaves. The small, oval leaves are opposite. It is found in moist meadows and on pond edges from valleys to mid-mountain heights.

Great mullein • *Verbascum thapsus*

FORM: 60–150 cm (2–5') tall. **Sometimes to 2 m (7').** Very thick, rough, erect stalk that **dries and stands all winter.**

BLOOMS: July onward. Blooms progressively on extending flower tip.

FLOWERS: 5 small, yellow, distinct petals, about 6 mm (1/4") across. Flowers are mostly **near top of thick, rough flowerspike** that may branch into several contorted stems.

LEAVES: Large, olive-green, flannel-like leaves form a rosette flat on the ground for the first year; stalk develops second year.

RANGE: Widespread and expanding. Most abundant east of Cascades in ponderosa pine and sagebrush ecosystems. Prefers alkaline soils. Low elevations to about 1200 m (4000').

NOTES: The ancient Romans rolled the thick, woolly stalks in tallow for use as torches. They were also used by early miners in the West as "miner's candles." Great mullein supposedly attracts moths.

MOTH MULLEIN (*V. blattaria*) has **green leaves** that are coarsely toothed or lobed. The flowers have **orange stamens**. It is rather rare and is found in ponderosa pine areas in Chelan County.

Yellow bell • *Fritillaria pudica*

FORM: 5–15 cm (2–6") tall. A single erect stem from a white bulb 2.5 cm (1") below ground.

BLOOMS: April to May.

FLOWERS: Usually 1, but sometimes to 3, nodding, fragrant, **yellow-orange flower** to 2 cm (3/4") long. A real jewel that appears to be scarce one season then more abundant the next.

LEAVES: 2–3 narrow, grass-like leaves start well up the stem and remain green while the flower blooms.

RANGE: Sagebrush and ponderosa pine ecosystems. East of Cascades. Okanogan County south to Columbia Gorge. Kamiak Butte. Steptoe Butte. Blue Mountains.

NOTES: The small bulbs had considerable value to Native Americans, who ate them fresh, steamed or boiled. Tribes in the Okanogan dried them for storage. Now, the best use of this beautiful flower is to leave it in the ground. Douglas encountered this species near the Spokane River in 1826.

Yellow glacier lily • *Erythronium grandiflorum*

FORM: 15–35 cm (6–14") tall. Erect stem with 1–3 flowers.

BLOOMS: May to July.

FLOWERS: 1–3 flowers on a stem. Reflexed petals.

FRUITS: Long seed capsule forms and marks the plant's location until winter.

LEAVES: The 2, sometimes 3, **glossy green**, basal leaves are attractive in themselves.

RANGE: Common at low elevations, often mixing into sagebrush areas and extending well up on mountain slopes. Ellensburg. Chelan County. Leavenworth. Steptoe Butte. Blue Mountains.

NOTES: Vast meadows are sometimes covered in blooming yellow glacier lilies.

Yellow iris • *Iris pseudacorus*

FORM: 30–90 cm (1–3') tall. Stout stems from a muddy or watery base.

BLOOMS: May to July.

FLOWERS: Resembles a garden iris. Light streaking of purple on 3 largest petals.

LEAVES: Wiry, long, green blades.

RANGE: Wide and spotty range. Ponds, marshes. Lower elevations. Ellensburg. Yakima Canyon.

NOTES: Yellow iris is an introduced species. Douglas said that the braided leaf of the native iris "will hold the strongest bullock and is not thicker than the little finger."

Gold star • *Crocidium multicaule*

FORM: 7.5–15 cm (3–6") tall. Slim stems carrying a single flower. Usually massed on suitable places.

BLOOMS: March to April. **Multitude of blooms** quickly coming and quickly going.

FLOWERS: Approximately 12 petals, creating a flower 2 cm (3/4") across. Button center.

LEAVES: Basal rosette of small, oval leaves. Stem leaves are alternate, narrow and about 1.3 cm (1/2") long. There may be small hairy tufts in leaf axils.

RANGE: Meadows, plains, rocky places. Lower elevations. Whidbey and Orcas islands. Vicinity of Ellensburg, through central Washington. Along Columbia River. Blue Mountains.

Yellow waterlily • *Nuphar polysepalum*

FORM: Usually assumed to be floating on water, but in shady, brushy shorelines, may climb 90 cm (3') into supporting vegetation. Large, scaly roots are anchored in the mud.

BLOOMS: May to August.

FLOWERS: A yellow cup, to 10 cm (4") across, of many, large, waxy sepals. **Small, greenish petals are mostly hidden by a circle of thick purple stamens.**

LEAVES: Long leaf stems reach up from root to large, floating leaves.

RANGE: Ponds, lakes. Low to middle elevations. Generally west of Cascades, but likely east of Cascades bordering foothills.

NOTES: The seeds were an important food source for Native Americans.

POND LILY (*N. variegatum*) is almost identical to yellow waterlily, but pond lily's stamens are yellow rather than purple. The leaves lie flat and have crinkled edges. It is generally found east of the Cascades, but its borders with yellow waterlily have not been determined.

Many-spined prickly-pear cactus • *Opuntia polyacantha*

FORM: 10–25 cm (4–10") tall. Spiny, mat-like.

BLOOMS: May to July.

FLOWERS: Beautiful **tissue-like flower,** ranges from yellow to pink and orange shades.

LEAVES: Unusual! Leaves have modified into fearsome spines, to 5 cm (2") long, and so conserve water. The thick, fleshy, pod-like stems, to 10 cm (4") long, do the work of leaves and also store water.

RANGE: Sagebrush ecosystem. Along Snake River from Clarkston westward to Columbia River. Abundant along Washington Highway 209 following Snake River southward and into tributary coulees and valleys.

Great quantities of a Kind of prickly pares much worse than any I have seen of a tapering form and attach themselves by bunches....Passed 20 Lodges of Indians drying fish & Prickly pares.
—Clark, October 16, 1805

NOTES: Native Americans ate the stems and fruit, after removing the spines. Remember that most of the travelers were wearing moccasins in those days, not sturdy leather boots.

Brittle prickly-pear cactus • *Opuntia fragilis*

FORM: 2.5–7.5 cm (1–3") tall. A spiny mat. May be inconspicuous or a large, spreading growth.

BLOOMS: June to July.

FLOWERS: Many **yellow, tissuey blossoms** with **red-stalked stamens.** At their best, flowers almost cover this spiny mat.

LEAVES: Reduced to spines. Fleshy, pod-like plant stems carry out function of leaves and store water. Spines rise from a common base—an areole.

RANGE: Random on dry, exposed slopes of San Juan Islands and easterly slopes of Puget Sound. Sporadic in drylands of sagebrush and ponderosa pine regions. Decreases in abundance southward from British Columbia border. Omak, Banks Lake.

NOTES: The red-stalked stamens are a quick feature to distinguish this species from many-spined prickly-pear cactus (above). The "brittle" part of the common name refers to the fact that the **upper stem**

segments break apart easily; there are usually a number of loose ones lying beside the plant. The spines are slightly barbed, which accounts for the strong pull needed to get them out of your shoes or skin.

Yellow monkey-flower • *Mimulus guttatus*

FORM: 5–60 cm (2–23 1/2") tall. Weakly erect.

BLOOMS: May to August.

FLOWERS: Large, yellow, tubular, "snapdragon" flowers to 2 cm (3/4") long. Lower broad petal lobed or 2-tipped, with **small, brown or crimson dots in a bearded throat**.

LEAVES: Short-stalked, lower leaves are in pairs, are almost round and have coarse teeth. Upper leaves are smaller and clasp stem.

RANGE: Widespread on **wet or seepage areas**. Common on wet roadside rocks.

CHICKWEED MONKEY-FLOWER (*M. alsinoides*) grows to 20 cm (8") tall. It blooms in March to May. **The lower lip has 1–2 purplish dots.** It is found west of the Cascades.

MUSK-FLOWER (*M. moschatus*) has a typical *Mimulus* flower that is to 2.5 cm (1") long. It has dark lines or spots and a hairy throat. There is sometimes a musky odor. The weak stems are **sticky, hairy and perhaps creeping**. The leaves are opposite and coarse. It grows in moist areas, ditches and **seepage areas**. It is widespread at low to medium elevations. Douglas found it on the "margins of springs [along the] River Columbia."

MOUNTAIN MONKEY-FLOWER (*M. tilingii*), also called "alpine monkey-flower," is a typical monkey-flower that grows in the **moist ground of the subalpine**. It is found in the Cascades, on Mt. Rainier and in the Olympics.

Common touch-me-not • jewelweed • *Impatiens noli-tangere*

FORM: To 1.2 m (4') tall. Stout stems are swollen at branching points.

BLOOMS: June to August.

FLOWERS: Beautiful! Flower is a complicated formation of 3 sepals, of which 1 forms a curled spur, and 4 petals.

FRUITS: *Impatiens* part of the scientific name refers to the way an "impatient" seed capsule explodes at a touch or when ripe.

LEAVES: Alternate, long-stemmed, coarsely toothed.

RANGE: Moist bottomlands. Very spotty distribution. Moist areas beside ponds, marshes, streambanks. Gray's Harbor and Spokane counties.

NOTES: This species is almost too scarce to include in this book, but it is too beautiful to leave out.

POLICEMAN'S HELMET (*I. glandulifera*) is an Asian introduction that usually **grows rankly in wet ditches and moist slopes**. It is 90–120 cm (3–4') tall and displays many "trumpet" flowers in white, pink and purple shades. Like common touch-me-not, it also has the **sharply twisted spur**. It is found west of the Cascades in Skagit, Mason and Pacific counties.

Policeman's helmet

Dalmation toadflax • *Linaria genistifolia*

FORM: To 90 cm (3′) tall. Stout, branching stem is erect or arching.

BLOOMS: July to August.

FLOWERS: Bright yellow, tubular flowers with a touch of orange in the throat. Sharp spur hangs from base of flower. Flowers form in loose rows on the topmost stems.

LEAVES: Important: Size and shape quickly separates this plant from butter-and-eggs (below). **Leaves in a symmetrical, alternate pattern.** Leaves are olive-green, clasping and about 4 cm (1 1/2″) long on the lower stem.

RANGE: Dry plains and hillsides. Conspicuous plant mostly east of Cascades and spreading rapidly. Stevens County.

NOTES: Dalmation toadflax is a Mediterranean import that is now a serious weed pest in some grazing areas. It spreads by creeping roots and seeds. Whole hillsides of it turn brilliant yellow and then an unattractive, stark brown. The "toad" part of the common name may reflect the way the squeezed blossoms open like a toad's mouth.

Butter-and-eggs • Common toadflax • *Linaria vulgaris*

FORM: 25–80 cm (10–31 1/2″) tall. Stout, erect, unbranched stalk, but may be several from a basal clump.

BLOOMS: Late spring into summer.

FLOWERS: Unmistakable! Yellow "snapdragon" flower with orange nose (butter-and-eggs) and long, straight spur. Flowers cluster densely along top section of stalk.

LEAVES: Alternate, narrow leaves, to 10 cm (4″) long, are quite different from symmetrically placed, much wider leaves of Dalmation toadflax.

RANGE: Spotty occurrence in fields, roadsides, foothill slopes of lower elevations. More common east of Cascades.

NOTES: This species has been a weed plant in eastern states since as far back as 1758.

Bird's-foot trefoil • *Lotus corniculatus*

FORM: 15–30 cm (6–12") tall. **Thin, wiry stems** that creep and climb to form a thicket or extensive patch along a roadside.

BLOOMS: July to September.

FLOWERS: Typical "pea" flowers. Yellow, sometimes with a pink tinge, 8–16 mm (1/3–2/3") long. **In compact clusters of up to 12.**

LEAVES: Important: **2 large, leaf-like stipules at the base of each stem.** Stipules are about same size as 1 of the 3 leaflets which form the stem leaves.

RANGE: Widespread. Favors moist places. Mostly west of Cascades. Not a native plant. Other trefoils in Washington have leaf characteristic mentioned above.

NOTES: Bird's-foot trefoil is an introduced species. The leaf-like stipules separate all Washington's trefoils from **clovers** (p. 128), **vetches** (pp. 151–152) and **peavines** (pp. 127, 151), which all have small, narrow stipules.

YELLOW CLOVER (*Trifolium aureum*), also called "hop clover," is a bushy plant that grows to 90 cm (3') tall. It blooms in June to August. The flower clusters form a **dense, elongated cone of**

Yellow clover

30 or more tiny, pea-like flowers. The leaflets are in 3s, with **2 sharp-pointed stipules close to the stem.** It is sporadic at low elevations. It is found in waste places and roadsides.

YELLOW SWEET-CLOVER (*Melilotus officinalis*) has yellow flowers, but it closely matches **white sweet-clover** (p. 57) in form and range.

Sulphur lupine • *Lupinus sulphureus*

FORM: To 75 cm (2 1/4') tall. Erect, finely hairy stems.

BLOOMS: April to June.

FLOWERS: Pale yellow, sometimes white, flowers less than 1.3 cm (1/2") long and irregularly arranged on flower stems.

LEAVES: Mostly basal, **silvery-gray,** very long-stemmed leaves. 9 very narrow, sometimes hairy leaflets.

RANGE: Widespread at lower elevations east of Cascades. Spokane. Benton and Klickitat Counties.

NOTES: This species is the only yellow-flowering lupine in Washington. Douglas recorded it in the "Blue Mountains of Northwest America."

MOUNTAIN FALSE LUPINE (*Thermopsis montana*), also called "mountain golden bean," has a showy head of **large "lupine" flowers,** about 2.5 cm (1") long, on an erect stem to 60 cm (2') tall. The leaves are divided into **3 large, oval leaflets** with a pair of **wing-like stipules at the leaf juncture.** It is sporadic in distribution, mostly east of the Cascades. It grows in ponderosa pine and adjacent mountain forest ecosystems. It is found at 900 m (2950') in the Blue Mountains.

Mountain false lupine

Bearded owl-clover • *Orthocarpus barbatus*

FORM: To 35 cm (14") tall. A number of stems from a common base.
BLOOMS: April to May.
FLOWERS: Very small, yellow flowers almost completely hidden by **large, lime-green bracts** in a dense, terminal tuft.
LEAVES: Many stem leaves, **each divided into 3–5 thin "fingers."**
RANGE: Sagebrush areas. Central Washington. Okanogan, Chelan, Grand Coulee, Clark counties.
NOTES: Bearded owl-clover is a leafy, lime-green plant that grows with sagebrush. There are several other white or yellowish owl-clovers in Washington. Owl-clovers are very similar to paintbrushes (below). YELLOW OWL-CLOVER (*O. luteus*) grows to 20 cm (8") tall. The leaves are alternate and wispy. The small, yellow, tubular flowers, 8 mm (1/4") long, are hidden behind 3-lobed, green bracts. It blooms in July to August. It is found on open ground, low meadows and adjoining slopes east of the Cascades.

Thompson's paintbrush • *Castilleja thompsonii*

FORM: 20–40 cm (8–16") tall. Erect, leafy, **yellow-green overall.**
BLOOMS: May to July.
FLOWERS: Small, yellow flowers are almost invisible behind broad, hairy bracts.
LEAVES: Important: **A tangle of narrow, twisting leaves. Lower leaves are single. Upper leaves are 3–5 lobed.**
RANGE: Sagebrush areas east of Cascades.
NOTES: Paintbrushes are much like owl-clovers (above), but paintbrushes are usually taller. In both plants, the tiny flowers are divided into an upper lip that narrows to a beak and a lower lip that is inflated and lobed. In paintbrushes, the upper lip is much longer; in owl-clovers, the upper and lower lips are equal in length.

GOLDEN PAINTBRUSH (*C. levisecta*) has erect, unbranched stems that are bent at the base. The yellow flowers are mostly hidden. The leaf design is important: the leaves are **alternate and almost rectangular, but the tip carries 1–3 short lobes**. It is found sporadically in open areas at low elevations west of Cascades.

Yellow sand-verbena • *Abronia latifolia*

FORM: A low plant with creeping stems from a central base.
BLOOMS: May to October.
FLOWERS: Bright yellow, 6-lobed flowers packed into a showy, rounded head.
LEAVES: Long-stalked, opposite, **thick**, **fleshy**, mostly round leaves. Leaves are sticky, so that grains of sand hold to them.
RANGE: Sand dunes and coastal beaches.

Bracted lousewort • *Pedicularis bracteosa*

FORM: 40–60 cm (15 1/2–23 1/2") tall. Erect, unbranched stems.

BLOOMS: July to August, **with other subalpine flowers.**

FLOWERS: Yellow, perhaps pinkish-tinged, small flowers with a hood. **May have sharp beak. Leaf-like bract at base of each flower.** The flower top is a series of little quaint "faces" peeping over each other.

LEAVES: Fern-like leaves, mostly on flowering stems, divided into **rows of saw-edged leaflets.**

RANGE: Subalpine flower meadows. Olympics. Mt. Rainier.

NOTES: There are **pink-flowered** louseworts on p. 131. "Lousewort" is a very old name that comes from the belief that grazing cattle picked up lice from a related European species.

COIL-BEAKED LOUSEWORT (*P. contorta*), also called "contorted lousewort," has soft yellow flowers, to 1.3 cm (1/2") long, with a **twisted beak** (resembling a pig's tail). The leaves are cut to the midrib between the leaflets. Its range is the same as that of bracted lousewort.

Common fiddleneck • *Amsinckia intermedia*

FORM: 20–80 cm (8–32") tall. Erect, sometimes branching.

BLOOMS: April to May, with other spring flowers.

FLOWERS: Small, **5-lobed, yellow flowers ride outside curve** of fiddleneck.

LEAVES: Leaves and stems covered with **bristly hairs.** Leaves alternate, slender, to 15 cm (6") long.

RANGE: Poor, dry soils. Mostly east of Cascades. Eastern section of Columbia Gorge and eastward.

NOTES: Some species of fiddleneck are only a few inches tall.

SMALL-FLOWERED FIDDLENECK (*A. menziesii*) is a smaller copy of common fiddleneck. It has small, pale yellow flowers and is found across Washington at low elevations.

Skunk cabbage • *Lysichiton americanum*

FORM: To 75 cm (2 1/2') tall. Large leaves tend to flatten.

BLOOMS: March to April. **First spring flower to show.**

FLOWERS: Small, greenish flowers on a thick, fleshy, club-shaped flower stem (spadix). Large yellow bract that partly sheaths flowers is what people notice.

LEAVES: Perhaps the largest leaves of any native plant—some to 1.4 m (4 1/2') long and 60 cm (2') wide.

RANGE: Wet ground. Most common west of Cascades, but in similar habitats inland.

NOTES: Native Americans used the leaves to line steam-cooking pits. Black bears may eat all or part of this plant.

Pacific sanicle • *Sanicula crassicaulis*

FORM: To 90 cm (3') tall. Several erect, stout, coarse stalks.

BLOOMS: May to July.

FLOWERS: Yellow flowers, **may be maroon-purple on some plants**, in uneven cluster of tightly packed flowerheads. **5 petals, almost too small to see.**

LEAVES: Long-stemmed, crinkled, **hairy**, **maple-like** leaves, as wide as long.

RANGE: Moist, shady places, often close to ocean. West of Cascades. Extends eastward through Columbia Gorge to Klickitat County.

NOTES: Pacific sanicle blooms with **camas** (p. 166), **sea blush** (p. 130) and **monkey-flowers** (pp. 89, 126).

Common tansy • *Tanacetum vulgare*

FORM: 60–90 cm (2–3') tall. Stout, erect, often massed stems.

BLOOMS: July to mid-September. **Late bloomer.**

FLOWERS: Flat-topped mass of small, flattish flowers. Each flower is 6 mm (1/4") across.

LEAVES: Dark green, "**carroty**," alternate leaves climb stem to top. Distinct, aromatic odor when crushed.

RANGE: Roadsides. Low elevations. Not in arid regions.

NOTES: Common tansy is an escape from Europe that is now spreading rapidly. Don't confuse it with **tansy butterweed** (p.108).
• Native Americans used it to make a yellow dye. In Britain it once had a reputation as an insecticide.

Canada goldenrod • meadow goldenrod • *Solidago canadensis*

FORM: Important: **90–120 cm (3–4') tall**. Stout, leafy stalk.

BLOOMS: July and August.

FLOWERS: Wide, diamond-shaped mass of small, yellow flowers.

LEAVES: Withering near base, but numerous above. Stemless, narrow leaves with a few teeth. Lightly 3-veined.

RANGE: Widespread in better soils. Lowlands, foothills.

NOTES: Goldenrod flowers were once a source of permanent dye, which was extracted by boiling. Despite their reputation, goldenrods don't produce hay fever.

SPIKE-LIKE GOLDENROD (*S. spathulata*) grows to 40 cm (15 1/2") tall. It usually has a single, erect stem with small, yellow flowers in a narrow spike on the top one-third. It often blooms with Canada goldenrod during August. It is widespread, except in arid areas.

DESERT-PARSLEYS • LOMATIUMS, BISCUITROOTS • *Lomatium* spp.

THE DESERT-PARSLEYS are a group of plants that can cause bewilderment and frustration to the amateur naturalist and professional botanist alike: 2 plants of the same species can have distinctly different flower colors, and the leaves are often so dissected that they can't be described by yourself or understood from technical references. The size and shape of the root may be diagnostic, and likewise the seeds may give a clue, but by the time the plant has gone to seed it has lost its attraction.

Some features, however, do allow a fair description. All desert-parsleys belong to the family Umbelliferae, as shown by the umbrella-like arrangement of the flowerhead. The small flower clusters at the end of each "umbrella" spoke often display this arrangement also. The individual flowers are small, and they have 5 petals, 5 stamens and no sepals. Desert-parsleys produce dry, 2-seeded fruits. Many species have divided, carrot-like leaves that resemble fern fronds. The leaf stems are swollen at the base and sheath the stem.

All parts of desert-parsleys are considered edible—roots, stems and seeds—but certain species were favored by Native American tribes. Many times in their journals, Lewis and Clark noted that desert-parsley roots were the only food available.

The **yellow**-flowered desert-parsleys are described on the following pages. There are also many desert-parsleys with **white** flowers (p. 66), and 1 with **purple** flowers (p. 154).

Spring gold • fine-leaved desert-parsley • *Lomatium utriculatum*

FORM: 7.5–30 cm (3–12") **tall.** A number of stems and leaves.

BLOOMS: Mid-March to mid-June. **Among the earliest!**

FLOWERS: Tiny, bright yellow flowers in a compact head that is part of overall, larger umbel.

LEAVES: Very **finely dissected (carroty)**. Leaves grow high on the stem.

RANGE: Mossy and rocky places at lower elevations. West of Cascades.

Martindale's desert-parsley • *Lomatium martindalei*

FORM: 5–25 cm (2–10") tall.

BLOOMS: April to August. Common in June.

FLOWERS: Yellow to whitish flowers in compact clusters on **umbel arms of varying length**.

LEAVES: Dull green, basal leaves are **so dissected that they look like lace**.

RANGE: Dry, open slopes, rocky places. Common in subalpine of Olympics. At lower elevations southward. West of Cascades.

NOTES: This species is often the first flower to bloom at high elevations.

cous (*L. cous*) grows to 15 cm (6") tall and has dissected leaves. The **ultimate leaf segments are rounded**. This fact and its occurrence in **southeastern Washington** are the best identifying features. The large, stout root, about 5 cm (2") long, was an important food and trade item among Native Americans.

> The soil is extremely fertile....and produces great quantities of the quamish [camas] and cows [cous] a root of which the natives are extremely fond.
> —Lewis, May 4, 1806
> ...a white meley root which is very fine in soup after being dried and pounded.
> —Clark, May 1806

Fern-leaved desert-parsley • *Lomatium dissectum*

FORM: To 1.2 m (4′) tall. **A very robust plant in full bloom.** Takes on rounded form from mass of leaves.

BLOOMS: April to May. Early in south, later in north.

FLOWERS: Small flowers in tight clusters on stems of unequal lengths, but forming a more or less flat-topped head to 15 cm (6″) across. Stout flower stem may rise 60 cm (2′) above foliage.

FRUITS: Masses of seeds, distinguished by narrow wings.

LEAVES: Basal leaves are large and finely dissected (i.e., *dissectum*). Olive-green in color.

RANGE: Exposed soils, rocky areas. Common roadside plant east of Cascades. Vantage, Yakima Canyon, Columbia Gorge.

NOTES: This species may have dark purple flowers with white anthers. The large woody taproot, young shoots and seeds were food items for Native Americans.

Narrow-leaved desert-parsley • nine-leaf biscuitroot • *Lomatium triternatum*

FORM: To 60 cm (2′), but most plants half that height.

BLOOMS: April to May.

FLOWERS: Typical *Lomatium* flowerheads provide dominant landscape color in early spring.

LEAVES: Important: Long, very thin, 9-segment leaves.

RANGE: Widespread in sagebrush-ponderosa pine zones. Columbia River benches, foothills.

NOTES: This species blooms with **sagebrush buttercups** (p. 78), **shootingstars** (pp. 116–117), **yellow bells** (p. 86) and **woodland stars** (p. 39).

BARESTEM DESERT-PARSLEY (*L. nudicaulis*), also called "Indian consumption plant," grows to 60 cm (2′) tall. It differs from many desert-parsleys in **not having** "**carroty**" **leaves**; instead it has **bluish-green** leaves that are **oval to somewhat narrower in shape**. Each flower cluster is on a stem of a different length. As common name indicates, the **flowering stem is leafless**, but so are most desert-parsley. There is sometimes a swollen hub at the main umbel juncture. This species is found on dry, rocky slopes on the San Juan Islands, but it is most abundant east of the Cascades (Klickitat County) in sagebrush and ponderosa pine ecosystems and higher into the foothills. It was a widely used food plant by Native Americans. A plant that looks like a dwarf variation of barestem desert-parsley is abundant in places on dry rocky slopes above 1200 m (3950′). It blooms with the earliest of flowers, in March to May. It is found at Harts Pass in the Cascades and in the Blue Mountains.

Gray's desert-parsley • *Lomatium grayi*

FORM: To 40 cm (15 1/2") tall. A rounded, thick, bushy plant. Old stems often create matting at base.

BLOOMS: April to May.

FLOWERS: Bright yellow flowers in typical *Lomatium* umbel.

LEAVES: Important: Leaves are so finely divided, and smallest segments are folded at edges, that **leaves seem unusually thick. Unpleasant pungent odor** when crushed.

RANGE: Open, dry hillsides. East of Cascades, except westward in Columbia Gorge. Rowena Lookout, Whitman and Garfield counties. Steptoe and Kamiak buttes and northward.

NOTES: This species is often a very showy and abundant plant on open, dry hillsides, where it may be the only yellow flower.

BUCKWHEATS • *Eriogonum* spp.

MANY BUCKWHEATS have a short, woody stem that could class them as a shrub. The stem is invariably hidden, however, and what is noticed is a colorful mass of flowers above a low thicket of leaves. There are a number of buckwheats that aren't in this book.

The sagebrush ecosystem can't outdo these plants in sheer color and abundance. At certain times, dry benchlands and rocky slopes are a profusion of bloom as far as you can see. Well-adapted to harsh conditions, buckwheats have deep taproots, and their leaves, either through size, coloring or covering, are designed to conserve moisture. The tiny flowers have very similar sepals and petals, 3 of each, and 9 stamens. The time of blooming could be an important clue to identification.

A problem in attempting color groupings is that a species may have white, cream, yellowish, pink or even reddish flowers. This color variation likely reflects such factors as soil composition, exposure and age. Be sure to check likely alternatives.

Buckwheats with **whitish** flowers are on pp. 64–65; **pinkish** on p. 132.

Douglas buckwheat • *Eriogonum douglasii*

FORM: 5–10 cm (2–4") tall. Compact, ground-hugging plant.

BLOOMS: Late April to May.

FLOWERS: Lemon-yellow, or possibly creamy, flowers in compact head to 1.3 cm (1/2") across. A mass of bloom about 5 cm (2") above leaves.

LEAVES: Important: **Whorl of leaves above center of stem. Small, paddle-like, tufted basal leaves on short stem.**

RANGE: Sagebrush-ponderosa pine regions. South-central Washington and southward. Brewster, Yakima Canyon, Vantage, east Columbia Gorge.

NOTES: This species is named in honor of David Douglas. It may be confused with **thyme-leaved buckwheat** (p. 132).

Heart-leaved buckwheat • *Eriogonum compositum*

FORM: 25–40 cm (10–15 1/2") tall. Stout, erect flower stems.

BLOOMS: May to July.

FLOWERS: Cream to pale yellow to sulfur flowers in cluster to 10 cm (4") wide.

LEAVES: Important: **Heart-shaped or triangular leaves are mealy green above, white-woolly below.** Stems to twice the blade length.

RANGE: Rocky areas, slides, cliffs. Mostly east of Cascades.

NOTES: In the Columbia Gorge west of The Dalles, heart-leaved buckwheat is **white**-flowered and resembles yarrow. Eastward it is **yellow**. It is a dominant plant in the spring landscape. Douglas collected this plant 150 years ago along the Columbia River.

SULPHUR BUCKWHEAT (*E. umbellatum*) grows to 10–25 cm (4–10") tall. The flowers may be **pale yellow to cream**, perhaps with a rosy tinge. There is a whorl of small leaves at the umbel juncture. It ranges mostly east of the Cascades, from arid landscapes to mountain heights.

ROUND-HEADED BUCKWHEAT (*E. sphaerocephalum*) grows to 40 cm (15 1/2") tall. It is tough and twiggy and has a round-headed arc of **mustard yellow** blooms **above a dull green leaf mass.** It blooms in May to July—it is often **the last yellow color on a parched sidehill.** Note the whorl of small leaves just below the flowers. It grows in rocky soils on dry banks in the sagebrush ecosystem and up into the ponderosa pine. It is found in south Chelan County, along the Vantage Highway to Ellensburg and in dry lands south of Vantage.

Sulpher buckwheat

Round-headed buckwheat

Hairy cat's-ear • *Hypochaeris radicata*

FORM: 15–40 cm (6–15 1/2") tall. **Wiry, dark green stems**, more or less erect, often branched.

BLOOMS: Abundantly in June, continuing to October.

FLOWERS: A single, yellow "dandelion" **flower** to 4 cm (1 1/2") across. Main stem may carry several flower stems. **Flowers regardless of sun or shade**.

LEAVES: Rough basal rosette of hairy, scalloped leaves.

RANGE: Low elevations west of Cascades.

NOTES: This species may be the **most common flower on roadsides, field borders and weedy lawns**.

SMOOTH CAT'S-EAR (*H. glabra*), which is smaller than hairy cat's-ear, grows to 30 cm (12") tall. **Its flowers only open in full sunlight**. Its leaves are not hairy. It is abundant on coastal roadsides.

AGOSERISES • *Agoseris* spp.

THERE ARE 7 species in Washington: 6 have yellow flowers, much like dandelions, and 1 has **orange** flowers (p. 113). The flowers tend to have a **ragged look**, and there are **so few ray flowers you could count them**. The leaves are mostly basal, they are very narrow, and, with the exception of pale agoseris, they have irregular teeth.

Large-flowered agoseris • *Agoseris grandiflora*

FORM: 15–45 cm (6–17 1/2") tall. A stout, erect stem with 1 flower. Stems and bracts woolly on young plants.

BLOOMS: June to September.

FLOWERS: A single, bright yellow flower about 4 cm (1 1/2") across. **Flower may age to pinkish**.

LEAVES: Narrow leaves, 10–25 cm (4–10") long, with several projecting lobes on the sides.

RANGE: Widespread across Washington, from bottomlands to slopes of the Cascades. Harts Pass. Subalpine in Olympics.

Pale agoseris • short-beaked agoseris • *Agoseris glauca*

FORM: To 60 cm (2') tall.

BLOOMS: April to July.

FLOWERS: Single, showy, **pale yellow** flower on a stout stem.

LEAVES: Long, narrow leaves, without any form of teeth—the only toothless agoseris.

RANGE: Valleys to alpine tundra. Olympics.

SPEAR-LEAVED AGOSERIS (*A. retrorsa*) grows to 40 cm (15 1/2") tall. Its stem branches several times. **The leaves are very unusual**: they are to 20 cm (8") long, are very narrow, and have **recurved teeth** to 1.3 cm (1/2") long. It is found in open Douglas-fir to ponderosa pine forests, in Okanogan and Chelan counties.

Silvercrown • cut-leaf luina • *Cacaliopsis nardosmia* • *Luina nardosmia*

FORM: To 1.2 m (4') tall. Stout, erect stem. Plants quickly wither and disappear by mid-July.

BLOOMS: May to July.

FLOWERS: A rather **bristly, bright yellow** flower about 1.3 cm (1/2") across. Held into a narrow head by 1 row of bracts. Flowers in a loose arrangement at stem top.

FRUITS: Loose cluster of "dandelion" seed heads.

LEAVES: Important: Long-stemmed basal leaves, looking much like **a dissected maple leaf, are to 25 cm (10") wide. Palmately veined.** These large leaves appear from mid-April to mid-May.

RANGE: Open Douglas-fir-ponderosa pine forests. East of Cascades. Okanogan, Chelan and Kittitas counties. Cle Elum. Satus Pass, Highway 97.

NOTES: The flowers of this species closely resembles those of ***Senecio* spp.** (pp.106–108), but **no** *Senecio*s **have large, palmate leaves.**

Slender luina • *Luina stricta*

FORM: To 90 cm (3') tall. A stout, erect, leafy stem.

BLOOMS: August.

FLOWERS: A long spike packed with **upward-pointing, yellow flowers**.

LEAVES: Long-stemmed basal leaves widen into narrow tongue-shaped leaves 30 cm (12") long. Higher leaves become progressively smaller.

RANGE: Moist subalpine areas on Mt. Rainier below Paradise Visitor Center. Sporadic southward in similar habitats.

NOTES: This species has limited range.

Yellow salsify • oyster plant • *Tragopogon dubius*

FORM: 30–60 cm (1–2') tall. Stout, usually branched stem.

BLOOMS: May to August.

FLOWERS: Pale yellow flowers **to 7.5 cm (3") across.**

FRUITS: Large "dandelion" seed heads in July.

LEAVES: Long, grass-like, alternate leaves.

RANGE: Common along roadsides, waste places. Lower elevations. Found across Washington, but more common east of Cascades.

NOTES: There is a salsify with **purple** flowers on p.146.

HAWKWEEDS • *Hieracium* spp.

HAWKWEEDS ARE easily confused with **hawksbeards** (below), and possibly with **hairy cat's-ear** (p. 99). All these plants supposedly have a milky juice to some degree when a stem is broken, and all produce a fluffy seed head. The seed bristles will be brown in a hawkweed and white in a hawksbeard. You can also check if it's a hawkweed by pulling it up: a hawkweed should come up easily, with a short, shallow root; a hawksbeard will have a stout taproot.

Only 2 hawkweeds are described here; there are several others that differ in the amount of hairiness and the shape of the basal leaves.

Western hawkweed • hairy hawkweed
• *Hieracium scouleri var. albertinum*

FORM: 30–90 cm (1–3') tall. Stout, erect, **silvery hairy** stem, branching near top.

BLOOMS: Late May to September.

FLOWERS: Before flowers show, head is **a white, soft, lumpy ball of buds.** Flowers, about 1 cm (3/8") across, are in a loose cluster. Each tiny ray flower has 5 minute teeth.

LEAVES: Important: Leaves, to 15 cm (6") long, are **very silvery hairy.**

RANGE: Open, dry slopes. Low to medium elevations. East of Cascades. Common in Palouse County, such as on Steptoe Butte.

HOUND'S TONGUE HAWKWEED (*H. cynoglossoides*) is a rather common plant that grows to about 75 cm (2.5') tall. Its smallish flowers—1.3 cm (1/2") across—are held in a loose cluster. The flower cluster and the **thin, narrow bracts covered with black hairs** are good clues to identification. The name "hound's tongue" comes from the tongue-like shape of the long, slender leaves. The leaves and stems are finely hairy. It is found in the valleys and foothills of eastern Washington.

Smooth hawksbeard • *Crepis capillaris*

FORM: 25–60 cm (10–24") tall. More or less erect, **much branched stem from taproot. Thin, milky juice from stem when broken.**

BLOOMS: May to September.

FLOWERS: Small "dandelion" flowers in a loose cluster.

LEAVES: Basal leaves are long-stemmed, generally narrow, to 10 cm (4") long. Variation in degree of toothing.

RANGE: A weedy looking plant that occupies typical weedy places west of Cascades.

NOTES: There are 6 or more hawksbeards in Washington; **all have leaves of such unusual design** that you notice the plant because of them. Hawksbeards grow to 75 cm (30") tall, and have branched, leafy stems.

SLENDER HAWKSBEARD (*C. atrabarba*) is common east of the Cascades. It blooms in June to July.

SHARP-LEAVED HAWKSBEARD (*C. acuminata*) is found in dry, exposed areas in southeastern Washington, from low elevations into the Blue Mountains.

LOW HAWKSBEARD (*C. modocensis*) is a low, bushy plant, **about 15 cm (6") tall**, with showy flowers to 5 cm (2") across. It often grows with **rigid sagebrush** and **balsamroots** (pp. 108–110). It is found in Chelan County.

SOW-THISTLES • *Sonchus* spp.

THERE ARE ONLY 3 species to identify in Washington. Sow-thistles are usually abundant in bloom in July to September. A broken stem should give a thin, milky juice. The leaves, which are often prickly, clasp the stem with 2 ear-like projections. The "dandelion" flower is supported by a series of narrow, uneven-length bracts. The seeds are topped by silky white hairs, creating a small, fluffy ball. The young leaves of all species are considered edible.

Perennial sow-thistle • *Sonchus arvensis*

Prickly sow-thistle

FORM: 60–150 cm (2–5') tall—**tallest** of Washington's sow-thistles. Stout, erect stem from extensive roots.

BLOOMS: July to September.

FLOWERS: Important: A showy, dark yellow flower to 3–5 cm (1–2") across—**almost twice as wide as either other sow-thistle**.

LEAVES: Large, irregularly and deeply toothed leaves to 25 cm (10") long. Very finely prickled.

RANGE: Widespread weed of roadsides and fields. Most common east of Cascades.

NOTES: Perennial sow-thistle is common along roadsides, where it is often the most abundant yellow flower.

PRICKLY SOW-THISTLE (*S. asper*) grows to 30–90 cm (1–3') tall from a short taproot. It blooms in July to September. Its yellow flowers, **to 2.5 cm (1") across**, are in several heads. The leaves, to 25 cm (10") long, are **irregularly lobed and distinctly prickly**. These features separate it from the other 2 sow-thistles. It is a wide-ranging weed of dry ground at lower elevations.

COMMON SOW-THISTLE (*S. oleraceus*) grows to 90 cm (3') tall. It is a much-branched, untidy looking plant. The flowers, to 2.5 cm (1") across, are in loose clusters. The leaves are to 20 cm (8") long. It is a widespread weed of waste places.

Lyall's goldenweed • *Haplopappus lyallii*

FORM: 5–15 cm (2–6") tall. Erect, sticky stems with single flowers from a clump of leaves.

BLOOMS: July to August.

FLOWERS: Symmetrical, small "daisy," to 2.5 cm (1") across, with **many ray flowers.**

LEAVES: Basal leaves, to 6 cm (2 1/4") long, are hairy and glandular. Leaves **continue well up stem.**

RANGE: Dry, rocky places in subalpine and alpine tundra.

NOTES: Lyall was a surgeon in the Royal Navy. His services were also required, however, on the International Boundary Survey. He discovered subalpine larch (*Larix lyallii*) and this goldenweed in the high mountains of the Pasayton Wilderness, Okanagon County.

Golden fleabane • *Erigeron aureus*

FORM: 5–15 cm (2–6") tall. An erect flower stem from a leafy base. **Stems not sticky.**

BLOOMS: May to September.

FLOWERS: Flowerhead is to 2.5 cm (1") across. **Many ray flowers. Spongy yellow center—mass of disk flowers. Pinkish to purple bracts.**

LEAVES: Long-stemmed and mostly basal.

RANGE: Subalpine and alpine terrain of Cascades. Harts Pass.

Narrow-leaved haplopappus • *Haplopappus stenophyllus*

FORM: 7.5–15 cm (3–6") tall. A number of flower stems from a spiny leaf mat.

BLOOMS: April onward.

FLOWERS: Miniature "sunflower" with **6–8 large, yellow ray flowers** and **a spongy yellow center with protruding yellow tubes—the disk flowers.**

LEAVES: Mat-like growth of narrow, pointed, dark olive-green leaves that are finely hairy and about 6 mm (1/4") long.

RANGE: Dry, rocky ground in sagebrush ecosystem. Wenatchee, Ellensburg and Yakima counties.

NOTES: This species often blooms with **thyme-leaved buckwheat** (p. 132).

The following 3 flowers make up most of the spring to summer gold in the landscape. Superficially, they can be very confusing, but each has a distinctive leaf design. Also note the differences in their ranges.

Woolly sunflower • *Eriophyllum lanatum* var. *lanatum*

FORM: 10–40 cm (4–15 1/2") tall. Twisted, hairy stems above a mass of olive-green leaves.

BLOOMS: April to September, depending on location.

FLOWERS: Completely yellow flowerheads, to 2.5–4 cm (1–1 1/2") across, single on long stalks. **8–13 broad ray flowers.**

LEAVES: Important: Either **alternate or opposite**, olive-green leaves. **Woolly beneath,** this sparser on interior plants. **Stem leaves divided into "fingers."**

RANGE: Sunny, open areas. Sea level to subalpine. San Juan Islands. Both slopes of Cascades. Chinook Pass at 1640 m (5340'). Olympics. Columbia Gorge.

Line-leaved fleabane • *Erigeron linearis*

FORM: 15–25 cm (6–10") tall. A number of stems branch from a stout root.

BLOOMS: April to June.

FLOWERS: 20 or more narrow ray flowers (typical of **fleabanes** [see pp. 70-71, 103, 134, 158-159, 174]). **Flowerheads are single and held high above leaves.**

LEAVES: Important: Leaves are mostly basal and all are **line-thin** (as name suggests).

RANGE: Sagebrush areas and foothills. East of Cascades. Grand Coulee. Vantage Highway. Yakima County. Steptoe Butte.

NOTES: Douglas found it along the Columbia River near The Dalles.

Oregon sunshine • *Eriophyllum lanatum* var. *integrifolium*

FORM: 15–40 cm (6–15 1/2") tall. Usually a number of stems together. Stems branching to each hold a flower.

BLOOMS: April to August.

FLOWERS: Yellow flowerheads, with darker center, to 4 cm (1 1/2") across. **7–8 ray flowers.**

LEAVES: Important: **Most leaves are opposite.** Narrow, **"paddle" leaves occur well up stem.**

RANGE: Sagebrush and ponderosa pine regions. Dominant on rocky slopes, coulees, bluffs. East of Cascades. Eastern section of Columbia Gorge.

ARNICAS • *Arnica* spp.

THERE ARE ABOUT 12 species of arnica in Washington, ranging from robust plants in lowland forests to dwarfed plants in alpine terrain. The shape of the leaves varies considerably, but they all have **opposite leaves**, which separates them from most other daisy-like flowers. The flowerheads, which are more than 2.5 cm (1") across, may be single or in a loose cluster. Medicinal arnica, so effective for cuts and bruises, is best used as a tincture from a European species.

Heart-leaved arnica • *Arnica cordifolia*

FORM: 25–45 cm (10–17 1/2") tall. Erect stem with 1–3 (usually single) flowers.

BLOOMS: April to July.

FLOWERS: Large and showy. 10–15 ray petals.

LEAVES: Important: Long-stemmed, **opposite**, lower leaves are **distinctly heart-shaped** and roughly toothed.

RANGE: Foothills to mid-mountain elevations. Mostly east of Cascades. Blue Mountains.

NOTES: Heart-leaved and **mountain arnica** are the most common arnicas in Washington.

MOUNTAIN ARNICA (*A. latifolia*) is **a treasured plant of subalpine meadows**, for it provides a brilliant yellow in the galaxy of colors. The showy blooms, sometimes 2–3 to a stem, have a light brown center. The petal tips are squared-off, but have prominent teeth. **The leaves are opposite, oval, coarsely toothed and not heart-shaped.** It is widespread from middle elevations through subalpine terrain.

Puget Sound gumweed • *Grindelia integrifolia*

FORM: To 90 cm (3') tall. A sprawling, bushy plant.

BLOOMS: Prolonged blooming. May to November.

FLOWERS: Bright yellow flowers, 1.3–4 cm (1/2–2") across, held in **gummy, green cup of bracts that curl outward at tips.**

LEAVES: Broad-stemmed basal leaves may be to 40 cm (15 1/2") long and resin-dotted. Stem leaves are alternate.

RANGE: Usually on coastal bluffs, but also inland. San Juan Islands. Puget Sound.

CURLY CUP GUMWEED (*G. squarrosa*) is "curly" because the **bracts are fully curved back**. Much like Puget Sound gumweed, except for leaves being toothed. It blooms in July to August. It is found east of the Cascades in dry, waste places, fields and roadsides.

BUTTERWEEDS, GROUNDSELS and RAGWORTS • *Senecio* spp.

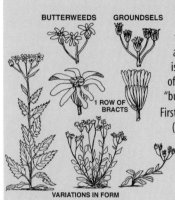

BUTTERWEEDS   GROUNDSELS

1 ROW OF BRACTS

VARIATIONS IN FORM

THERE IS PROBABLY no other group of plants that can add so much confusion in identification. *Senecio* species range in size from 7.5 cm (3") to 1.8 m (6') tall. Some are locally abundant and showy; others are dwarf plants in the alpine tundra. There is a seemingly endless number of species and varieties. Some of the more distinct species are included here. For the others, "butterweed, I suppose," may be the best way to go.

First, what is a *Senecio*? They all have **yellow or orange "flowers"** (made up of ray and disk flowers) that are **less than 2.5 cm (1") across**. The flowerhead is held in a receptacle, a **row of sharp-pointed bracts of equal length.** There is usually a sparse, much shorter row of bracteoles as well. Also note that *Senecio*s have **alternate leaves**, which separates them from **arnicas** (p. 105), which have opposite leaves and larger flowers.

Most *Senecio* species have **few ray flowers** and **a button center**—the **butterweeds**. Others have **tightly clustered heads of many ray flowers**—the **groundsels**. "Ragwort" is another common name of some species.

Common groundsel • *Senecio vulgaris*

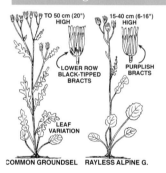

TO 50 cm (20") HIGH

15–40 cm (6–16") HIGH

LOWER ROW BLACK-TIPPED BRACTS

PURPLISH BRACTS

LEAF VARIATION

COMMON GROUNDSEL   RAYLESS ALPINE G.

FORM: To 50 cm (19 1/2") tall. Weedy looking. Branched stem.

BLOOMS: Year-round at the coast.

FLOWERS: No ray flowers (petals). **Head of tightly packed disk flowers.** Row of **narrow bracts** with a **sparse, much shorter, black-tipped row.**

LEAVES: Basal leaves are alternate, few, rounded. Stem leaves deeply lobed. Stem leafy to top.

RANGE: Common roadside and garden weed. Most common west of Cascades.

NOTES: This species was introduced from Europe.

RAYLESS ALPINE GROUNDSEL (*S. pauciflorus*) is 15–40 cm (6–15 1/2") tall. It is an erect plant with **a cluster of orange flowers.** The top half of the bracts is usually purplish. The leaves are sparse. Lower leaves are long-stemmed; upper leaves are small and divided. This species is limited to damp subalpine and alpine tundra terrain.

Canadian butterweed • *Senecio pauperculus*

FORM: 10–50 cm (4–19 1/2") tall. Erect stem with high branching into few to several flower stems.

BLOOMS: May to September, depending on altitude.

FLOWERS: Center is yellow. Green bracts.

LEAVES: Few basal leaves are long-stemmed and usually toothed to near base. Upper leaves are much smaller and deeply serrated.

RANGE: Moist ground, swamps, meadows. Valley bottoms to medium elevations.

Woolly butterweed • *Senecio canus*

FORM: 15–45 cm (6–17 1/2") tall. Usually a number of untidy stems from a clump of leaves. Stems are **dull silver** from extensive **white hairs**.

BLOOMS: Late May to July.

FLOWERS: In widely branched clusters. **5–8 rather ragged ray flowers** around a button center.

LEAVES: Important: Tufts of leaves are so **white-hairy they are a dull silver color**.

RANGE: Dry, open slopes exposed to sun. Foothills to sub-alpine. Mostly east of Cascades.

Elmer's butterweed • *Senecio elmeri*

FORM: 15–50 cm (6–20") tall. Stout stem is usually curved at base.

BLOOMS: May to July.

FLOWERS: A tight cluster of up to 10 flowerheads, each with **8–10 ray flowers** (petals). **Bracts are black-tipped**.

LEAVES: Thick, coarse basal leaves, to 15 cm (6") long, are **hairy beneath**. Leaves continue up stem.

RANGE: Rocky, well-drained slopes in subalpine. Cascades. Wenatchee Mountains. Harts Pass.

NOTES: This species is representative of a number of butterweeds. It springs up as soon as the snow is gone and blooms with **fan-leaved cinquefoil** (p. 82).

Arrow-leaved butterweed • giant ragwort • *Senecio triangularis*

FORM: 60–90 cm (2–3') tall. A leafy, erect stem. Usually abundant.

BLOOMS: June to August.

FLOWERS: Orange-yellow flowerheads, less than 2 cm (3/4") across, in **flat-topped clusters**.

LEAVES: Important: Symmetrically **triangular leaves**. Lower leaf blades, 4–20 cm (1 1/2–8") long, are **regularly saw-toothed**. Stem leafy all the way to flowers.

RANGE: Damp ground. Valley bottoms to subalpine. Most common in subalpine. At higher elevations in Columbia River Gorge.

NOTES: This butterweed is **an important flower of subalpine flower meadows**.

Western butterweed • *Senecio integerrimus*

FORM: To 90 cm (3') tall, **placing flower well above most other spring blooms.**

BLOOMS: April to July.

FLOWERS: In a large, showy head. 5–12 individual ray flowers. **Bracts in 1 main row**, with **tiny triangular black tips.**

LEAVES: Basal leaves are long-stemmed, mostly round-tipped and to 20 cm (8") long. Leaves are smaller and narrower higher up stem. They are irregularly toothed.

RANGE: Widespread. Sagebrush and ponderosa pine ecosystems and continuing up mountainsides beyond 900 m (2950') in elevation.

NOTES: This species and arrow-leaved butterweed (p.107) are the 2 most abundant butterweeds in Washington. Western butterweed is so **widespread and noticeable** while it is in bloom that it seems to be everywhere east of the Cascades.

Tansy butterweed • ragwort • *Senecio jacobaea*

FORM: To 1.2 m (4') tall. Usually a number of stout, erect stems in a clump.

BLOOMS: July to August.

FLOWERS: Large, **very showy** heads to 15 cm (6") across. Prominent ray flowers (petals). **Bracts are black-tipped.**

LEAVES: Large, **alternate**, **dark green** leaves that are very deeply dissected, giving a fern-like appearance. Uniform leaf design all the way up stem.

RANGE: Widespread. San Juan Islands and low coastal areas.

NOTES: Don't confuse this species with **common tansy** (p.94). Tansy butterweed is a vigorous, introduced weed that is rapidly spreading. It is the most common roadside flower on lower Olympic roads during August. It is toxic to horses and cattle.

BALSAMROOTS • *Balsamorhiza* spp.

BECAUSE OF THEIR large size, showy blooms and abundance—they mass on hundreds of acres of benchland or foothill slopes—balsamroots really are plants to know. Fortunately, the main species are fairly easy to recognize. Many plants are a real puzzle, however, since **hybridization can create weird and wonderful varieties.** Three rather obscure balsamroots in Washington are not mentioned in this book.

Native Americans ate the rich, oily seeds either raw or mixed with deer fat and boiled. The deep-growing roots were eaten raw or were roasted with much care in large pits.

The **true sunflowers** (*Helianthus* spp.) are on p.111. **Mule's-ears** (p.110) is quite similar to balsamroots.

Arrow-leaved balsamroot • spring sunflower
• *Balsamorhiza sagittata*

FORM: To 75 cm (2 1/2') tall. Many leaves and flowers.
BLOOMS: May to June.
FLOWERS: Important: **Only 1 flowerhead to a stem**, to 10 cm (4") across.
LEAVES: Important: Large, arrow-shaped, **velvety** leaves, **olive-green on both sides**. Dry to twisted parchments visible for several months.
RANGE: East of Cascades. Southward from British Columbia border to Wenatchee area, where Carey's balsamroot (below) takes over, and on to Columbia River. Eastward it forms a wide strip with its eastern border running from Coulee Dam to Waitsburg near Oregon border.

Deltoid balsamroot • *Balsamorhiza deltoidea*

FORM: To 90 cm (3') tall. Many leaves, many flowers.
BLOOMS: April to May.
FLOWERS: Showy flowerhead to 10 cm (4") across. **1 main bloom** with smaller 1 below.
LEAVES: Triangular leaves. **Same green color on both sides**. May have 1–2 small stem leaves.
RANGE: Important: **Very limited, spotty distribution west of Cascades**. Usually with Garry oak on open sidehills, meadows in Puget Sound. Scatter Creek Wildlife Area in Thurston County. Eastward in Columbia Gorge to about mile 74.

Carey's balsamroot • *Balsamorhiza careyana*

FORM: To 90 cm (3') tall. Many leaves, many flowers.
BLOOMS: April to June. Seems to bloom longer than others.
FLOWERS: Important: **Usually 2–3 flowerheads** at top of stem, but **often only 1**.
LEAVES: Important: **Large, triangular** leaves are **dark, shiny green on both sides**, variable in shape. Color remains into summer.
RANGE: East of Cascades. Generally above sagebrush zone. Adjoins range of arrow-leaved balsamroot (above). Westward into Columbia Gorge to around mile 73. Eastward to Waitsburg (near Walla Walla). Northward to Cle Elum.

Hooker's balsamroot • *Balsamorhiza hookeri*

FORM: Averages 50 cm (20") tall. Basal spray of long leaves.

BLOOMS: April to May.

FLOWERS: Single, showy flower to 7.5 cm (3") across on each leafless stem.

LEAVES: Important: To 50 cm (20") long. **Twisting, dark green, deeply cut to the midrib.**

RANGE: With sagebrush and ponderosa pine. Coulees above Vantage, southern third of Yakima Canyon, Klickitat County.

NOTES: This plant has a number of variations in leaf shape.

HOOKER'S DWARF BALSAMROOT, the author's designation for a possible variety of the above. Only to 30 cm (3") across. Leaves are to 10 cm (4") long, cut to the midrib, twisted and **often form a rosette pattern.** It is the **primary flowering plant from April to May** in a tiny ecosystem of thin, rocky soils within the bordering sagebrush zone. Rigid sagebrush (*Artemesia rigida*) is a companion and Carey's balsamroot may also be there. See it at the turn-off to Sun Lakes from the Vantage Highway, on open slopes above the Cle Elum-Ellensburg #10 Road and in the Blue Mountains.

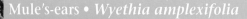

Mule's-ears • *Wyethia amplexifolia*

FORM: To 75 cm (2 1/2') tall. Single, stout stems. Often forming a small meadowland of plants.

BLOOMS: Late May, into July at higher elevations.

FLOWERS: 1 large sunflower, to 10 cm (4") across, at stem top, with several smaller ones below.

LEAVES: Glossy green leaves to 40 cm (15 1/2") long. Thick yellow midrib on both sides. **Stem leafy all the way to top.** Leaves are obvious source of common name.

RANGE: Wide, spotty range in ponderosa pine ecosystem. Leavenworth. Hills east of Coulee City. Colfax. East of Goldendale. Medium elevations in Blue Mountains. Anatone.

Brown-eyed Susan • *Gaillardia aristata*

FORM: 35–50 cm (14–19 1/2") tall. Usually several stems from a leaf clump.

BLOOMS: May to August.

FLOWERS: Bright yellow "sunflower" with a reddish-brown center. Flowerhead is 4–5 cm (1 1/2–2") across. Yellow **ray flowers** are **deeply notched into 3 segments.**

LEAVES: Sparse, lower leaves are narrow, long-stemmed and to 12 cm (4 3/4") long. Stem leaves may be lobed or toothed.

RANGE: Usually in bunchgrass and ponderosa pine ecosystems.

NOTES: Lewis and Clark noted brown-eyed Susan as they crossed the Rocky Mountains.

BLACK-EYED SUSAN (*Rudbeckia hirta*) has a central button that is **so deep brown or purple** that it **appears black. The ray flowers are not notched.** It is wide-ranging at lower elevations, but never abundant.

Cusick's sunflower • *Helianthus cusickii*

FORM: To 60 cm (2') tall. Usually a number of branching stems.
BLOOMS: May.
FLOWERS: Several **pale yellow** flowerheads to a stem, to 7.5 cm (3") across. **8–15 sharp-pointed ray flowers form a bowl-shape.** Bracts are hairy.
LEAVES: May have opposite or alternate leaves to 7.5 cm (3") long. Look for a **faint 3-veined pattern**.
RANGE: Dry, open plains and foothills in south-central Washington. Vantage to Ellensburg. Yakima Canyon. Sunnyside. Steptoe Butte.
NOTES: Compare this species to Rocky Mountain helianthella (below). Cusick's sunflower blooms with **Hooker's onion** (p. 124) and **Douglas buckwheat** (p. 97).

Rocky Mountain helianthella • *Helianthella uniflora*

FORM: 20–90 cm (8"–35.5") tall. **Several unbranched stems** from 1 base.
BLOOMS: May to August.
FLOWERS: **1 flowerhead on a stem**, 4–6 cm (1.5"–2.25") across, **About 13 sharp-pointed ray flowers. Bracts are narrow, not noticeably hairy.**
LEAVES: Lowermost leaves are opposite. Higher leaves are alternate. **Lower leaves with 3-veined pattern. All leaves are sandpapery.**
RANGE: Common roadside plant along eastern slope of Cascades to 1200 m (3940'). Leavenworth. Mazama. Eastern Washington.
NOTES: Douglas recorded this species in the "subalpine range of the Blue Mts." He was the first white man to explore those mountains.

Common sunflower • Kansas sunflower • *Helianthus annuus*

FORM: Important! 90 cm–2.1 m (3–7') tall. Stout, branching stem.
BLOOMS: June to October.
FLOWERS: Typically **to 7.5 cm (3") across.** Bright yellow ray flowers (petals) surround **a rich brown center.** Flowerheads single at end of stout stems.
LEAVES: Large, triangular leaves are sandpapery and hairy.
RANGE: East of Cascades and especially at lower elevations in south-central region. Associated with sagebrush and ponderosa pine. Wenatchee, Okanogan, and Chelan areas. Naches. Steptoe Butte.
NOTES: Common sunflower is a native plant that has had some attempts at cultivation for many centuries. The seeds are edible and highly nutritious. It is the state flower of Kansas.

ORANGE — *4 PETALS*

California poppy • *Eschscholzia californica*

FORM: 10–50 cm (6–19 1/2") tall. A number of flower stems from a large clump of leaves.
BLOOMS: April to December at the coast.
FLOWERS: Bowl-shaped, orange and gold flowers open wide when sun is shining. About 5 cm (2") across.
FRUITS: Long seed pods, which split to scatter seeds.
LEAVES: So finely dissected as to **resemble carrot leaves**.
RANGE: Widely distributed and locally abundant. Mostly west of Cascades. Columbia Gorge.

NOTES: This genus is named for Johann Friedrich Eschscholz, a physician and naturalist who was part of the Russian exploration team that visited the California coast in 1816.

ORANGE — *5 PETALS*

Munro's globemallow • desert mallow • *Sphaeralcea munroana*

FORM: 20–45 cm (8–17 1/2") tall. Rather sprawling plant with branching stems.
BLOOMS: May to June.
FLOWERS: Unusual **orange or brick-red color**. Flowers and buds form clusters in leaf axils. Flowers to 2 cm (3/4") across, held by a 5-parted calyx. Many stamens.
LEAVES: Rather **maple-like** leaves, to 5 cm (2") long, with 3–5 lobes and **mealy texture**.
RANGE: Sagebrush habitat. Grant County. Yakima. Wenatchee. Bickleton.
NOTES: Douglas found this species on "the plains of the Columbia."

ORANGE — *6 PETALS*

Tiger lily • Columbia lily • *Lillium columbianum*

FORM: 25–75 cm (10–30") tall. Stout stem from a scaly, white bulb.
BLOOMS: June to August.
FLOWERS: Much **like a garden lily**, with reflexed "petals" and a projection of long stamens. **Bright yellow to deep orange** and **spotted with maroon dots**. Few to many flowers hanging from long stems.
LEAVES: Narrow leaves in **rough whorls on lower stem**. Upper leaves more scattered.
RANGE: Sea level to 1200 m (3940') in damp rich soils. Meadows, forest openings. Both sides of Cascades. Often very abundant.

Orange agoseris • *Agoseris aurantiaca*

FORM: 10–30 cm (4–12") tall. Single stem with milky juice.

BLOOMS: June to August.

FLOWERS: An orange "dandelion"—color provides good identification. **Head may turn brown or pink.**

LEAVES: All basal, narrow, mostly upright, with wavy margins or shallow teeth.

RANGE: A fairly common flower over wide areas. Open ground, forest openings, meadows. Medium elevations to subalpine. Olympics, Cascades and other mountain systems.

Orange hawkweed • devil's paintbrush • *Hieraceum aurantiacum*

FORM: 20–60 cm (8–24") tall. Usually a thick growth from spreading roots.

BLOOMS: June to August.

FLOWERS: Vivid orange-red flowers with streaked yellow centers are sure identification. Flowers to 2.5 cm (1") across. A single bloom when young above a cluster of buds. Later a flower cluster.

LEAVES: Basal rosette of narrow leaves covered with fine hairs.

RANGE: Mostly east of the Cascades, fields, roadsides. Ferry County. East slope of Snoqualmie Pass.

NOTES: Other **hawkweeds** are on p.101.

Spotted coralroot • *Corallorhiza maculata*

FORM: 20–40 cm (8–15 1/2") tall. **Erect, "orangy" stem** from gnarled, knobby (coral-like) roots.

BLOOMS: May to June.

FLOWERS: Small orchids, each with 6 petals, spaced along stem. Flowers have **white lip petal with crimson spots.**

LEAVES: Small scales on stem.

RANGE: Rich forest soils at lower elevations. Klickitat County.

NOTES: These coralroots are color coded as "orange" based on the overall color of the flower and stem. Coralroots are saprophytes that feed on decaying organic matter, so they lack the green color of most other plants.

WESTERN CORALROOT (*C. mertensiana*) is very similar, but the **lip petal is marked with red lines.** It blooms in summer. It is found in moist forests.

STRIPED CORALROOT (*C. striata*) is very similar, but the **lip and other petals are striped with red.** It is found in moist forest soils.

Oaks toothwort • *Cardamine pulcherrima* var. *pulcherrima*

FORM: 7.5–25 cm (3–10") tall.

BLOOMS: March to June.

FLOWERS: Flowers, about 1.3 cm (1/2") across, in loose clusters. **4 pale pink petals** are sometimes **veined with rose lines**.

LEAVES: Unusual design of leaves on upper part of stem is significant. **Leaves are 3–5 lobed.** No basal leaves.

RANGE: West of Cascades. Shady woods of Klickitat and Yakima counties. Columbia Gorge.

NOTES: The common name "oaks" refers to this species' preferred habitat under Garry oak (*Quercus garryana*). It blooms with other spring flowers, including **satin-flower** (p. 123), **shootingstars** (pp. 116–117), **white fawn lily** (p. 49) and **woodland stars** (p. 39).

American searocket • *Cakile edentula*

FORM: To 50 cm (19 1/2") tall. **Sprawling on beach edges**.

BLOOMS: July to August.

FLOWERS: Several tiny, pinkish-purple flowers in clusters. 4 petals (typical of mustard family).

LEAVES: Thick, fleshy leaves. Leaf stems arise from branches that may be partly buried in sand.

RANGE: Very abundant beach plant along coast. Common on Long Beach.

Pink fairies • clarkia • *Clarkia pulchella*

FORM: 15–40 cm (6–15 1/2") tall. Plants often abundant.

BLOOMS: Mid-June to mid-August.

FLOWERS: Brightness of flowers is only matched by their flamboyant design. Take a close look to see that there really are only **4 petals**. **Each petal has 3 broad fingers**.

LEAVES: Alternate, dull green leaves, 2.5–5 cm (1–2") long, are overshadowed by flowers.

RANGE: Often with ponderosa pine and open Douglas-fir. 900–1500 m (2950'–4920'). East of Cascades. Okanogan County. Spokane County. Steptoe Butte. Eastern section of Columbia Gorge.

NOTES: This species was named for Clark by Lewis, who found it "on the Kooskoosky and Clarck's rivers [Clearwater and Snake rivers]."

Farewell-to-spring • *Clarkia amoena*

FORM: To 50 cm (10") tall. Strong, thin, erect stems.

BLOOMS: May to June.

FLOWERS: Beautiful! Generally **pink with blotches of deeper red** on each petal. To 6 cm (2 1/4") across.

LEAVES: Alternate, narrow, lance-like.

RANGE: Rocky slopes close to the ocean to moderate elevations. Olympics, Columbia Gorge west of The Dalles. Catherine Creek.

NOTES: Douglas collected seeds from this plant "along the northwest coast of America" and sent them to England for further study.

Fireweed • *Epilobium angustifolium*

FORM: 60–120 cm (2–4') tall. Erect, leafy stem from spreading roots.

BLOOMS: June to August.

FLOWERS: Pink-rose-purple, as *you* see them. **4 large petals. Protruding 4-lobed stigma.** Flowers 2.5–5 cm (1–2") across, in a dense, spike-like cluster.

FRUITS: Seed pods split open and disgorge thousands of tiny, fluffy seeds that can be carried on winds for great distances.

LEAVES: Alternate leaves, to 20 cm (8") long, paler beneath.

RANGE: Common, except immediate coastal strip and arid regions. Low to high elevations. Old burn and logging areas. Roadsides.

NOTES: Native Americans ate the pith of young shoots raw or boiled the entire stem. They also used the roots, bark and seed fluff. Fireweed honey rates high with bee-keepers.

Broad-leaved willowherb • alpine fireweed, river beauty • *Epilobium latifolium*

FORM: 20–40 cm (8–15 1/2") tall. A leafy, sprawling plant.

BLOOMS: June to August.

FLOWERS: Large, **reddish-purple** flowers, 3–6 cm (1 1/4–2 1/4") across, in loose clusters.

LEAVES: Distinctive, soft blue-green leaves. Lower leaves opposite. Upper leaves alternate, fleshy. Leaves supposedly resemble those of a weeping willow.

RANGE: Most frequent on gravel bars, stream edges, slopes of subalpine and alpine regions, but will turn up at lower elevations.

SMALL WILLOWHERB (*E. glaberrimum*) is less than 30 cm (12") tall. The flowers have 4 notched, pinkish petals. **The flower stems are pink**, like the main stalk. **A powdery bloom makes leaves grayish green.** It is found in wet places, from high forests to the alpine. Olympics.

Smooth douglasia • cliff douglasia • *Douglasia laevigata*

FORM: 4–6 cm (1 1/2–2") tall. Short stems above a leafy mat cluster.

BLOOMS: June to July.

FLOWERS: Large number of deep pink to red flowers on a mat-like growth. **2–10 flowers,** to 1 cm (3/8") across, **in a tight umbel cluster**.

FRUITS: Attractive, reddish seed head in August.

LEAVES: Basal rosettes of small, sharp-tipped, mostly untoothed leaves.

RANGE: A moist rockery plant favoring coastal slopes from lowlands to alpine. To subalpine in Olympics, where it is fairly common.

NOTES: The genus name honors David Douglas. "Smooth" refers to the leaves not being toothed, but they may actually carry a few teeth.

SHOOTINGSTARS • PEACOCKS • *Dodecatheon* spp.

THERE ARE 7 shootingstar species in Washington, enough to cause confusion in identification, since most shootingstars are subject to considerable variation.

Such a flamboyant flower requires a special pollination technique: a visiting bumble bee hangs upside-down from the yellow ring on the flower; a buzz of its wings shakes pollen from the anthers (the dark tubes) onto its abdomen; the bee scratches the pollen back into sacs on its legs, but some pollen is left on its abdomen; when the bee visits another flower, the protruding stigma is placed perfectly to rub on the pollen.

White shootingstar (*D. dentatum*) is found on the eastern slopes of the Cascades.

Henderson's shootingstar • broad-leaved shootingstar • *Dodecatheon hendersonii*

FORM: 7.5–20 cm (3–8") tall.

BLOOMS: Late March to May.

FLOWERS: One white to yellow ring. Reddish-purple stamen tube.

LEAVES: Almost stemless, oval leaves.

RANGE: Meadows, open forests. San Juan Islands. Coastal Washington.

NOTES: The oval-leaf-shape gives a positive identification of this species. It blooms with **spring gold** (p. 95), **trillium** (pp. 27, 140), **satin-flower** (p. 123), **field chickweed** (p. 35) and **gold star** (p. 87).

FEW-FLOWERED SHOOTINGSTAR (*D. pulchellum*) is identified by its pale green leaves, which **narrow to a long, thin leaf stem not more than 3 mm (1/8") wide**. (In Jeffrey's **shootingstar** [p.117], the leaf stem is 6 mm [1/4"] wide.) This shootingstar is 10–50 cm (4–19 1/2") tall and has **2 rings on its flowers**: both yellow, or 1 white and 1 yellow. It blooms in April to August, depending on the elevation. It is found in moist meadows and streamsides from lower elevations to the subalpine . Mt. Rainier.

Desert shootingstar • *Dodecatheon conjugens*

FORM: 5–20 cm (2–8") tall.

BLOOMS: Early April to May. With first arrow-leaved balsamroots and sagebrush buttercups.

FLOWERS: Flower has **a yellow ring often bordered by a narrow, reddish ring.** There **may be a further yellowish ring around the anther tube.**

LEAVES: Light green, narrow, several times as long as broad.

RANGE: In sagebrush and ponderosa pine ecosystems in the foothills. **Likely the only shootingstar** in the sagebrush and ponderosa pine ecosystem.

JEFFREY'S SHOOTINGSTAR (*D. jeffreyi*), also called "tall mountain shootingstar," can be **immediately separated** from other shootingstars by its **white**, rather than yellow ring. It can grow to 50 cm (19 1/2") tall. The dull green leaves may be 15 cm (6") long, and **they narrow to a wide leaf stem**, 6 mm (1/4") wide. It blooms in April to August. It is found in damp, mountain meadows and on streambanks in the subalpine of the Olympics and Cascades, and in the Columbia Gorge.

Poet's shootingstar • *Dodecatheon poeticum*

FORM: To 30 cm (12") tall.

BLOOMS: March to April.

FLOWERS: Bright, pink-purple petals, yellow ring with red base, purple stamen-stem.

LEAVES: 4–15 cm (1 1/2–6"). May be entire or weakly toothed. **Leaves and stem with fine glandular-pubescence.**

RANGE: Moist soil on eastern slope of the Cascades from Satus Pass south, Columbia Gorge, both sides. Tom McCall Nature Preserve area.

NOTES: This is difficult to identify for it depends greatly on the amount of glandular-pubescence you see on leaves and stem. Range is important.

Twinflower • *Linnaea borealis*

FORM: 5–10 cm (2–4") tall. Slender stems from a trailing, fine vine. Technically a shrub.

BLOOMS: May to August.

FLOWERS: Thin stems carry **"twin" pink flowers**—sometimes more white than pink—and only 6 mm (1/4") long. Delicate fragrance.

LEAVES: Small, evergreen, paired leaves, to 1.3 cm (1/2") long. **Scattered teeth on top half of leaves.**

RANGE: Cool, moist woods from sea level to timberline.

NOTES: Linnaeus, the Swedish botanist who was the founder of the system of botanical classification, chose twinflower as his favorite plant.

GERANIUMS • *Geranium* spp.

THERE ARE MANY geraniums in the state and except for a white-flowered one, they are all pinkish to purple in color. All have 5 petals, 5 sepals and 10 stamens. The styles (central flower stem) are elongated and finely beaked. A general division can be made on the size of the flowers, the small-flowered being 3–10 mm (1/8–3/8") long, others twice as large or more.

SMALL-FLOWERED GERANIUMS

BICKNELL'S GERANIUM (*G. bicknellii*) has pink-purple flowers. Seeds in pairs, **bristle-tipped sepals. Leaves deeply 5-parted.** East of Cascades and San Juan Islands.

CAROLINA GERANIUM (*G. carolinianum*) has small, **pink flowers with slightly notched petals. Style tips yellowish-green.** San Juan Islands and east of Cascades in dry, rocky places.

DOVEFOOT GERANIUM (*G. molle*) has small flowers with **deeply notched petals, seed pod stems with a downward twist.** Dovefoot supposedly relates to leaf shape. Lowlands mostly west of the Cascades.

Dovefoot geranium

ROBERT'S GERANIUM (*G. robertianum*) has **bristles on sepals,** entire petals. **Flowers and seeds in twos.** Stems often reddish. Blooms with buttercups. Dry places, roadsides, mostly west of the Cascades at lower elevations.

Robert's geranium

Sticky geranium • *Geranium viscosissimum*

FORM: 30–50 cm (12–20") tall. Coarse appearance from branching of stout stems.

BLOOMS: May to July.

FLOWERS: Attractive rose-purple flowers with **petals finely veined.** They are from 2.5–4 cm (1–2") across.

LEAVES: Large, almost circular, but with 5–7 deeply parted segments, **all finely hairy** and possibly glandular.

RANGE: Open grassy forests of ponderosa pine, aspen and Douglas-fir. Widespread east of the Cascades. Steptoe Butte, Blue Mountains. Ranges to 1200 m (4000') elevation.

Common stork's-bill • filaree, heron's-bill • *Erodium cicutarium*

FORM: 7.5–50 cm (3–20") tall. Sometimes a sparse mat or a bushy, fern-leaved plant.

BLOOMS: March to August.

FLOWERS: 2–10 small, bright, pink to purplish flowers per stem. The 5 petals are matched by 5 stamens.

FRUITS: Long, sharp, seed pods 2.5–4 cm (1–1 1/2") long are a distinctive feature (stork's-bill).

LEAVES: May be a small basal grouping flat on dry ground or a robust growth of fern-like leaves.

RANGE: Common on dry ground, road edges and waste places. A Mediterranean import now widespread.

Small-leaved montia • streambank springbeauty, little-leaf montia • *Montia parviflora*

FORM: To 30 cm (12") tall. Stems may lie flat or be in an arching spray. There are many plants because they sprout from runners.

BLOOMS: May to August.

FLOWERS: Generally pink with darker veins, but on the San Juan Islands often with white flowers. Petals slightly notched on a flower 1.3 cm (1/2") across.

LEAVES: Basal leaves are oval to lance-shaped. Stem leaves are alternate and smaller.

RANGE: Moist, shady places at lower elevations of Olympics and Cascades.

Smooth woodland star • smooth prairie star • *Lithophragma glabra*

FORM: To 25 cm (10") tall. Slender erect stem.

BLOOMS: March to June. With gold stars and shootingstars.

FLOWERS: Pink, but can age to white. 5 petals each 3–5-lobed.

LEAVES: Important: Lowest leaves branch from slightly above ground level. Deeply cut into segments. Usually 2 small stem leaves.

RANGE: Dry, grassy slopes east of the Cascades. Lower elevations. Chelan and Klickitat counties. Columbia Gorge.

NOTES: 3 other *Lithophragmas* keyed as white, p.39.

Spreading phlox • carpet pink • *Phlox diffusa*

FORM: 2.5–7.5 cm (1–3") **A spiny-leaved mat** covered with flowers.

BLOOMS: May to August depending on elevation.

FLOWERS: 5-petalled flowers **(not notched)** are about 1.3 cm (1/2") across and lie flat. **Color variations of pink and lavender** are common **and white** may be seen.

LEAVES: Form a ground-hugging mat. They are **spiny and fused into pairs at their bases.**

RANGE: Widespread in dry, open areas to alpine terrain. Olympics, Cascades, Mt. Adams.

TUFTED PHLOX (*P. cespitosa*) is sometimes **white**, see p.34. Similar to the above, but **loosely erect. Range is different!** Found with ponderosa pine, sagebrush areas, and adjacent foothills.

Long-leaved phlox • *Phlox longifolia*

FORM: 7.5–25 cm (3–10") tall. Branched to form a leafy clump.

BLOOMS: April to June.

FLOWERS: Most phloxes have a **long flower tube.** Green sepals are close to the **same length as the flower tube.** Small, pink or lavender flowers, but sometimes white.

LEAVES: Opposite, narrow and up to 5 cm (2") long. Leaves join at base, but appear as opposite.

RANGE: On dry rocky terrain from low to mountainside elevations east of the Cascades. Ellensburg, Blue Mountains.

Showy phlox • *Phlox speciosa*

FORM: To 40 cm (16") tall. Many branched, bushy plant.

BLOOMS: April to June.

FLOWERS: The bright pink flowers to 1.3 cm (1/2") across have **notched petals** and are carried in stem top clusters. Flowers are so abundant they cover the plant. They give off a faint perfume.

LEAVES: Narrow and opposite.

RANGE: Sagebrush and ponderosa pine areas. Widespread.

WHITE PHLOX: Judging by the notched petals, this flower must be related to showy phlox, but reference books don't seem to mention it. Plants are about 30 cm (12") tall with large flowers to 2.5 cm (1") across. They form a domed mass of bloom 40 cm (16") across. So abundant and showy that near Chelan you can see massed bloom on the hillsides 450 m (1/4 mile) away. They bloom in early May with arrow-leaved balsamroot. Also found between Cle Elum and Ellensburg on the old road and high in the mountains east of this road. I can find no reference to this plant.

Moss campion • *Silene acaulis*

FORM: A low mat of green leaves and bright flowers.
BLOOMS: June to August.
FLOWERS: Bright pink flowers less than 1.3 cm (1/2") across. Petals almost rectangular, yellow stamens.
LEAVES: Short, thin, stiff, spiny. Persist over the years.
RANGE: Usually on rocky places **in the alpine tundra.** High mountains except the Olympics. A circumpolar species.

Pink wintergreen • *Pyrola asarifolia*

FORM: 5–35 cm (2–14") tall. Erect stem from leaf rosette.
BLOOMS: July to August.
FLOWERS: The only pink *pyrola,* see p. 36 for others. The **lovely flowers are drooping and arranged singly** along a pinkish stem. Thick waxy petals range from greenish-white to red. **The style is protruding and has a downward twist.**
LEAVES: A basal rosette of thick, glossy green leaves, may be purplish beneath. They retain their color all winter hence "wintergreen."
RANGE: Shady, moist sites from low to high elevations.

Prince's pine • pipsissewa • *Chimaphila umbellata*

FORM: 12.5–25 cm (5–10") tall. Stout, greenish, woody stem.
BLOOMS: June to August.
FLOWERS: Pink to white, waxy flowers with faint perfume and in a loose cluster of 3–8.
LEAVES: A rough whorled appearance on lower half of stem. They are **evergreen, teeth on the upper half.**
RANGE: Usually in humus under shady coniferous trees. Most common at middle mountain elevations.
NOTES: Technically a shrub. The roots and leaves were used by Native Americans for various medicinal purposes.

> *I have been only three nights in a house since my arrival [4 months before]. I have a tent when it can be carried, which rarely can be done.*
> — **Douglas, April 16, 1825**

Showy milkweed • *Asclepias speciosa*

FORM: 60–90 cm (2–3′) tall.

BLOOMS: June to August.

FLOWERS: Light pink-to-purplish flowers bunch into a knobby head. 5 purple petals have 5 curved horns protruding from the central stamen tube. In fall long pods release thousands of silky parachutes.

LEAVES: Opposite, **thick, fleshy and velvety. To 15 cm (6″) long.**

RANGE: Field edges, roadsides. East of the Cascades. Associated with ponderosa pine and sagebrush.

NOTES: This is a host plant for the monarch butterfly. Native Americans ate the tender, young shoots like asparagus. This plant was once named after Douglas who recorded it in the Rocky Mountains.

Henderson's sidalcea • Oregon checker-mallow, marsh hollyhock • *Sidalcea hendersonii*

FORM: To 1.5 m (5′) tall. **Spindly stemmed.**

BLOOMS: June to August.

FLOWERS: Large, showy about 2.5 cm (1″) across, **light to a deep pink with darker veins.** In stem-top clusters.

LEAVES: Basal, round in outline, but **deeply lobed into 7 segments and all coarsely toothed.** Stem leaves much smaller and finely fingered.

RANGE: Associated with ponderosa pine and sagebrush areas east of the Cascades. Draws leading to the Snake River, base of Steptoe Butte.

Old man's whiskers • long-plumed avens • *Geum triflorum*

FORM: 15–50 cm (6–20″) tall. Usually locally abundant.

BLOOMS: May to July.

FLOWERS: Ranges from **pink to purple.** An unusual design! The **globe of 5 almost unnoticeable yellow petals is enclosed by 5 arching sepals and other, shorter ones.**

LEAVES: Tufts of bright green leaves, **deeply and finely lobed.**

RANGE: On grassy slopes to high forest openings east of the Cascades ranging widely in association with ponderosa pine. Blue Mountains to 1500 m (5000′).

NOTES: A little known plant before being recorded by Lewis on the banks of the Clearwater River, which flows into the Snake River near Lewiston.

> *Colter's horse fel with him in passing hungry creek and himself and horse were driven down the creek a considerable distance rolling over each other among the rocks. Fortunately [he] escaped without injury or loss of his gun.*
> —Lewis, Wednesday, June 18, 1806

Grass widow • *Sisyrinchium inflatum* • *Olsynium inflatum*

FORM: 15–40 cm (6–16") tall.

BLOOMS: March to April with camas, stonecrop, shootingstars, grass widows, fawn lilies and some violets.

FLOWERS: May range from pale purple to blue, pink or white. Petals are narrow and pointed, **not rounded as in satin-flower.**

LEAVES: Grass-like. Shorter than stem.

RANGE: Ranging from sagebrush lowlands upwards into the ponderosa pine ecosystem east of the Cascades. Spokane, Coulee Dam southwards, Kamiak Butte, Columbia Gorge, lower slopes of the Blue Mountains.

NOTES: Don't confuse with satin-flower (below). This has sharp-pointed petals.

March 24. Mayer State Park, Oregon. Columbia Gorge. This small park and the much larger Tom McCall Nature Preserve to the west, on or close to Oregon State Highway 30, has a beautiful display of spring wildflowers.

Satin-flower • *Sisyrinchium douglasii* • *Olsynium douglasii*

FORM: 10–25 cm (4–10") tall. Erect stem with 1–2 flowers.

BLOOMS: March to April with camas, stonecrop, shootingstars, grass widows, fawn lilies and some violets.

FLOWERS: Reddish-purple with satiny petals. Bloom 2.5–4 cm (1–1 1/2") across. They only last a few days, but likely are replaced by new flowers.

LEAVES: A spray of long, thin leaves that look like stout grass blades.

RANGE: On rocky, open situations west of the Cascades. Often in the thousands! San Juan Islands and southwards. Very abundant in western section of Columbia Gorge.

NOTES: David Douglas (*douglasii*) found this plant in 1826, near the Columbia River's historically famous fishing area of Celilo Falls (now flooded). It continues to grow in abundance today near there.

I purchased a dog and some wood made a fire on the rocks and cooked the dogs on which the men breakfast...wind hard all day cold from the N.W.
—Clark, April 20, 1806

Nodding onion • *Allium cernuum*

FORM: To 30 cm (12") tall. Upright to arching with **nodding neck.**

BLOOMS: Mid-May to mid-July.

FLOWERS: Nodding flower head is main feature. A definite twist in the stem holds a dozen or so pink blooms. **6 stamens protrude** far out of the pink cup.

LEAVES: 3–7 short, grass-like leaves are seen **at time of flowering.**

RANGE: Middle mountain to subalpine, coastal and central Washington. Most common and widespread of the many onions. Olympics, west Columbia Gorge.

DOUGLAS' ONION (*A. douglasii*) is an onion to 35 cm (14") tall with a densely clustered pink, flower head. Strong onion smell. Usually 2 thin, flat, leaves to two-thirds of stem height persist during blooming period. Border of Columbia Basin and southwards. Kittitas County, Columbia Gorge, Blue Mountains.

> *The chief set before me a large platter of onions which had been sweeted. I gave a part of these onions to my party and we all eate of them, in this state the root is very sweet and the tops tender.*
> —Clark, April 16, 1806, near The Dalles

Hooker's onion • *Allium acuminatum*

FORM: 15–45 cm (6–18") tall. Erect stem from a bulb.

BLOOMS: April to June. Best during May.

FLOWERS: Pink to rose-purple. A close cluster with most flowers erect. **Sepals and petals, sharp-pointed and curl back. Best clue!**

LEAVES: At flowering the **1–2 leaves have withered.**

RANGE: Dry, rocky sites at lower elevations from the San Juan Islands and southward. Columbia Gorge. Also east of the Cascades at low to medium elevations. Vantage region.

NOTES: So abundant in places as to give hillsides a reddish blush and an onion fragrance.

GEYER'S ONION (*A. geyeri*) 20–60 cm (8–24") is tall with rose-colored flowers **often mixed with pink-tinged bulblets.** Stamens are shorter than the tiny triangular petals. Note that the 2–3 leaves are to 3 mm (1/8") wide and to 30 cm (12") long. They are **green at the time of flowering.** Moist to dry soils. East of the Cascades. Yakima, Kittitas counties.

SCALLOPED ONION (*A. crenulatum*), also called "Olympic onion," is a ground hugging plant to 10 cm (4") tall. Blooming May to July the flowers are white-pink-rose in a clustered head. Leaves unmistakable, 2 curling leaves lie flat. Dry, rocky places of subalpine. Olympics, Cascades, Wenatchee Mountains.

Columbia lewisia • *Lewisia columbiana*

FORM: To 25 cm (10") tall. A number of slender flower stems from a thick, leaf clump.

BLOOMS: June to August.

FLOWERS: A symmetrical flower to about 1.3 cm (1/2") across with **6–9 petals, pinkish to white, but with veins of a deeper pink**. Flowers and buds on branching stem tops.

LEAVES: Thick **tuft of narrow, fleshy leaves** anchored by stout roots in rocky crevices.

RANGE: Often a considerable number of plants on an area of **exposed, thin, rocky soils**. Both sides of Cascades at high mountain elevations up to and including subalpine terrain. Harts Pass and northward to the British Columbia border, but not beyond.

Bitterroot • rock-rose • *Lewisia rediviva*

FORM: 2.5–7.5 cm (1–3") tall.

BLOOMS: April to August depending on elevation.

FLOWERS: Very large pink to rose flowers, sometimes white, have many petals. Sometimes a single flower, but more often several in a group. On or close to the ground.

LEAVES: Thick, fleshy in a rosette before the flower appears. Withers as flower comes into bloom.

RANGE: East of the Cascades. Sporadic on dry rocky places on edge of sagebrush and ponderosa pine regions. Okanogan County south. Grand Coulee region. Limited near mile 74, Columbia Gorge.

NOTES: The thick fleshy roots once were highly prized by Native Americans. A sack of roots would buy a good horse.

> *…it had a bitter taste which was nauseous to us, although the Indians seemed to relish it.*
> —Lewis and Clark, August, 1805

Tweedy's lewisia • *Lewisia tweedyi*

FORM: 10–20 cm (4–8") tall. Several flower stems from basal clump of leaves.

BLOOMS: June to July. **This is a relatively scarce plant. Do not disturb.**

FLOWERS: Overall, possibly **the most beautiful wildflower you will find.** They may be pale pink, salmon or pale yellow. The 8 (7–9) petals create a striking bloom about 4 cm (1 1/2") across. There can be buds and blooms on the same stem.

LEAVES: A clump of **thick, basal leaves** to 20 cm (8") long. They appear to come directly from the ground. Leaves **have wide stems.**

RANGE: Rocky slopes, crevices. Mostly east of the Cascades and associated with ponderosa pine and sagebrush. Leavenworth region. Wenatchee Mountains. Chelan County and northern Kittitas County.

Broad-leaved starflower • *Trientalis latifolia*

FORM: 10–20 cm (4–8") tall. Slender stem carrying leaf-top whorl of leaves.

BLOOMS: May to July.

FLOWERS: Usually pinkish, but sometimes white. 5–9 petals, usually 7, star-like. One or several short stems from center of leaf whorls, each holding a flower.

LEAVES: A whorl of 4–7 oval leaves near top of stem.

RANGE: Shady and open forests at lower elevations west of the Cascades. Also in forests of eastern Washington.

Pink monkey-flower • red monkey-flower • *Mimulus lewisii*

FORM: 30–60 cm (1–2') tall. A cluster of erect, unbranched stems. **Plants often in a mass.**

BLOOMS: July to August.

FLOWERS: In opposite pairs, pink-to-rose or purplish-red **"snap-dragon" flowers** 2.5–5 cm (1–2") long. There are **5 petals, 2 turn up and 3 down.** The **throat has a touch of yellow** and may be hairy.

LEAVES: Large, opposite leaves with wavy-toothed margins are to 10 cm (4") long. Notice the **parallel veining.**

RANGE: Streamsides, gravel bars, wet meadows from middle to high mountain elevations.

NOTES: Another plant attributed to Lewis of the Lewis and Clark Expedition.

Foxglove • *Digitalis purpurea*

FORM: 0.6–2.1 m (2–7') tall. A stout, erect stem.

BLOOMS: June to August.

FLOWERS: A flaring, drooping tube that, with dozens of others, covers the top third of the stem. Flowers to **whites, pinks, reds and purples**. In Olympics, flowers are pink to rose-purple.

LEAVES: Basal leaves are long-stemmed and finely toothed. Stem leaves decrease in size with height.

RANGE: Roadsides and old burns. Most common west of the Cascades. Adaptable. Hoh rain forest, subalpine Mt. Baker.

NOTES: This plant is the source of digitalis, a heart stimulant used for over a century. It also contains poisonous substances.

Woolly-pod milk-vetch • Pursh's locoweed • *Astragalus purshii*

FORM: 5–15 cm (2–8") tall. A flower stem from a spray of greenish-woolly basal leaves. Often mat-forming.

BLOOMS: An early bloomer-April. **Fuzzy white seed pods** in May are the easiest identification.

FLOWERS: Shades of pink, but possibly white, yellow or purple.

LEAVES: Leaflets in pairs. A total of 7–19 grayish-woolly leaflets.

RANGE: Grasslands and sagebrush areas. Vantage.

NOTES: A white-flowered species is found on p. 56. True vetches, *Vicia* spp., pp. 151–152, and locoweeds, see p. 56, are similar. **Milk-vetches and locoweeds lack twisting tendrils** at stem-ends. Both have a small flower beak.

Broad-leaved peavine • everlasting pea • *Lathyrus latifolius*

FORM: A climber on shrubs and fences. Easy to identify.

BLOOMS: June to September.

FLOWERS: Pink-rose-purple in large, showy clusters.

LEAVES: Important: **Unusual wide wings border the stems.** Leaves end in tendrils.

RANGE: Most abundant west of the Cascades, but often near settlements throughout.

NOTES: Purple peavine, see p. 151.

Giant vetch • *Vicia gigantea*

FORM: A climber on logs and shrubbery.

BLOOMS: May to August.

FLOWERS: In a tight, **faded pink-brown cluster. Sometimes pink-purple.**

LEAVES: 18–26 leaflets, opposite or alternate, **main stems thick and zigzagging and ending in tendrils.**

RANGE: Common on beach logs and over adjoining vegetation, clearings, old logged areas. Coastal areas.

NOTES: Douglas recorded it in "...open woods of the Columbia."

Sand clover • *Trifolium tridentatum*

FORM: 5–30 cm (2–12") tall. Often forming a **mat-like growth.**

BLOOMS: April into May.

FLOWERS: Small, pea-like flowers, perhaps 8–12, forming a rounded cluster about 1 cm (1/2") across. Pink to purplish with a white blaze on the face. **Note the saucer-shaped involucre (cup holding the flowers)** with its **spiny margin.**

LEAVES: Made up of 3 very narrow, sharp-pointed leaflets each about 1 cm (1/2") long.

RANGE: On grassy open slopes west of the Cascades. Abundant in the Catherine Creek area of Columbia Gorge.

NOTES: David Douglas recorded this in 1827 along the Columbia River.

Springbank clover • *Trifolium wormskjoldii*

FORM: Long creeping roots and flowers on short stems.

BLOOMS: May to September.

FLOWERS: Red-purplish usually white-tipped. **Tiny flowers,** 2–60, **form a tightly packed head.** This cluster **sits on a spike-pointed, circular bract.**

LEAVES: Typical clover, 3-foliate, finely toothed.

RANGE: Stream banks and damp meadows of coastal Washington.

NOTES: This is the most abundant and colorful of the native clovers. Highly valued for their nutritious roots which were dug in the fall and steamed or dried. Native Americans considered patches of springbank clover to be private ground.

Big-head clover • giant's head clover • *Trifolium macrocephalum*

FORM: 7.5–25 cm (3–10") tall. Often a mat-like growth with flowers on short stems.

BLOOMS: Mid-April to mid-May. Often with Howell's triteleia.

FLOWERS: An **eye-catching pinkish ball to 5 cm (2")** across is made up of **tiny pea flowers** in shades of white, cream and pink.

LEAVES: Resembling a small lupine leaf with 5–7 hairy leaflets.

RANGE: Abundant locally, usually in dry, rocky or thin soils. Wide

ranging, but sporadic. Mostly in sagebrush and ponderosa pine regions. High plains southwest of Bickelton. High slopes above Vantage-Ellensburg Highway, Dalles Mountain Road, Columbia Gorge. 1,200 m (4,000') Blue Mountains.

Water smartweed • water knotweed • *Polygonum amphibium*

FORM: 7.5–15 cm (3–6") tall. Short flower stems above a mass of floating leaves. **Often a floating mat.**
BLOOMS: June to August.
FLOWERS: Tiny, rose-pink flowers in a globe or column.
LEAVES: Alternate, leathery leaves attached to a thick stem to 1.2 m (4') long.
RANGE: Widespread, in ponds and lakes. Low to mid-elevations.
NOTES: Under favorable conditions this plant can almost cover a small lake, giving the impression of the lake having pink water.

Thin-leaved owl-clover • *Orthocarpus tenuifolius*

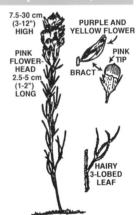

FORM: 7.5–30 cm (3–12") tall. Erect, unbranched stem.
BLOOMS: May to June.
FLOWERS: Pink bracts hide tiny yellow and purplish flowers 1.3 cm (1/2") long. **These have a hooked nose or beak.**
LEAVES: With 3–5 thin fingers.
RANGE: Dry, exposed soils of the bunchgrass and sagebrush regions. Okanogan, Douglas and Spokane counties. Lewis recorded it on the banks of Clark's River (now called the Snake River).
NOTES: Yellow Owl-clovers, see p.92.

Mountain owl-clover • *Orthocarpus imbricatus*

FORM: 10–20 cm (4–8") tall. Erect stem, usually a number of plants in their special habitat.
BLOOMS: July to September.
FLOWERS: Tiny, pink and white almost hidden by **large, pink-purplish bracts** that color the top one-third of the stem.
LEAVES: Sparse, narrow.
RANGE: Common in the subalpine in the Olympics. Doubtful occurrence in northern Cascades, but is found in Oregon Cascades.

Rosy pussytoes • *Antennaria microphylla*

FORM: From 2.5–40 cm (1–16") tall. Erect from a sparse mat of dense, woolly leaves.

BLOOMS: May to August.

FLOWERS: Pink to rosy bracts. Several heads in a cluster.

LEAVES: Sparse, basal, paddle-shaped to 2.5 cm (1") long. Stem leaves small, alternate.

RANGE: Widespread from low to subalpine.

NOTES: Most pussytoes are **white**, see p. 59.

Sea blush • Rosy plectritis • *Plectritis congesta*

FORM: 7.5–30 cm (3–12") tall. Slim erect stems.

BLOOMS: April to May with blue-eyed Mary, satinflower, stonecrops, shootingstars and white fawn lily.

FLOWERS: Tiny, pink flowers are clustered together to form a **compact, rounded head.**

LEAVES: Opposite, oval leaves on tall plants may be to 5 cm (2") long, but on dwarfed plants may be only 6 mm (1/4") long.

RANGE: Open, rocky, mossy places, forest edges. Southward at lower elevations from the San Juan Islands through coastal Washington to an abundance in the Columbia Gorge.

NOTES: A close relative, **white plectritis**, is on p. 58. An early botanical description of this plant was described from specimens grown from seed collected by David Douglas in his early travels.

Thrift • sea-pink, sea lavender • *Armeria maritima*

FORM: 10–20 cm (4–8") tall. Stiff stems from a **basal clump of spiny leaves.** Resembles the garden variety.

BLOOMS: March to July.

FLOWERS: A pinkish dome, to 1.3 cm (1/2") across, **of tiny flowers.** The parchment-like petals dry and may last for months.

LEAVES: A basal clump of narrow, spiny leaves.

RANGE: Grassy bluffs along the coast and grassy meadows inland.

Elephant's head • *Pedicularis groenlandica*

FORM: 15–60 cm (6–24″) tall. Single, erect, **purplish stem** from a spray of basal leaves.

BLOOMS: July to August, usually ahead of lupines and paintbrushes. **A treasured part of the high flower meadows.**

FLOWERS: Strangely-shaped flowers, reddish-purple and clustered in a long floral arrangement at the stem top. The flower, 1.3 cm (1/2″) long, has an upper lip with a dome-shape and long extended spur giving it the popular name, elephant's head.

LEAVES: Finely divided with **each leaflet toothed.**

RANGE: Moist places, meadows, streamsides from middle to subalpine areas where it is at its best. Most mountain systems.

BIRD'S BEAK LOUSEWORT *(P. ornithorhyncha)* is only to 30 cm (12″) tall. Resembles the above in flower arrangement, but the flowers are pink to reddish-purple. The hood is the shape of a bird's head with **a straight spur (like a bird's beak).** Leaves are fern-like. Subalpine meadows in the Cascades.

Sickletop lousewort • parrot's beak • *Pedicularis racemosa*

FORM: 20–50 cm (8–20″) tall. A mass of reddish stems giving a **pinkish-brown blush to a hillside.**

BLOOMS: June to September.

FLOWERS: In shades of pink and white. Flowers grow 1 above another and have 2 lips. The upper is hooded and encloses 4 stamens. The twisting, curved head resembles a hand sickle. The broad lower lip is an insect's landing pad putting it in contact with the stamens above.

LEAVES: Alternate, narrow, toothed or scalloped. **Larger leaves on the upper part of the stem**, the reverse of most plants.

RANGE: Shady slopes in the subalpine. Wide range in mountain systems. Olympics, Cascades, Columbia Gorge.

NOTES: A very noticeable plant because of its pink-brown coloration and abundance. Perpetually on the go, Douglas climbed the mountains north of the Columbia River and about September 1-3, 1825 recorded, "…one of the most laborious undertakings I have ever experienced the way was so rough…very little paper could be carried." However, he did collect sickletop lousewort "…at the summit…."

Mountain sorrel • *Oxyria digyna*

FORM: 5–35 cm (2–14″) A number of stems from a cluster of leaves.

BLOOMS: July to September.

FLOWERS: Small **pink-to-green**, but changing to **small, flat, circular seeds with pale red wings** which give the long flower stems a pinkish tinge.

LEAVES: A rough rosette of long-stemmed, bright green, oval leaves. **They have a sour acid taste—a curiosity.**

RANGE: Open, rocky slopes. Middle to subalpine elevations. Steptoe Butte.

Spreading dogbane • *Apocynum androsaemifolum*

FORM: To 75 cm (30"). tall. Smooth, **reddish stems exude a milky juice** when broken.

BLOOMS: May to July.

FLOWERS: Small, pinkish, "bell" blossoms in twig-end clusters. They produce curved seed pods to 12.5 cm (5") long.

LEAVES: Opposite, egg-shaped leaves hang down as if tired in the summer's heat. **By early August they turn yellow** and so mark their place in the landscape.

RANGE: Most common in the ponderosa pine ecosystem. Okanogan, Ferry, Pend Oreille counties.

NOTES: Dogbanes have stout, fibrous flower stems, but **die down each year**. They are included with flowers.

HEMP (*A.cannabinum*), also called "common dogbane," is a light green, erect shrub, to 1.2 m (4') tall. Reddish stems, **narrow leaves point upright**. Sporadic in the ponderosa pine ecosystem. Yakima, Conconully. Hemp provided a valuable fiber for Native Americans. It was used in weaving, rope and net making. It was an item of trade carried over long distances. Douglas, in June 1825, was watching the Indians catch salmon in the Columbia River, "The net is made from the bark of a species of *Apocynum* which is very durable."

Thyme-leaved buckwheat • *Eriogonum thymoides*

FORM: 5–15 cm (2–6") tall. **A compressed, twiggy little shrub**, but included with the flowers since most people would think of it as a flower and other *Eriogonums* are in this classification.

BLOOMS: April to June.

FLOWERS: May be white, pink, red or yellow. Tiny flowers form a tightly packed cluster about 1.3 cm (1/2") across. Typical umbel formation. Buds often reddish-tinged.

LEAVES: Circlet of leaves on stem near center point. Narrow basal leaves are in tufts on twig ends, grayish and often hairy beneath.

RANGE: On dry, rocky soils at lower elevations east of the Cascades and southward from Chelan County. Often with sagebrush. Vantage area. Cliffs, mid-Columbia Gorge.

NOTES: White buckwheats are on pp.64–65 and **yellows** on pp.97–98.

Spotted knapweed • *Centaurea maculosa*

FORM: 30–90 cm (1–3') tall. A much branched plant covered with blooms.

BLOOMS: June to August.

FLOWERS: Pink-purple and about 2 cm (3/4") across. Note that **the involucre (cup beneath the petals) is formed of triangular scales.** The **tips are black and tufted with hair** (the easiest identification).

LEAVES: With spare, narrow segments.

RANGE: On dry soils, fields, range areas and foothills mostly east of the Cascades.

NOTES: This alien from Europe is a serious weed pest now blanketing vast areas of field and range land. Chemical sprays aren't feasible. The emphasis now is on finding biological controls.

RUSSIAN KNAPWEED (*C. repens*) has the same general form, blooming time and flower color as above. But the **scales are thin and papery**. Leaves are alternate and entire. East of the Cascades in drier areas.

DIFFUSE KNAPWEED (*C. diffusa*) **is smaller than the above two plants**. Only 30–60 cm (1–2') tall. Flowers pink-purple or sometimes white and to 1.3 cm (1/2") across. **Scales distinctive being sharp-pointed and fringed with bristles**. Blooms July to August. Ranges in dry areas east of the Cascades.

Subalpine daisy • *Erigeron peregrinus*

FORM: 15–60 cm (6–24") tall. Single, erect stem from a leafy base. Often a single plant, but sometimes massed.

BLOOMS: July to September. At its best during mid-July to mid-August in the subalpine.

FLOWERS: A beautiful flower **and a treasured part of the subalpine floral display.** Usually **one bloom to a stem**, and about 5 cm (2") wide. The color varies **from pale to deep pink or red-purple** with a **yellow button center**. You find it with arnicas, paintbrush and lupines.

LEAVES: Mostly basal, paddle-shaped and to 20 cm (8") long.

RANGE: Widespread in moist soils from middle to alpine heights. **All high mountain parks.**

NOTES: See leafy aster, p.157, for a similar plant. Douglas was collecting plant specimens day after day. How could one keep a record? His system was simple in that he started with #1 and recorded everything in numerical order along with whatever botanical name, usually generic, he believed it to be. If his name tag had an "S" beside it, it meant he had also collected seed.

Philadelphia fleabane • *Erigeron philadelphicus*

FORM: 30–90 cm (1–3') tall. Erect stem branching near the top.

BLOOMS: May to July. **Fleabanes bloom in early summer, asters later.**

FLOWERS: Usually an attractive pink, but **sometimes white.** Up to 2 cm (3/4") across. **A great number, 150–400, ray petals**, yellow button center. Can be **a dozen or more flowers on branching stems.**

LEAVES: Basal leaves broadly lance-shaped and possibly a few teeth. Stem leaves clasping.

RANGE: Favors moist ground from valleys to middle mountain elevations. Relatively common except for the more arid regions.

NOTES: Height and petal count are distinctive. Plants often massed. The name "fleabane" was first used for European species. It was thought that bunches of dried leaves would repel fleas.

Fairy-slipper • calypso • *Calypso bulbosa*

FORM: 10–15 cm (4–6") tall. Single stem from a buried bulb.

BLOOMS: April to June.

FLOWERS: Rose-purple in color, it has varying shades. The "slipper" is a softer color and **streaked and spotted with purple.** The single flower is about 2.5 cm (1") long and has a faint fragrance.

LEAVES: One shiny, dark green leaf at the base of a reddish stem. The leaf withers during summer, but grows again to remain during the winter.

RANGE: Cool, coniferous forests rich in humus. Widespread, sea level to 1,500 m (5,000').

NOTES: Named after the sea nymph, Calypso, who long ago way-laid Odysseus. This lovely "orchid-looking" plant will capture your attention. The stem rises from a small, lightly buried, marble-sized corm. These were a meager source of food at one time but today deserve all protection.

Pacific bleeding heart • *Dicentra formosa*

FORM: 20–40 cm (8–16") tall. Usually stout stems with a mass of foliage.

BLOOMS: May to June.

FLOWERS: Loose cluster of **4–10 drooping, pinkish "hearts,"** sometimes white. Petals are held together near their tips.

LEAVES: All leaves basal on long stems. So fringed as to **look fern-like.**

RANGE: In moist forest areas, lowlands, shady glades west of the Cascades. Low to middle elevations, Olympics, Cascades, Columbia Gorge.

STEER'S HEAD (*D. uniflora*) is a small plant from 4–10 cm (1 1/2–4") with an unusual pinkish flower. Two sepals are curved to give an impression of a steer's horns. Somewhat rare, but most common east of the Cascades in moist soils below, and in, the subalpine ecosystem.

Flower slopes in the Blue Mountains

Candy stick • barber's pole, sugar stick • *Allotropa virgata*

Both of these plants are saprophytes. They lack green leaves because they feed on dead and decaying vegetation. The vestiges of leaves occur as pale scales on the stem. Indian pipe, see p.40, is a **white** saprophyte.

CANDY STICK (*A. virgata*) is a plant to 45 cm (18") tall, its stout stem striped in white and red. Small urn-shaped flowers have 5 sepals and **10 red stamens**. Look for it July to August in rich humus soils. Most common west of the Cascades, but also on the eastern slope.

PINEDROPS (*Pterospora andromeda*) is recognized by a **stout, orange-red stem** 30–90 cm (1–3') tall. Small "bell" flowers adorn it with a loose arrangement. It blooms June to August in humus soils beneath ponderosa pine and Douglas-fir.

Pinedrops

Scarlet gilia • *Gilia aggregata* • *Ipomopsis aggregata*

FORM: 20–45 cm (8–18") tall. Slender upright stem perhaps branching near top to hold **a dozen or so blooms.**

BLOOMS: Mid-May to mid-July.

FLOWERS: Light scarlet trumpets to 2.5 cm (1") long, flare into 5 petals with **small white dots.**

LEAVES: Drab, thin-fingered, alternate. Rather sparse.

RANGE: In dry exposed places **favoring sandy soil** east of the Cascades. Often along roadsides in the ponderosa pine ecosystem, but will range higher.

NOTES: Favorite plant of hummingbirds which carry out pollenization. Douglas found this species on the banks of the Spokane River, near its junction with the Columbia. This plant is a biennial. During its first year as a clump of leaves it produces food to be stored in the enlarged taproot. The second year it quickly becomes a vigorous plant.

Common hound's-tongue • burgundy hound's-tongue • *Cynoglossum officinale*

FORM: 25–80 cm (10–32") tall. A stout, erect stem from a **basal clump of large leaves**.

BLOOMS: May to June.

FLOWERS: An **unusual red-purple or burgundy** about 6 mm (1/4") across with a **darker center from a circle of short teeth.** Top section of stems in a spray of arching branches, carry one to many flowers at the tip.

LEAVES: Mostly basal, paddle-shaped. 50 cm (20") long with half in stem.

RANGE: Mostly east of the Cascades at lower elevations. Common on open disturbed ground, old pastures, fields, roadsides.

Brown's peony • *Paeonia brownii*

FORM: 15–50 cm (6–20") tall. A plant forming a tangled mass of leaves perhaps 75 cm (30") across.

BLOOMS: April to June with arrow-leaved balsamroot, paintbrush and phlox.

FLOWERS: An **off-red color, maroon perhaps.** A flower to 2.5 cm (1") across appearing thick and heavy and usually nodding. Appears to have **a double row of petals, but the outer row are 6 greenish to purple sepals.** The inner row is formed by 5–6 slightly larger, dull brownish-red petals creating a partly closed cup. Inside are a great mass **of worm-like golden stamens.**

LEAVES: Stems and leaves are thick and fleshy. Leaves divide into several leaflets which divide again into broad lobes.

RANGE: Open slopes from ponderosa pine to high mountains east of Cascades. Chelan County, Leavenworth, Spokane, Blue Mountains 1200 m (4000') and higher.

NOTES: This plant and one in California are the only species of peony native to North America. It is relatively obscure in Washington. Douglas considered finding this peony one of the more important events of his travels. He referred to it a number of times in his writings.

> *I...arrived from a fatiguing trip journey on the Blue Mountains....*
> *I found on those alpine snowy regions a most beautiful species of Paena.*
> —Douglas, July 9, 1826
>
> Later he collected it again and recorded the official location:
>
> *...Near the confines of perpetual snow, in the subalpine range of Mt. Hood, North-West America....*
> —Douglas, 1826

PAINTBRUSHES • *Castilleja* spp.

THE PAINTBRUSH flower is almost hidden by large, showy bracts, usually reddish, which relate to the name paintbrush. Color coding is based on bract colors. Flowers, usually overlooked, are thin tubes which have a slit on the outer side quite evident to a hummingbird or long-tongued insect. There are several dozen paintbrushes in the state with colors ranging through white, cream, yellow, pink and various shades of red. Paintbrushes are partially parasitic on the roots of other plants.

Scarlet paintbrush • *Castilleja miniata*

FORM: To 75 cm (30") tall. Usually several stems and branched.
BLOOMS: July into August. Often massed with lupines.
FLOWERS: Very bright red or scarlet bracts. Tiny, greenish flowers show their tips from behind **bracts with several sharp tips.**
LEAVES: Alternate, narrow and often show a faint 3-vein pattern. Upper leaves may have 3 shallow lobes.
RANGE: Widespread in mountain systems from low to subalpine where it is most abundant. Blue Mountains.

Harsh paintbrush • *Castilleja hispida*

FORM: 10–40 cm (4–16") tall. Single erect stems.
BLOOMS: From mid-April at the Coast to August elsewhere.
FLOWERS: Usually **red on coastal slopes** but **orange-red east of the Cascades.** Tiny flowers are greenish.
LEAVES: Leaves and stem covered with hairs. Stem leaves divide into 3–7 fingers. The highest have 5 red-tipped lobes.
RANGE: Open, rocky places in coastal areas. Common east of the Cascades around 900 m (3000') or middle mountain elevations.

Small-flowered paintbrush • *Castilleja parviflora*

FORM: To 35 cm (14") tall. Usually a clump. Stems unbranched.
BLOOMS: May to August.
FLOWERS: Bracts pink to red. Lobed and hairy.
LEAVES: Alternate, **3–5 narrow lobes.** Slightly hairy. Sometimes white especially in the north Cascades.
RANGE: A common **paintbrush of the subalpine** especially in damp areas.
NOTES: When the plant ages and dries it turns black.

Magenta paintbrush • *Castilleja parviflora* var. *oreopola*

FORM: 15–35 cm (8–14") tall. Stout, erect stems, but not massed.

BLOOMS: June to August. **Among the earliest** in the subalpine.

FLOWERS: Bracts definitely an **off-red color, magenta, red-purple.** Plants stand singly and dot a slope or meadow with color.

LEAVES: Alternate, 3–5 lobed.

RANGE: Along higher roadsides and subalpine meadows. **Mt. Rainier National Park and southward.**

OLYMPIC MAGENTA PAINTBRUSH (*C. parviflora* var. *olympica*) **closely resembles the above**, but for shades of color and minute floral differences. Note range difference. Common in meadows around Hurricane Ridge and Obstruction Point in Olympic National Park.

ALPINE PAINTBRUSH (*C. rhexifolia*) is a close relative to scarlet paintbrush. **Crimson to scarlet bracts** and **less than 30 cm (12") tall. Upper leaves are lobed.** Subalpine paintbrush of eastern Washington. Cascade Mountains north of Lake Chelan. Blue Mountains.

Red columbine • western columbine • *Aquilegia formosa*

FORM: 60–90 cm (2–3') tall. An erect plant, much branched to carry sprays of flowers.

BLOOMS: May to August.

FLOWERS: An amazing floral design. **5 scarlet petals arch backward to look like 5 perched doves.** The name, columbine, is derived from the Latin, "*columba,*" which means "dove." The spurs end in a bulbous tip (a honey gland reachable only by hummingbirds and long-tongued butterflies). The **center** of the flower is **yellowish** with a central tuft of stamens and styles.

LEAVES: Mostly basal. Twice divided into 3s.

RANGE: Shady sites coastal to subalpine in coastal mountains. Relatively abundant.

YELLOW COLUMBINE (*A. flavescens*) flowers are mostly yellow, but may be tinted pink. Moist areas, mostly in high open forests to the subalpine. North-central Washington, Sherman Pass. Cascades to Kittitas County.

Sagebrush mariposa lily • green-banded mariposa lily • *Calochortus macrocarpus*

FORM: 20–50 cm (8–20") tall. Single, erect stem.

BLOOMS: May to July.

FLOWERS: 1–3 pale purple or lavender blooms, often 5 cm (2") across. 3 large petals, each marked on the inside with a central green band. Thin sepals are longer than the petals.

LEAVES: 1–3 thin grass-like leaves while blooming.

RANGE: Abundant in low lands east of Cascades. Usually associated with **sagebrush and ponderosa pine.** Benches of Okanogan and Columbia rivers. Nighthawk to Loomis, Okanogan County.

NOTES: Douglas was the first person to record this plant near The Dalles. He also noted it near Okanogan. Lewis and Clark passed the same area over 20 years before, but not during the blooming season. Its once great abundance has been severely reduced by expanding agriculture and grazing animals. It is almost impossible to transplant and the several years to produce plants from seed are seldom successful.

Round-leaved trillium • *Trillium petiolatum*

FORM: 10–25 cm (4–10") 3 large leaves and a small, purple flower.

BLOOMS: April to May.

FLOWERS: Cradled in a cup where the leaves join. **A 3-petalled flower**, soft purple or maroon, with 6 dark purple anthers.

LEAVES: 3 almost round, bright yellow-green leaves on long stems.

RANGE: Low elevations, bunchgrass and ponderosa pine regions of eastern Washington. Spokane, Pullman.

MOTTLED TRILLIUM (*T. chlropetalum*), also called "giant trillium." To 60 cm (2') tall. 3 large stemless **leaves, dark green mottled with purple.** Erect, stemless **flower with 8 narrow white-to-pink-to purple petals.** West of the Cascades. Pierce County southwards.

Alpine speedwell • veronica • *Veronica wormskjoldii*

FORM: 10–20 cm (4–8") tall. Slim, erect, hairy stems.

BLOOMS: July to August. Often near Jacob's ladder, see p.162.

FLOWERS: A cluster at stem top of buds and flowers with **4 violet to blue petals surrounding a cream center. 2 stamens and a style protrude** beyond the petals and make the small flower distinctive. Note that one petal is smaller than the others.

LEAVES: Opposite pairs of small, ovalish leaves. They may be hairy and slightly toothed.

RANGE: Moist meadows and streambanks, middle mountain to subalpine heights. Most mountain parks, Mt. Rainier.

Sagebrush violet • *Viola trinervata*

FORM: 5–10 cm (2–4") tall. **Much like a small pansy.**

BLOOMS: March to May.

FLOWERS: 2-toned, **2 deep purple, upper petals, others mauve-white and vein-streaked.** May be a yellow spot in the center.

LEAVES: Bluish, deeply cut into 3–5 narrow lobes.

RANGE: Gravely soils of bunchgrass and sagebrush ecosystems. Widespread southward from Grand Coulee. Yakima Canyon, Fort Simcoe.

NOTES: White violets, see p.41, **yellow,** see p.81, **blue,** see p.61.

Naked broomrape • one-flowered cancer root • *Orobanche uniflora*

FORM: 5–15 cm (2–6") tall. A single, erect, finely hairy stem.

BLOOMS: April to May with other spring flowers.

FLOWERS: From **1-3 single purplish flowers with a white throat.** Usually a single flower. Rather unusual among other spring flowers.

LEAVES: Leafless, but a few scales near bottom of a finely hairy stem.

RANGE: Moist areas, seepages, small water courses. Lowlands and foothills across the state. Klickitat and Skamania counties, Columbia Gorge.

NOTES: Naked broomrape is parasitic on certain plants such as saxifrages and stonecrops. The name, "naked," refers to the lack of leaves.

Clustered broomrape • *Orobanche fasiculata*

FORM: 5–20 cm (2–8") tall. A mass of fleshy stems growing in a cluster.

BLOOMS: May to July.

FLOWERS: A number of **long-stemmed flowers form a cluster. May be purplish-tinged or yellow.** Flower with 2 upper lobes and 3 below.

LEAVES: A few scale-like.

RANGE: Exposed bluffs. San Juan Islands but more common in drylands of eastern Washington with sagebrush and buckwheats.

NOTES: A parasitic plant, particularly on sagebrush and buckwheats.

Field mint • Canada mint • *Mentha arvensis*

FORM: 30–90 cm (1–3') tall. Stout, leafy, squarish stem.

BLOOMS: July to August.

FLOWERS: Tiny, 5-petalled flowers, **pale purple to pink, in tight clusters** in uppermost leaf axils.

LEAVES: Opposite leaves to 7.5 cm (3") long. Coarsely toothed. **Minty smell even before being crushed.**

RANGE: Moist places, stream edges, low to middle elevations.

NOTES: Several other mints are garden escapes (unlike the above which is a native plant). You can make herb tea by using fresh or dried leaves. In 1826, Douglas arrived at Okanogan (a small post near the present town). He also collected birds and animals in his travels.

The first night of my arrival I had the great misfortune to get a pair of my grouse devoured, the skins torn to pieces by the famished dogs....Grieved beyond measure. Carried the cockbird 457, and the hen 304 miles on my back and then unfortunately lost them.

—Douglas, February 6, 1826

Thread-leaved phacelia • *Phacelia linearis*

FORM: 12.5–50 cm (5–20") tall. Sometimes a single stem, but often branching. Mulleins and sagebrush often nearby.

BLOOMS: Mid-May to June.

FLOWERS: Soft mauve or lavender to 2 cm (3/4") across. **In a tightly coiled head.**

FRUITS: Flowers leave a row of seed capsules in a loose coil formation.

LEAVES: Lower leaves are very narrow, **thread-leaved,** but **upper are larger and 5-pronged.**

RANGE: In open low lands and foothills, most common east of the Cascades. Abundant in various locations.

Silky phacelia • *Phacelia sericea*

FORM: 15–30 cm (6–12") tall. A number of short flower stems from a thick clump of leaves.

BLOOMS: July to September.

FLOWERS: Spikes of fuzzy, violet flowers. Long, protruding stamens tipped by yellow anthers. **Long stamens are characteristic of phacelias.**

LEAVES: Alternate, grayish green, deeply divided, and have a **silky** appearance and texture from a covering of fine hair.

RANGE: Rocky ridges, slopes. Subalpine and into the alpine tundra. Most high mountains.

European bittersweet • *Solanum dulcamara*

FORM: Vigorous, twining climber to 2.1 m (7') tall.

BLOOMS: June to September.

FLOWERS: Purple flowers with a yellow cone. Much like tomato and potato blooms. Followed successively by berries.

FRUITS: Green, yellow and shiny red berries. Considered mildly poisonous.

LEAVES: Lower ones have a twist in the stem that holds them upright. Higher ones have 1–2 ear-like lobes at the base.

RANGE: Moist areas at lower elevations. Usually near settlements.

On crossing Cedar River...my horse in gaining the other side, which is steep and slippery, threw back his head and struck me in the face and I was plunged head foremost in the river. I...received a good ducking and got wet what seed I had collected during the day....
—Douglas, August 4, 1826 near Kettle Falls

Marsh cinquefoil • *Potentilla palustris*

FORM: Flower stems rising to 30 cm (12") above **floating or partially submerged creeping stems.**

BLOOMS: June to August.

FLOWERS: Bowl-shaped, purplish-red flowers about 2 cm (3/4") across. Large sharp-pointed sepals, petals are smaller. A fetid nectar attracts pollinating insects.

LEAVES: Mostly on flowering stems, alternate, carrying **5–7 regularly toothed leaflets.**

RANGE: Swamps, marshes from seashore to subalpine. Widespread, but not too noticeable.

NOTES: Another cinquefoil in wet areas has **yellow** flowers, pp.82-83.

Columbia monkshood • *Aconitum columbianum*

FORM: Varies from 75 cm (30") to 1.5 m (5') tall.

BLOOMS: June to August depending on altitude.

FLOWERS: Color varies from **blue–violet-purple**. Each flower, 4 cm (1 1/2") long, is on an upward-arching stem. Topmost sepal forms a hood. **2 large side petals arch upwards to help form a "monk's hood"** and 2 petals form the bottom lip.

LEAVES: Large, alternate leaves deeply divided, forms 3–5 sections, coarsely toothed.

RANGE: In moist areas, marshes from low elevations to the subalpine. East of Cascades.

NOTES: All parts are poisonous.

BLUE-EYED GRASSES • *Sisyrinchium* spp.

A NUMBER OF plants have been generalized as blue-eyed grasses. These are very difficult to separate and label without expert knowledge. Hybridization adds to the puzzle. Close relatives, coded under **PINK**, are on page 123.

Idaho blue-eyed grass • *Sisyrinchium Idahoense*

FORM: 10–40 cm (5–16") tall.

BLOOMS: May to June.

FLOWERS: Purple sometimes shading to blue. **Petals pleated and tipped with a short spine.** Flowers 1.3–2 cm (1/2–3/4") across.

LEAVES: Leaves are narrow and shorter than the flower stem.

RANGE: Moist grassy slopes from lowlands into low mountains. East of the Cascades. Ellensburg, Pullman.

MOUNTAIN BLUE-EYED GRASS (*S. montanum*) to 35 cm (14") tall, this flower of **pale to deep purple, is held erect or horizontally.** The filaments (stems holding the anthers) are held together to near their tips. **The plant stems are usually broader than the thin leaves.** This species is the most common east of the Cascades. Moist areas in the dry interior region.

Harvest brodiaea • *Brodiaea coronaria*

FORM: 5–25 cm (2–10") tall. Single, erect stem from a deeply buried bulb.

BLOOMS: Late May to June.

FLOWERS: Usually a showy **cluster of 3–5 purple-pink flowers** about 4 cm (1 1/2") across. Each petal striped with a dark purple line. **3 white, petal-like anthers stand vertically** from the center giving the flower a distinct "white eye." Flower stems originate from the same place (umbel design), but vary greatly in length.

LEAVES: The 1–3 grass-like leaves wither before the flowers appear.

RANGE: On open, grassy slopes and high, rocky soils of western Washington, **sometimes by the thousands.** Penetrates into the Columbia Gorge and northwards into Yakima County.

NOTES: At one time, coastal tribes gathered these bulbs as a food item. A **white** relative, see p.51, **blue** ones, see p.165. *Triteleia* is an alternative name for several of the *brodiaeas.*

Ball-head cluster lily • ookow • *Brodiaea congesta*

FORM: To 1.2 m (4') tall.

BLOOMS: Mid-May to June.

FLOWERS: The small, dark purple flowers form a tight ball. Flower head over 5 cm (2") across. Perhaps a dozen 6-petalled flowers in each cluster.

LEAVES: Likely the long green leaves are lying on the grass.

RANGE: Dry, grassy slopes, meadows in the coastal forest ecosystem. Columbia Gorge as far east as The Dalles.

NOTES: Very showy since there are usually a number of plants.

Purple loosestrife • *Lythrum salicaria*

FORM: 0.9–1.8 m (3–6') tall. Many upright stems.

BLOOMS: July to September.

FLOWERS: Massed spikes of pink-purple flowers. Tubular in shape with 5–6 petals.

LEAVES: Opposite, stemless and without teeth.

RANGE: Lowland sloughs, marshes and ditches.

NOTES: Here is a beautiful villain! This European introduction has spread from coast to coast invading ponds and ditches. It can take over the habitats of fish, muskrats, nesting birds and indigenous plants, thereby eliminating them. Chemical controls are impractical, but there is some experimentation with biological controls. The best control is to pull up invasive plants and burn all parts.

Pasqueflower • prairie crocus • *Anemone patens*

FORM: 20–45 cm (8–18") tall. Erect, hairy stems holding 1 flower.

BLOOMS: April to May.

FLOWERS: Violet or purple-blue flowers to 4 cm (1 1/2") across. The **cup-shaped bloom, with a golden center,** is formed by **6–7 large sepals.** After blooming **the stem extends** to 45 cm (1 1/2') to produce a silky-white seed head.

LEAVES: Many long-stemmed, basal, grayish and hairy. Divided into many narrow segments, 1–2 tight whorls on the stem.

RANGE: Plains and foothills east of the Cascades. Wenatchee Mountains eastward to the Rockies. Also northeastern Washington.

Simpson's cactus • hedgehog thistle • *Pediocactus simpsonii*

FORM: 5–12.5 cm (2–5") tall. A blunt sphere covered with a pattern of prominent bumps each with a cluster of needle-like spines.

BLOOMS: April to May. Blooms with bighead clover, dwarf *Eriogonums* and spreading phlox. Bitterroot, often with it, will bloom a week or two later.

FLOWERS: Purple-rose or sometimes yellow. Several rows of delicate, tissue-like petals. The center is a mass of golden stamens.

RANGE: East of the Cascades. Favors rocky, exposed ground with embedded stone. Apparently quite rare except in limited local areas—usually associated with rigid sagebrush—where it is quite plentiful. Most prolific between 600–1050 m (2000–3500') elevations. Kittitas and Douglas counties. The Vantage Highway.

NOTES: Yellow-flowering cacti are on p. 88.

Common salsify • *Tragopogon porrifolius*

FORM: 30–75 cm (1–2 1/2') tall. Stout stem.

BLOOMS: May to June.

FLOWERS: Deep purple and to 7.5 cm (3") across.

FRUITS: Large seed head follows flowers.

LEAVES: Alternate. Long, grass-like.

RANGE: Valley roadsides. Widespread.

NOTES: Yellow salsify, *T. dubius*, has yellow flowers, see p. 100. This is a sun-sensitive plant that tends to close the flower during cloudy weather.

Common butterwort • *Pinguicula vulgaris*

FORM: 5–12.5 cm (2–5") tall. **A single, leafless stem with a single flower.**

BLOOMS: June to September.

FLOWERS: A lovely violet-purple about 1 cm (1/2") or more long. **The petals create a tube** which ends in a spur. Notice how the upper stem clasps on to the flower spur.

LEAVES: A rosette of **unusual basal leaves, yellowish-green, thick and slimy** to trap insects.

RANGE: Most abundant on edges of bogs, wet meadows, seepage areas. Wide ranging. From lower mountain slopes to subalpine, Alaska to California.

Cooley's hedge nettle • *Stachys cooleyae*

FORM: To 90 cm (3') tall. An erect, coarse, weedy plant with a square stem typical of the mint family.

BLOOMS: June to July.

FLOWERS: Red-purple flowers to 4 cm (1 1/2") long **in open, terminal clusters**, also several flowers in leaf axils. Note that the **lower petal (lip) is broadly 3-lobed.**

LEAVES: Opposite, hairy both sides, rank smell, coarsely blunt-toothed.

RANGE: In damp ground at low elevations. West of the Cascades. San Juan Islands and coastal zone.

NOTES: All of the plants collected by David Douglas would be studied by eminent botanists in Great Britain. This meant that all significant parts had to be collected: roots or bulbs at one end and flowers and seeds at the other. These would be pressed and dried and fastened in some fashion to a sheet of heavy paper about 16" x 22" in size. Noted would be pertinent details, a name (if identified), date and place of collection, elevation and habitat and anything else deemed important. This system of collection is called a herbarium. Douglas' specimens are still seen in various herbaria and are regarded as excellent examples of craftsmanship.

PENSTEMONS • BEARD TONGUES • *Penstemon* spp.

ALL PENSTEMONS have a **funnel-like flower with a 5-lobed calyx.** Petals fuse into a tube with 5 lobes: 2 tilt upwards while the lower 3 slope outwards and create a landing strip for bees. When a bee crawls into the tube its back brushes the overhanging stigma and receives pollen deposited by a previous bee. More pollen also falls on the bee's back and the process is repeated. The bee's reward is the nectar in the rear of the tube. There are 5 stamens, but only 4 anthers are fertile. The lack of, or the amount of, hair in the throat or tongue may be a distinguishing factor.

Only about half of the penstemons that may be found in the state are described here. These are the most common and recognizable.

Three common penstemons, **Davidson's, shrubby** and **Scouler's,** technically can be classed as shrubs because of their woody growth. However, they differ so little in appearance they have been grouped with the others. They separate from others by having very **noticeable woolly-tipped anthers.** An exception is woodland penstemon, see p. 150. Recognize them by the differences in leaves.

DAVIDSON'S PENSTEMON (*P. davidsonii*): Evergreen leaves short, stubby. Forms a mat-like growth.

SHRUBBY PENSTEMON (*P. fruticosus*): Leaves usually not toothed, relatively broad. To 6 cm (2 1/4") long and to 1.2 cm (1/2") wide. Not mat-like.

SCOULER'S PENSTEMON (*P. fruticosus* var. *scouleri*): Leaves usually fine-toothed, narrow, about 6 mm (1/4") wide. Not mat-like.

Two penstemons, because of their unusual color, are noted here.

YELLOW PENSTEMON (*P. confertus*) **may be white to cream to pale yellow.** Associated with the ponderosa pine ecosystem.

WHITE PENSTEMON (*P. deustus*) **is the only true white penstemon.** It favors the dry lands of central Washington.

Davidson's penstemon • Menzies' penstemon • *Penstemon davidsonii*

FORM: 20–30 cm (8–12") tall.

BLOOMS: June to August.

FLOWERS: Long, deep blue-purple flowers appear flattened. Flower throat bristly, anthers woolly-tipped.

LEAVES: Evergreen, opposite, thick and blunt to 6 mm (1/4") long and forming a mat.

RANGE: High, rocky places in the subalpine.

NOTES: This plant ranges to California where it was first collected by Dr. George Davidson.

High, rocky places in the subalpine

Shrubby penstemon • *Penstemon fruticosus*

FORM: 20–30 cm (8–12") tall. A shrubby loose growth **(not mat-forming)** with short flower stems.

BLOOMS: May to August. Blooms later than Scouler's.

FLOWERS: Long-tubed, bright blue-lavender or light purple. **White hairy on base of lower lip,** anthers woolly-tipped. Flowers in pairs to 4 cm (1 1/2") long.

LEAVES: Opposite, smooth or sometimes finely toothed. To 4 cm (1 1/2") long and 6 mm (1/4") wide.

RANGE: On open, rocky slopes. East of the Cascades to the Rockies. Wide elevation range from low to high mountains. Common along steep roadsides.

NOTES: Douglas found it near Kettle Falls and in the Blue Mountains and Lewis found it in the Rocky Mountains.

Scouler's penstemon • *Penstemon fruticosus* var. *scouleri*

FORM: 20–30 cm (8–12") tall. **Twiggy, low, shrub-like** growth with short flower stems.

BLOOMS: April to July.

FLOWERS: To 4 cm (1 1/2") long, in showy purple clusters. Anthers woolly-tipped.

LEAVES: Usually **fine-toothed**, thick, narrow, **about 6 mm (1/4") wide.**

RANGE: East of the Cascades. Blooming on steep banks, rocky places, roadside cliffs in April to July. From low to subalpine. Wide range in elevation.

NOTES: Named after John Scouler, M.D., a geologist/surgeon/ naturalist who accompanied David Douglas on his first trip to the Northwest.

Small-flowered penstemon • *Penstemon procerus*

FORM: To 60 cm (2') tall. Noticeable because of the **several, upright, flower stems.**

BLOOMS: May to August depending on elevation.

FLOWERS: Dark blue-purple often tinged with pink. A whitish throat. About 1.3 cm (1/2") long. In **distinctive whorls** between higher, opposite leaf axils. Flowers point upward.

LEAVES: A loose mat or tuft with stem leaves opposite and narrow.

RANGE: East of the Cascades. Dry, open ground from low, open forests to rocky ridges near the subalpine ecosystems.

Woodland penstemon • *Nothochelone nemorosa*

FORM: To 60 cm (24") tall. One to several stems.

BLOOMS: June to September.

FLOWERS: Rose-purple to blue-purple. About 3 cm (1 1/4") long. **Upper lip much shorter than the lower. Stamens have hairy anthers.** See pp.148–149 for other penstemons with woolly anthers.

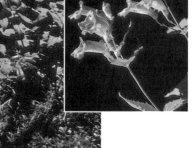

LEAVES: Opposite, coarsely toothed from 4–10 cm (1 1/2–4") long.

RANGE: Cascades and eastward. Open forests, meadows. A woodland plant often in shade. Low to subalpine. Olympics.

NOTES: A minor variation in flower structure gives this a different genus name.

Coast penstemon • *Penstemon serrulatus*

FORM: 20–70 cm (8–28") tall. Erect stems forming a bushy plant.

BLOOMS: June to August.

FLOWERS: Flowers to 2.5 cm (1") long, **1 to several whorl-like clusters near stem tops. No woolly anthers.**

LEAVES: Important: Stem leaves opposite, **oval with sharp-pointed teeth.**

RANGE: West Cascades. Moist areas low to medium elevations.

NOTES: References often say, **"deep blue to purple"** but it can be quite pinkish. The name, "penstemon," is derived from the Greek *pente* (five) and *stemon* (a stamen) referring to the five stamens.

PEAVINES AND VETCHES • *Lathyrus* spp. and *Vicia* spp.

THE PEAVINES and vetches are very similar and include many introduced species. Both have weak stems and depend largely on twining tendrils for support. **Peavines have 3–5 pairs of opposite leaflets per leaf, most vetches have 4–13 pairs.** The experts say to take a flower apart and look at the style. This requires a magnifying glass and imagination! Peavine flowers have fine hairs arranged on one side of the style, vetches have hairs that surround it.

Purple peavine • *Lathyrus nevadensis*

FORM: A stout vine with angled stems to 1.2 m (4') long. Climbs on vegetation.

BLOOMS: May to July.

FLOWERS: Red-purple to blue. To 2 cm (3/4") long and in clusters of 2–7. Almost lost in supporting vegetation.

LEAVES: 4–12 narrowly oval, alternate leaflets per leaf. Tipped with **unbranched tendrils.**

RANGE: Open woods at low to middle elevations. Widespread. Olympics, coastal Washington, Columbia Gorge. East slope of Cascades bordering ponderosa pine ecosystem.

Beach pea • *Lathyrus japonicus*

FORM: Stems to 1.2 m (4') tall. Trailing or climbing.

BLOOMS: May to August.

FLOWERS: Reddish-purple to dark purple, in loose **clusters of 2–8.**

FRUITS: The pea seeds are considered edible.

LEAVES: Important: A key feature is the **2 large leaf-like stipules of unusual triangular-shape** at the base of a leaf stem. **Each leaf has 3–6 pairs of leaflets** and a stem is tipped with curling tendrils.

RANGE: On debris of coastal beaches and on adjoining slopes. Always near the ocean.

American vetch • *Vicia americana*

FORM: Climbs over other vegetation, but may be unsupported as individual plants. A perennial like most peavines.

BLOOMS: April to June.

FLOWERS: Purple-pink to lavender. Flowers 2 cm (3/4") long, in loose **terminal clusters of 3–9.**

LEAVES: 8–18 opposite leaflets ending in tendrils.

RANGE: Widespread, but mostly east of the Cascades. Chelan, Klickitat counties. Columbia Gorge.

Woolly vetch • *Vicia villosa*

FORM: Branching form creates thickets of vine on other vegetation. Tendrils are branching.

BLOOMS: May to August (dependent on location).

FLOWERS: Important: Flowers light or dark purple, often fringed with white, **fine white hair from stem and leaves to part way up the keel.** (But you really need a magnifying glass to see this hair.) Flowers appear to **droop in 2 rows.** Pea pods about 2.5 cm (1") long with 4–5 peas.

LEAVES: With narrow leaflets opposite and in 8–12 pairs.

RANGE: Widespread, but most abundant east of the Cascades. **Sometimes covering whole hillsides with a soft purple shade.** Okanogan, Ferry and Klickitat counties.

TUFTED VETCH (*V. cracca*) has dark, bluish-purple flowers, with a touch of white, that **grow in a row from 1 side of the stem. 12–18 leaflets twice the length of the flowers.** Blooms June to August. Masses in fields and lower mountain slopes. Widespread at lower elevations.

COMMON VETCH (*V. sativa*) provides a dab of bright, red-purple to pink amid the green grasses of spring along coastal Washington. A slender vine with short **flower stems holding 1–3 flowers** 2.5 cm (1") long. **Leaves have 8–16 leaflets.** They are opposite and about the same length as the flowers. Note there is a little bristle at the tip of each leaflet.

Self-heal • heal all • *Prunella vulgaris*

FORM: 7.5–40 cm (3–16") tall. A single stem or several stems from a leaf clump.

BLOOMS: Spring and summer.

FLOWERS: Varying from a **dark purple to almost pinkish.** A small flower rather resembling an orchid with its upper and lower lips. They form **an elongated cluster at the top of the stem.**

LEAVES: Sparse, opposite pairs, not toothed.

RANGE: From fields and roadsides to high on the mountainside. Wide range.

NOTES: Widespread use for medicinal purposes started a long time ago in Europe. Coastal natives used it for various reasons in the past.

Pacific waterleaf • *Hydrophyllum tenuipes*

FORM: 20–80 cm (8–32") tall. Very leafy.

BLOOMS: April to July.

FLOWERS: Pale to dark purple, **sometimes white to greenish,** in tight clusters of a dozen or more at end of a stalk. 5 small petals and 5 projecting stamens tipped with a golden anther.

LEAVES: Alternate, large, deeply divided into sharply toothed segments, usually 5.

RANGE: East of Cascades. Damp, shady places at lower elevations in coastal forests. West Columbia Gorge.

NOTES: See p.47 for a closely related species.

Burdock • dock • *Arctium minus*

FORM: 0.9–1.5 m (3–5') tall. Coarse, much branched.

BLOOMS: June to August.

FLOWERS: Purplish to pinkish, tuft-like, **surrounded by rough, hooked bristles.** They develop by fall into hard, round burs with hooked spines.

LEAVES: In spring, they form a rosette of **huge leaves, white-woolly beneath and about the size of rhubarb.** A stout, dead stem on the ground would suggest there will be a tall plant.

RANGE: A native of Eurasia now common on wastelands at lower elevations.

NOTES: They are often listed as the origin for Velcro.

Teasel • *Dipsacus sylvestris*

FORM: 0.9–1.8 m (3–6') tall. Single, thorny, erect stem.

BLOOMS: July to September.

FLOWERS: Almost **overlooked in the large, spiny head of bracts.** They are tiny, 4-lobed and **form a collar around the head.** Colors vary from pink, rose-purple and pale purple. Immediately below are **several thin, twisting leaves.** By early autumn the **familiar cone-like head of stout bristles is hardening.**

LEAVES: Opposite and to 30 cm (12") long.

RANGE: Low, moist areas. Mostly west of the Cascades. Columbia Gorge. Also widespread to the east. Steptoe Butte, Garfield, Pullman, Dayton, Prosser.

NOTES: The large burs were once used to card or tease wool in Europe. It was probably introduced to America for the same purpose. Some say it was teasel that provided the inspiration for Velcro.

Fern-leaved desert-parsley • chocolate tips, carrot leaf •
Lomatium dissectum

FORM: To 1.2 m (4'), but can be taller. The tallest, **most robust of the desert-parsley species. Stems extend high** above the bright, green thicket of foliage.

BLOOMS: April to June.

FLOWERS: Tiny, in cluster heads and held in umbel formation. **Dark purple in this case, but a yellow form is common. White anthers contrast sharply against the chocolate-colored background.**

LEAVES: So dissected as to deserve the name "fern-leaved."

RANGE: Rocky areas and exposed soils. East of the Cascades. Often in ponderosa pine regions or edge of sagebrush zone. Vantage, Yakima Canyon, Columbia Gorge.

NOTES: Young shoots and roots were considered food by some Native Americans, but left alone by others. This desert-parsley has also been included with the **yellow** blooming ones, see pp.95-97. • Both Lewis and Clark and David Douglas made reference a number of times to "the Canadians." Often they were French-Canadians, adventurous and self-reliant. They explored routes, trapped and helped the Hudson's Bay Company to establish small trading posts. They were were the experts on raft, canoe and horse travel. Douglas met them in his explorations and was glad to have their company and assistance.

THISTLES • *Cirsium* spp.

WITH ABOUT 50 thistles in North America and a dozen in Washington, how do you know you are seeing a thistle? Beyond the technical details of a flower head all species in Washington have **leaves spiny to some degree.** Plants are immune from grazing animals and spread widely through roots.

COMMON THISTLE (*C. vulgare*) has a **single blossom on a bristly green bur which may be 5 cm (2") across. Stem has spiny wings.** Leaf stems are clasping. **Leaves spiny.** Blooms July to August. Widespread at low to middle elevations. A favorite of bumble bees.

CANADA THISTLE (*C. arvense*) has **spine-tipped leaves, but not the spiny stem wings of the** above. Flowers are pale purple-pink, **about 1.3 cm (1/2") across. Flowers in loose clusters** from many branching high stems. Leaves lobed to various degrees, **prickly everywhere.** Summertime blooms may form extensive patches and later great masses of fluffy seed heads. Found throughout.

The roots of the thistle [edible thistle] is from 9–15 Inches in length and about the size of a man's thumb...when first taken from the ground is white and nearly as crispt as a carrot. When prepared for use it becomes black, and is more shugery there any fruit or root that I have met with in uce among the natives....
—Lewis, January 21, 1806

EDIBLE THISTLE (*C. edule*) has **one to several large rose-purple blooms each on a pedestal of a many-spined white, woolly mass.** Leaves may be 25 cm (10") long, **deeply incised and spiny.** The plump root about 30 cm (12") long can be boiled and eaten. A showy plant of higher elevations and into the subalpine.

WAVY-LEAVED THISTLE (*C. undulatum*) has **an overall silvery-white color** and flowers from rose to lavender to white. **A single flower at each branch tip. Wavy edges to leaves protected by long, yellowish spines.** Widespread on exposed, dry soils.

Silver thistle • *Carduus nutans*

FORM: To 1.8 m (6') tall. A very stout, spiny stem **and leaves with a silvery appearance.** The **size and this coloration** provide positive identification.

BLOOMS: May to July.

FLOWERS: Large, purple flower head may be 6 cm (2 1/4") wide.

FRUITS: Forms a tuft of white seeds after flowering.

LEAVES: A basal rosette of very large, lobed, spiny leaves. They are up to 30 cm (12") long and half as wide. Equally **ferocious spiny leaves continue up the stem.**

RANGE: A native of Europe and western Asia, it was recorded several decades ago as being "sparingly abundant." Now it is a wide-ranging pest especially along the Snake River and its tributaries. Steptoe Canyon road.

NOTES: Failing to find a common name for this giant silvery thistle, the author has used the obvious "silver thistle."

ASTERS AND FLEABANES

FOR NOTES ON these species and differences, see p.70. There are over 2 dozen asters in the state so expect some confusion. **All asters with blue and purplish-color tones are grouped here.**

Alpine aster • *Aster alpigenus*

FORM: 10–25 cm (4–10") tall. Several, **short, flower stems** from a clump of leaves.

BLOOMS: July to August.

FLOWERS: Showy, **purple to lavender, with a bright yellow button center. One bloom to a stem** and about 4 cm (1 1/2") across. Rather tousled, ray petals droop and twist.

LEAVES: Mostly basal, narrow and to 6 cm (2 1/4") long.

RANGE: Subalpine to alpine. Olympics, Cascades. Mt. Rainier.

NOTES: A dwarf aster of the subalpine.

Showy aster • large purple aster • *Aster conspicuus*

FORM: To 40–90 cm (16–36") tall. Stout, erect, branching near top. **Resembles a garden-variety, Michaelmas daisy.**

BLOOMS: August to September.

FLOWERS: Showy heads of many smallish, light purplish, ray petal flowers. Flowers to 2.5 cm (1") across. There is a golden button center. Bracts stick out.

LEAVES: Alternate, thick, rough, coarse-toothed to 15 cm (6") long. **Distinguished by many large, rough, sharp-toothed leaves.**

RANGE: Coarse soils in open forests. East of the Cascades.

NOTES: A plant favored by Native Americans for its medicinal properties. A preparation from water and roots was used to treat infections.

Douglas' aster • *Aster subspicatus*

FORM: 40–90 cm (10–36") tall. Stout stems usually branching to give a rounded top outline and a loose, open flower grouping.

BLOOMS: August to September.

FLOWERS: Showy heads of 16–20 purple ray flowers with a yellow center. Flowers 2.5–4 cm (1–1 1/2") across. Overlapping bracts have a thin, transparent margin and a yellow-brown base coloration.

LEAVES: Long, narrow, lower leaves have short stems, those above are stemless, sharp-pointed.

RANGE: Well-drained soils, open coniferous forests, roadsides. Most common west of the Cascades. At low to middle elevations. Puget Sound area and Columbia Gorge.

NOTES: Several other asters (not in this book) are similar. In this, the **overlapping bracts have a thin transparent margin. Use a magnifying glass.**

Great northern aster • *Aster modestus*

FORM: 45–90 cm (1 1/2–3') tall. Stems single or branched.

BLOOMS: August to October. **Late blooming is significant, a characteristic of asters.**

FLOWERS: Light purple to violet. **Long, thin, ray petals, about 30, around a small dull yellow button center.** Note that the **bracts are narrow, greenish and glandular.** This is **the best key** in identification. Use a magnifying glass.

LEAVES: Basal leaves small, usually withered by blooming times. Others broadly lance-shaped, to 5–12 cm (2–5") long. Leaves often irregularly toothed.

RANGE: Widespread on moister ground, streambanks, lowlands to higher open forests. Columbia Gorge.

LEAFY ASTER (*A. foliaceus*), also called "leafy-headed aster," which is significant in identification. **Many large, green, leaf-like bracts support the flower head.** This aster of moderate height, 30–75 cm (1–2 1/2'), has a rather small flower cluster on a stem branch. These may be rose-purple to violet with a yellow center. **Ray petals are thin and numerous** for an aster. Lower leaves wither quickly, others are stemless and 5–12 cm (2–5") long. Wide range in moist forests from valley to subalpine. Harts Pass, Columbia Gorge.

COMMON CALIFORNIA ASTER (*A. chilensis*) has a common aster height of 30–90 cm (1–3'). Often bushy. Check that **bracts are shingle-like, green-tipped and rounded.** Flowers pale bluish or violet, to 2.5 cm (1") wide with large button center. *A. chilensis* var. *hallii* has white rays and is fairly common. Basal leaves soon withering. Others long and narrow. Dry, open areas near the coast. Generally west of the Cascades.

PURPLE ASTER (*A. ledophyllus*) has large, lavender-purple flowers. Single or several. **Bracts narrow, sharp-pointed.** Lower leaves reduced, others **gray-woolly beneath.** Cascades and Mt. Rainier.

Great northern aster

Leafy aster

Typical terrain for asters

FLEABANES • *Erigeron* spp.

THERE COULD BE over 2 dozen in the state and many with minor differences. The **differences between fleabanes and asters** are found on p.70. **Cut-leaved daisy**, on p.70, may be **purple** and similar to a fleabane, so check it. *Erigerons* can be **white**, see pp.70–71, **yellow**, pp.103-104, **pink**, pp.133–134, and **blue**, p.174. The name, fleabane, comes from a belief that these plants repelled fleas. **Most bloom in early summer.**

Cushion fleabane • *Erigeron poliospermus*

FORM: 5–15 cm (2–6″) tall. A loose mat of leaves with short, flower stems.

BLOOMS: April to May.

FLOWERS: Soft purple-violet, sometimes white. About 2.5 cm (1″) across with 25–30 ray flowers, yellow center.

LEAVES: Basal tufts of narrow, paddle-shaped leaves. Dull green and finely hairy. You need a hand lens to see them. Several, small, stem leaves.

RANGE: East of the Cascades in sagebrush regions, often associated with rigid sagebrush. Spokane, Wenatchee, Ellensburg, Vantage, Sunnyside, Walla Walla, Kittitas County.

Long-leaved fleabane • *Erigeron corymbosus*

FORM: 15–50 cm (6–20″) tall. Erect, hairy stems, leafy base.

BLOOMS: June to July.

FLOWERS: Usually several, light purple, bluish or pinkish flowers per stem. **Ray flowers, 40–60, wider than most.**

LEAVES: Basal tuft of paddle-shaped hairy leaves. Note a 3 vein pattern on larger leaves. A few small stem leaves.

RANGE: Sagebrush ecosystem and into the foothills.

NOTES: This is a particularly attractive fleabane because of its bloom of wide ray flowers contrasting with a golden center of disk flowers. The fact that it blooms in spring is a good indication that it is a fleabane rather than a daisy.

Sagebrush ecosystem and into the foothills

Showy-fleabane • large purple fleabane • *Erigeron speciosus*

FORM: To 75 cm (30") tall. Erect stems. Plants are massed.

BLOOMS: May to September. **A late-blooming fleabane.**

FLOWERS: Purple to blue ray flowers and golden center. Blooms may be to 5 cm (2") or half that across. Several to a stem. **About 100 very narrow, ray flowers.**

LEAVES: Long, thin, entire leaves with only small change in size, climb almost to the top. To 5 cm (2") long.

RANGE: Foothills to moderate elevations. Mostly western Washington but also on the east slope of the Cascades.

NOTES: David Douglas collected seed that was successfully grown in England.

Western meadowrue • *Thalictrum occidentale*

FORM: 30–90 cm (1–3') tall.

BLOOMS: May to August. **Male and female on separate plants.**

FLOWERS: Male flowers are delicate and attractive with tassels of silky, purple anthers. Female flowers are greenish-white and drooping. This plant is wind-pollinated.

LEAVES: A definite **soft bluish-green**. Divided several times with each round leaflet lobed again.

RANGE: Shady, moist locations from ocean side to the subalpine. Widespread.

NOTES: Different native tribes attributed various medicinal properties to the same plant. The western meadowrue was such a one.

Female flowers

Cusick's speedwell • mountain veronica • *Veronica cusickii*

FORM: 5–20 cm (2–8") tall. Slim, erect stems. Plants often clustered.

BLOOMS: July to August.

FLOWERS: In a terminal cluster. Large for such a tiny plant, to 1.3 cm (1/2") long, blue-violet. **Broad upper petal marked with lines of purple dots.**

LEAVES: Bright green, opposite leaves.

RANGE: Moist meadows to rocky areas. Adaptable. Mountain forests to subalpine. Common in the Cascades and Olympics.

COMMON SPEEDWELL (*V. officinalis*) is often flat on the forest floor and partly covered by conifer needles. Short flower stems branch up. **Tiny flowers** are miniature gems with **light blue petals tinged with lavender stripes.** Leaves are opposite and **finely toothed.** It ranges widely both sides of the Cascades to middle mountain elevations.

Sugar bowls • *Clematis hirsutissima*

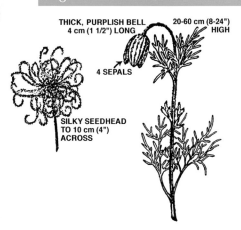

THICK, PURPLISH BELL
4 cm (1 1/2") LONG

20-60 cm (8-24") HIGH

4 SEPALS

SILKY SEEDHEAD
TO 10 cm (4")
ACROSS

FORM: 20–60 cm (8–24") tall.

BLOOMS: April to May.

FLOWERS: Unusual! 4 rather ragged sepals (no petals) create a leathery, **nodding, dark blue-purple "bell"** ornamented by ridges padded with white hair. Tightly clustered stamens give it a yellow throat.

FRUITS: Eventually there is a beautiful, white, feathery seed head.

LEAVES: Opposite, finely divided, hairy, and to 12.5 cm (5") long adorn the flower stem to near the single flower.

RANGE: Usually with sagebrush and ponderosa pine.

Whitestem frasera • shining frasera • *Frasera albicaulis*

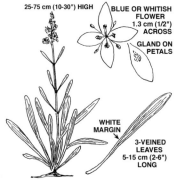

25-75 cm (10-30") HIGH

BLUE OR WHITISH
FLOWER
1.3 cm (1/2")
ACROSS

GLAND ON
PETALS

WHITE
MARGIN

3-VEINED
LEAVES
5-15 cm (2-6")
LONG

FORM: 25–75 cm (10–30") tall. Stout, erect stems with flower spikes.

BLOOMS: May to July.

FLOWERS: Pale blue, sometimes white, and in **an elongated cluster.** Not very noticeable. 4-petal flowers and 4 stamens alternate. There is a **gland at the base of each petal.**

LEAVES: Important: Shiny, green basal leaves to 15 cm (6") long **have white margins and 3 faint veins.** Smaller leaves on the stem.

RANGE: East of Cascades and often with ponderosa pine. Klickitat County. Pullman. Douglas recorded this species in the mountain valleys between Spokane and Kettle Falls.

Clustered frasera • *Frasera fastigiata*

FORM: To 1.5 m (5') tall. Single or several stout stems.
BLOOMS: May to July.
FLOWERS: Conical plumes of pale blue to mauve flowers. Almost colorless from a distance, but beautiful close-up. Flowers are about 1.3 cm (1/2") across. They are cup-like with **1 short, spiny bract between the petals.** 4 stamens stand erect.
LEAVES: Large and oval to 25 cm (10") long and in a series of whorls around the stout green stem.
RANGE: High, meadows and forest openings, Blue Mountains. Big Butte Lookout, Asotin County.
NOTES: Giant frasera, a larger edition with **green** flowers, is on p.177.

Oregon anemone • blue anemone • *Anemone oregana*

FORM: 7.5–20 cm (3–8") tall. **Slender stem and 1 flower.**
BLOOMS: April to May.
FLOWERS: 5 soft, sky-blue sepals. About 2.5 cm (1") across.
LEAVES: The 3 leaves, each 3 divided into lobed segments.
RANGE: Mostly east of the Cascades. Chelan County south to the Columbia Gorge. Blue Mountains, high open forests about 1500 m (5000') elevation.

Early blue violet • blue violet • *Viola adunca*

FORM: To 15 cm (6") tall. Leafy plant with short flower stems.
BLOOMS: April to August.
FLOWERS: Pale to dark blue or violet **flowers less than 1.3 cm (1/2") across.** The **lower 3 petals** often **white-throated with purple veins.** The upper 2 petals form a slender, backward-projecting spur half as long as the lower petal.
LEAVES: Round, heart-shaped leaves have long stems. There are 2 sharp bracts where a leaf joins the main stem.
RANGE: Moist woods, meadows. Low to subalpine.

Showy Jabob's-ladder • polemonium, blue jacob's-ladder
Polemonium pulcherrimum

FORM: 7.5–30 cm (3–12″) tall. A spray of leaves and flower stems from a common base. Height varies greatly with elevation.

BLOOMS: May to July.

FLOWERS: 5-petalled, **light blue with a yellow throat and 5 white stamens.** About 1 cm (3/8″) across. Flowers and buds cluster at stem ends.

LEAVES: Important: **A ladder-like arrangement of 11–25 leaflets,** each about 1.3 cm (1/2″) long. Combined leaves **look like a tufted, fern foliage.** May be greatly dwarfed at high elevations.

RANGE: Cascade Mountains from middle elevations to the alpine. Mt. Adams. Probably in the highest areas of the Blue Mountains.

NOTES: Two varieties of this plant account for **a tall form at lower elevations** and **a dwarfed form in the subalpine** and alpine.

Western blue flax • *Linum perenne*

FORM: 30–60 cm (1–2′) tall. Slender, erect stems from a common base.

BLOOMS: June to August.

FLOWERS: Saucer-like flowers of brightest blue. Flower parts are in 5s with a flower about 2 cm (3/4″) across. Flowers along tops of high branchlets.

LEAVES: Alternate, narrow and to 2.5 cm (1″) long.

RANGE: Random occurrence on well-drained open soils. Mostly east of the Cascades. Often with ponderosa pine, altitudinal tolerance.

NOTES: This is a very close relative to the European flax whose fibrous stems have been made into thread since time immemorial.

Common harebell • bluebell • *Campanula rotundifolia*

FORM: 15–45 cm (6–18") tall. Slender, erect and branching. Often grows in a tight clump.

BLOOMS: June to August.

FLOWERS: 5 distinct petals on beautiful, blue bells. These to 2 cm (3/4") long. Several, one above another. Bluebells of Scotland.

LEAVES: Young basal leaves wither before flowers appear. Then stem leaves are sparse and very narrow.

RANGE: Dry, open ground, meadows, forest edges from low to the subalpine. Olympics.

MOUNTAIN HAREBELL (*C. lasiocarpa*), also called "alpine harebell," has **a single bluebell** about 2 cm (3/4") long only **a few inches above the tuft of leaves** less than 2.5 cm (1") long. Narrow sepal lobes are toothed. High, rocky places in the northern Cascades.

OLYMPIC HAREBELL *(C. piperi)* is found **only in the Olympics.** Bright blue, bowl-like, to 2.5 cm (1") across. High elevations, the subalpine mostly. Crevices in the rocks. Can be abundant in a suitable localized habitat. Hurricane Ridge, Olympics. Discovered by an early botanist, C.V. Piper, in the Olympics, 1901.

Mountain harebell

Olympic harebell

Blue stickseed • false forget-me-not • *Hackelia micrantha*

FORM: To 90 cm (3') tall. Many stems from the root base and branchlets create a **loose, rounded outline**.

BLOOMS: June to August.

FLOWERS: Small, typical forget-me-not flowers with a yellowish or white eye. The small clusters originate at the end of stems from the upper leaf axils.

LEAVES: Paddle-shaped to 20 cm (8") long. Alternate and smaller stem leaves.

RANGE: Low forest meadows to the subalpine east of the Cascades. Mingles with Fendler's waterleaf and other subalpine meadow plants. Harts Pass.

Larkspurs • *Delphinium* spp.

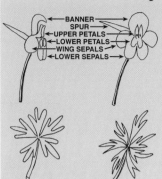

BANNER
SPUR
UPPER PETALS
LOWER PETALS
WING SEPALS
LOWER SEPALS

NUTTALL'S L.   MENZIES' L.

THE **UNUSUAL flower shape and its intense color** brings larkspurs to the attention. **Colors vary in shades of purple and blue,** but all are grouped under **BLUE.** The 5 large petals you see are actually sepals. The uppermost is prolonged backward into a spur. It encloses 2 small, nectar-bearing petals—usually appears to be only 1. The lower 2 petals, both quite small, have a cluster of stamens behind them.

This state has about a dozen larkspurs. Some may be poisonous to grazing cattle. Larkspurs are confusing because leaf shapes are rather similar and there is variation even within a single species. Use the range differences to separate the two most common. In short, Menzies' larkspur is west of the Cascades, Nuttall's larkspur to the east.

NUTTALL'S LARKSPUR (*D. nuttallianum*): **East of the Cascades.** Usually less than 40 cm (16") tall, **the common larkspur of early spring to early summer.** The bluish sepals give an **impression of a "dirty face" because of the whitish smudge of small petals.** It is a quick way of identification even if the leaves appear different on some plants. (If these central petals are clear-white then see rockslide larkspur below.) This larkspur favors dry soils associated with sagebrush and ponderosa pine and subsequently has a wide range.

MENZIES' LARKSPUR (*D. menziesii*): **West of the Cascades.** To 40 cm (16") tall. Leaves are variable but generally resemble Nuttall's larkspur. The common larkspurs on bluffs, rocky openings and dry meadows. Blooms mid-May to mid-July. Western section of Columbia Gorge.

PALE LARKSPUR
(*D. glaucum*): **Recognizable by its height**, to 1.8 m (6'). Purple to pale blue flowers with a long spur. Leaves palmately lobed and lobes coarsely toothed. Seeks moist places in the subalpine.

Nuttall's larkspur

ROCKSLIDE LARKSPUR
(*D. glareosum*): Usually less than 40 cm (16") tall and found in gravel or rocky places. Tiny, clear, white petals otherwise much like Nuttall's above. Subalpine zone in the Olympics and Cascades. Harts Pass.

NOTES: Several larkspurs with white flowers have a limited range in the Okanogan and Chelan counties. They favor dry hillsides at valley elevations. *D. xantholeucum* may be the robust plant growing along the Entiat River Road south of Chelan.

Menzies' larkspur

Howell's triteleia • *Triteleia howellii*

FORM: To 50 cm (20") tall. Single, erect stem.

BLOOMS: May to June.

FLOWERS: The tubes are dark blue with occasional paler lobes. There is a **dark blue line down each tube and petal. Up to a dozen flowers and buds in a head.** Note that the **anthers are on a filament smaller than they are.**

LEAVES: Usually **2 thin, grass-like leaves** about half the height of the plant.

RANGE: On coastal bluffs and meadows west of the Cascades. San Juan Islands and through Puget Sound. Columbia Gorge and eastward into Klickitat County. Along the lower eastern slope of the Cascades into Grant and Chelan counties.

NOTES: This triteleia can also be white, see p.51. Related **purple** Brodiaeas are on p.144.

Large-flowered triteleia • Douglas's brodiaea • *Triteleia grandiflora* • *Brodiaea douglasii*

FORM: To 75 cm (30") tall. Slender stem, topped by a large flower cluster.

BLOOMS: April to June.

FLOWERS: Blue "trumpets" point out horizontally. They have a darker blue line down them. Flowers about 2 cm (3/4") long. **Note that petal margins are wavy.**

LEAVES: 1–2 narrow leaves almost as long as the flower stem.

RANGE: In sagebrush and ponderosa pine habitats east of the Cascades. Chelan County, Steptoe Butte, Columbia River benchlands south of Pasco, Columbia Gorge east, Idaho's U.S. 95.

NOTES: An early English scientific journal states, "Found in North-west America by Mr. Douglas. It is growing in the garden of the Horticultural Society, where it flowers in July." • Several Native Americans harvested these bulbs for food. They were especially valuable because they could be dug in early spring.

> Their [Douglas's journals] *greatest interest lies in the accounts of the travels of a most observant man through a primitive wilderness— of journeys by canoe or on horseback —of icy rivers and freezing wind— and long portages across terrible terrain. He was often in danger from Indians, or bears, or starvation. He was content to travel on his own for long periods, but he was also a social animal and a good companion. Enormously tough and singleminded, he never lost a sense of wonder at the riches of Creation.*
> —Douglas of the Forests
> *by John Davies*

CAMASES • *Camassia* spp.

LIKELY CAMAS would rate, within its range, as the most valuable and abundant of all the native plants used for food by Native Americans. Tribes or families laid claim to certain beds or fields where a rough form of cultivation was used to enhance the annual crops. When bulbs were properly cooked they were sweet and digestible. When formed into cakes and dried they could be stored for months.

Common camas • *Camassia quamash*

FORM: 30–60 cm (1–2′) tall. Flower stems and leaves from a large bulb.

BLOOMS: April to June. May cover large meadows.

FLOWERS: Blue-purple to 4 cm (1 1/2″) across. Sometimes white. **Many buds and flowers to a stem. 3 sepals and 3 petals very similar**, i.e., 6 petals or sepals.

LEAVES: Long, narrow, grass-like, shorter than flower stem.

RANGE: Widespread, but sporadic occurrences in moist, grassy areas. Columbia Gorge.

NOTES: Death-camas has white flowers (see p.61).

GREAT CAMAS *(C. leichtlinii)* is much like common camas. Only **1–3 flowers at a time** and blooming later than common camas. Later **the sepals and petals twist together.** West of the Cascades on lowlands.

During April the slopes above the Columbia River are a mass of bloom.

...The quamish [camas] is now in blume and...at a short distance it resembles lakes of fine clear water...and there always in open grounds and glades...it delights in a rich black rich moist soil... a truncated bulb...shape and appearance of the onion, glutanous or somewhat slimy when chewed and almost tasteless in its unprepared state...this bulb is from the size of a nutmeg to that of a hen's egg.

—Lewis, June 12, 1806

Lewis also noted that eaten in quantity they could affect the bowels:

...when in the Indian hut, I was almost blown out by the strength of the wind.

Reached the old establishment at Spokan at eleven oclock. Mr. Finley...regretted exceedingly he had not a single morsel of food to offer me. He and his family were living for the last six weeks on the roots of the Phalangium quamash called by the natives all over the country Cannass...."

—Douglas, May 11, 1826

Western blue iris • blue flag • *Iris missouriensis*

FORM: 30–90 cm (1–3′) tall. Resembles a garden iris.

BLOOMS: May to June.

FLOWERS: 1–4 lovely violet-blue flowers to 7.5 cm (3″) across. The 3 sepals and 3 petals give it a 6-petalled appearance. The broad sepals usually stand upright. A yellowish intrusion in throat has spreading, violet lines, extending to the edge of the sepals.

LEAVES: Stout, grass-like.

RANGE: Frequent in ponds, marshy areas of the sagebrush and ponderosa pine regions. Infrequent in Puget Sound. Ellensburg, Yakima Canyon, Steptoe Butte, Pullman.

Bachelor's button • *Centaurea cyanus*

FORM: 30–90 cm (1–3′) tall. Stout stem branching near top.

BLOOMS: June to October.

FLOWERS: Usually bright blue, but can range to white, pink and purple. The flower is an attractive circle of disk flowers. The outer are larger. Flowers are carried singly at branch tips, a quick clue in separating it from chicory.

LEAVES: Alternate, narrow.

RANGE: An alien locally common along roadsides, waste areas.

NOTES: Closely related to knapweeds, see p.133.

Chicory • blue sailors • *Cichorium intybus*

FORM: 0.6–1.2 m (2–4′) tall. A branching, leafy stem.

BLOOMS: June to October.

FLOWERS: Usually 1–3 blooms in the axils of upper leaves. (Compare to bachelor's button which is single at stem tips.) Light blue, but sometimes white. The petals (ray flowers) are slightly toothed.

LEAVES: Alternate, lower ones deeply toothed and lobed.

RANGE: Roadsides and waste places across the state. An introduced plant from Eurasia and now a weed pest in some regions.

NOTES: Chicory brings to mind that the deep, tap root is used as a coffee substitute. The name, "blue sailors," comes from an old legend concerning a sailor's sweetheart who was deserted, but nevertheless kept faithful watch for him. The gods took pity on her and changed her into a blue-eyed plant to haunt roadsides.

Large-flowered blue-eyed Mary • innocence • *Collinsia grandiflora*

FORM: To 30 cm (12") tall. **Erect or sprawling.**

BLOOMS: Mid-March to mid-June. One of the earliest to bloom.

FLOWERS: Important: **Length of about 1.3 cm (1/2") long** distinguishes them from flowers half that size (small-flowered blue-eyed Mary). Upper petals are white, the others blue. **Flowers in rough whorls** from upper leaf axils.

LEAVES: Opposite, narrow, but variable in shape.

RANGE: Mossy bluffs, meadows at low to medium elevations. Mostly west of the Cascades.

SMALL-FLOWERED BLUE-EYED MARY (*C. parviflora*): Compare flower size to the above. **Quite small, about 6 mm (1/4") long.** Blue flowers with upper lips tipped with white or purple and nearly hidden in narrow leaves. Wide ranging on mossy rocks, open ground to shady forest edges across the state.

Gentians • *Gentiana* spp. and *Gentianella* spp.

THERE ARE A number of gentians in the state that aren't included here. **Gentians with folds between the petals are *Gentianas*, those without are *Gentianellas*.** Most gentians are a beautiful shade of blue or blue-purple. **All have erect flowers.** Leaves are opposite or whorled. Gentians favor **moist and boggy places.**

King gentian • swamp gentian • *Gentiana sceptrum*

FORM: 30–60 cm (1–2') tall. Stout erect stem.

BLOOMS: July to September.

FLOWERS: Dark blue with **dark, green dots on inside of petals** (really sepals). Flower to 4 cm (1 1/2") long, **no folds between sepals.** Flowers single or several at top of stem. Others in upper leaf axils.

LEAVES: 10–15 pairs, lowest may be scale-like.

RANGE: Coastal bogs, damp areas. West of the Cascades.

MOUNTAIN BOG GENTIAN (*G. calycosa*) is 10–30 cm (4–12") tall. (Wet ground in the subalpine.) **Each stem with a single, dark blue flower. Forked filament between each petal lobe.** High Olympics, Cascades.

PRAIRIE GENTIAN (*G. affinis*): To 30 cm (12") tall. **Flowers deep blue streaked with green.** Either a single or a small cluster. Note a **single, short tooth between petal lobes.** Ranges east sides of the Cascades. Damp soils, meadows. From valley to medium elevations.

Fuzzy-tongued penstemon • *Penstemon eriantherus*

FORM: To 40 cm (16") tall. A number of stems from a common base.

BLOOMS: May to July.

FLOWERS: Extra large, extra vibrant, **bulbous flowers** with vari-colored faces. Stem-top clusters of flowers, light blue to pinkish or purple. **The fuzzy tongue is very noticeable** and the 4 dark stamens above it.

LEAVES: Basal leaves of various sizes, but up to 12 cm (5") long, most toothed. Upper leaves narrow and entire.

RANGE: East of the Cascades. Associated with sagebrush and ponderosa pine regions. Okanogan and Ferry counties and southward.

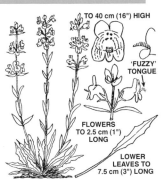

TO 40 cm (16") HIGH

'FUZZY' TONGUE

FLOWERS TO 2.5 cm (1") LONG

LOWER LEAVES TO 7.5 cm (3") LONG

TAPER-LEAVED PENSTEMON (*P. attenuatus*): Difficult to find good distinguishing features. Note the **height of up to 75 cm (30").** Locally it can be very abundant as along U.S. 12 west of Yakima. Flowers are **variable in color, blue, purple or pinkish.** They form in definite **tight whorls on the upper stem.** Stem leaves are opposite, stemless and taper to a sharp point. Eastern slope of Cascades. Low mountain forests.

Elegant penstemon • *Penstemon venustus*

FORM: To 75 cm (30") tall. Usually branching from base with arching stems to form a rounded clump.

BLOOMS: June to August. In June with white and purple fleabanes, Hooker's onion, as balsamroot fades.

FLOWERS: Very large, dark blue. Twin leaf axils produce a short stem with a **cluster of 3–5 flowers** each to **4 cm (1 1/2") long.** Flowers all face the same way.

LEAVES: Cluster of long-stemmed leaves at base, then opposite, clasping, serrated leaves.

RANGE: In sagebrush and ponderosa pine zones east of the Cascades. Walla Walla and Douglas counties. Douglas recorded it "...on dry channels of rivers among the mountains of North-West America."

NOTES: See p.148 for general notes on penstemons and **other colors.** There are a number of other penstemons you may find.

Long-flowered bluebell • *Mertensia longiflora*

FORM: 5–20 cm (2–8") tall. A short, slim stem with a **top-heavy flower cluster.**

BLOOMS: April to June. Blooms with buttercups, yellow bells, shootingstars and prairie stars.

FLOWERS: A clump of long-tubed blue flowers. Usually buds and young flowers have **a pinkish tinge.** Flowers are to 2 cm (3/4") long.

FRUITS: Seeds have a long appendage.

LEAVES: Several, alternate, rather broad stem leaves.

RANGE: East of the Cascades at lower elevations. Often with ponderosa pine, but also below and upward of this.

Tall bluebell • *Mertensia paniculata*

FORM: 0.3–1.2 m (1–4') tall. The height is a **distinguishing feature.** Usually several or a thicket of stems.

BLOOMS: April to August.

FLOWERS: Long, bell-shaped blue to pink flowers about 2 cm (3/4") long. **They hang in drooping clusters. Bracts flare out.**

LEAVES: Basal leaves are long-stemmed, but shorten further up.

RANGE: East of the Cascades except for the Olympics where it is found from high forests to subalpine. Stevens Pass, eastern slope. Ellensburg. Chelan County, Mt. Rainier.

WESTERN MERTENSIA (*M. platyphylla*) is much like the tall bluebell, but not as tall, with a single stem, not several. Blue flowers in a tight drooping cluster. Ranges west of the Cascades.

LUPINES • *Lupinus* spp.

LUPINES ARE variable in color, but for simplicity **those that look violet, magenta or purple have been grouped here.** Look for whites, p.57, and yellows, p.91. Lupines, about 2 dozen, are confusing unless a professional study is made of flower parts and seeds. These are the most common and identifiable. For others say, "Oh my, what a beautiful lupine!"

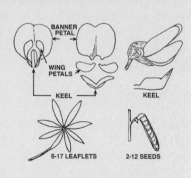

Lupines have 5 petals as shown on the diagram. The shape and hairiness of the keel are often used as clues. 10 stamens unite at the base. A pod dries out and twists open to disperse 2–12 seeds with toxic alkaloid properties. **5–17 leaflets radiate from a central point. They are never toothed.** As legumes, lupines enrich the soil with nitrogen from the air.

Field of lupines and balsamroot, east of Chelan

Prairie lupine • *Lupinus aridus*

FORM: 10–20 cm (4–10") tall. Flower spikes, on very short stems.

BLOOMS: May to June. Often massed and so creating rich color on the open slopes it favors.

FLOWERS: Light to dark purple with a definite **white rectangle on the banner petal.**
Important: **Flower spikes appear to sit among the leaves.** The variety, *lepidus,* below, has flower spikes well above them.

LEAVES: Mostly basal, 7 narrow **leaflets.**

RANGE: South-central Washington. Eastern Columbia Gorge. Goldendale. "From the Great Falls of the Columbia in North America to the sources of the Missouri" (recorded Douglas).

ELEGANT LUPINE (*L. lepidus*), to 35 cm (14") tall, has **flower spikes definitely above the leaves.** Prairie lupine has flowers among the leaves. Leaves basal, long-stemmed. **7 narrow leaflets.** Usually associated with sagebrush and ponderosa pine. High, exposed side hills. Ellensburg, Vantage.

BICOLORED LUPINE (*L. bicolor*) is **a small lupine** to 25 cm (10") tall with a small flower cluster of several **deep purple-blue flowers clearly marked with a white square** on the banner petal. **Leaves and stems hairy,** leaflets mainly 7. Blooms April to June. Ranges west of the Cascades at low elevations and on dry ground. Columbia Gorge east. Klickitat County.

Mountain valleys…near the Kettle Falls and very abundant along the course of the Columbia….
—Douglas, 1833

Arctic lupine • broad-leaved lupine • *Lupinus arcticus*

FORM: 30–60 cm (1–2′) tall. Usually a many-stemmed bushy plant.

BLOOMS: Mid-April, Columbia Gorge, late August, Mt. Rainier.

FLOWERS: Important: **Double, rectangular white blazes on the banner petal.** The same on silky lupine below, but note overall silky color of that plant. In the Olympics it is the main lupine but the white blazes aren't as clearly defined. Arctic lupine has a white keel, but this requires a close look.

LEAVES: 6–9 light green leaflets many with sharp-pointed tips.

RANGE: A common roadside lupine in forested areas. 3 varieties continue to give wide coverage to western Washington. Both slopes of the Cascades. Mt. Adams, Mt. Rainier, Olympics.

NOTES: The most common and widespread lupine.

Dwarf mountain lupine

DWARF MOUNTAIN LUPINE (*L. lyallii*) is a small lupine **flourishing on high, dry ridges.** Bright blue-purple flowers with a white blotch. **Silky-hairy leaves, usually 6 leaflets.** The only other lupine, except for the above, in the subalpine and alpine areas of the Olympics. Probably in northern Cascades.

Spurred lupine • *Lupinus arbustus* • *Lupinus laxiflorus*

FORM: To 60 cm (2′) tall. Slim, erect.

BLOOMS: April to June.

FLOWERS: A plume about 12.5 cm (5″) long of **blue, purple, violet or whitish small flowers 1 cm (3/8″) in length.** Note the double white spot on the banner petal like arctic and silky lupines, but **this has a spur, or hump** at the base of the flower.

LEAVES: Dark green, usually with **11 pointed or rounded leaflets.** Leaves climb high on the stem.

RANGE: East of the Cascades and mostly along the base of the Cascades with sagebrush and ponderosa pine. Easterly Columbia Gorge.

Silky lupine • *Lupinus sericeus*

FORM: 30–90 cm (1–3′) tall. A large, much-branched, bushy plant.

BLOOMS: April to August.

FLOWERS: Soft blue with lavender tinge, thickly clustered **on erect spikes** reaching **well above the leaves. Flowers with 2 white markings on the banner petal. This densely hairy on back.** Use a magnifying glass.

LEAVES: Important: **An overall gray or silvery sheen** caused by silky-white hairs on stem and leaves. (Use a magnifying glass to view.) **7–9 very narrow leaflets.**

RANGE: Important: East of the Cascades. **The most abundant lupine in the sagebrush and ponderosa pine ecosystem.**

NOTES: See p. 57 for a **white**-flowering variety. BIG-LEAF LUPINE (*L. polyphyllus*) is the largest of the lupines, except for tree lupine. **Often to 1.2 m (4′) tall.** Big leaves to 20 cm (8″) across. Typically 10–17 sharp-pointed leaflets. **Flower spike to 50 cm (20″) long.** A roadside lupine favoring moist areas, ditches. West of the Cascades. Low to middle mountain elevations.

> ...Nor can I pass the beauty, not to say grandeur of Lupinus grandiflora [a former name for the above]...on the border and lowland of streams....
> —Douglas, 1825

Big-leaf lupine

Ballhead waterleaf • *Hydrophyllum capitatum*

FORM: 10–23 cm (4–9″). One or several erect or bending flower stems.

BLOOMS: April to May.

FLOWERS: Tiny, **5-petalled flowers in a clustered ball** to 6 cm (2 1/4″) across. Usually a shade of blue. It **can vary from white to light pink.**

LEAVES: Only a few, with some appearing to come out of the ground at the base of the plant. **Long-stemmed with 5–7 lobes** each **divided into several fingers.** Young leaves made excellent greens for the pioneers.

RANGE: Widespread east of the Cascades in moist areas, shady slopes, open forests. Often associated with ponderosa pine areas. Columbia Gorge under Garry oak and ponderosa pine. Douglas recorded this species in fissures in moist rocks in the interior of the Columbia.

Columbia kittentails • *Synthyris stellata*

FORM: 15–40 cm (6–16") tall. Slender stems from a clump of distinctive leaves.

BLOOMS: Mid-March to mid-April.

FLOWERS: Columnar clusters of small, blue to purple flowers. These have **4 petals with 2 long, protruding anthers** which give them a rather fuzzy appearance.

LEAVES: Important: Leaves quickly recognizable when flowers are gone. They are **long-stemmed, kidney-shaped with large lobes each with 3 teeth.**

RANGE: Shady sidehills. Most abundant along the scenic "falls" section of the highway on the Oregon side of the Columbia. 50 years ago, Columbia kittentails didn't occur in Washington, but are now found about mid-section of the Columbia Gorge in shady woods.

...some handsome cascades are seen on either hand tumbling from the stupendious rocks of the mountain into the river....
—Lewis, April 14, 1806

Thread-leaved fleabane • *Erigeron filifolius*

FORM: To 25 cm (10") tall. Slender, erect stem from basal leaf tuft. Sometimes dwarfed to half this height.

BLOOMS: April to June.

FLOWERS: Usually considered **blue, but could be pink or white.** Usually **several flowers on a stem.** About 2.5 cm (1") across. Many narrow ray petals and yellow button center.

LEAVES: Important: **Leaves are very narrow, thread-thin-like.**

RANGE: Sagebrush habitat.

Typical sagebrush-bunchgrass habitat

Wild ginger • *Asarum caudatum*

FORM: 5–20 cm (2–8") tall. An evergreen, short, trailing plant. A loose cluster of leaves. Faint ginger smell when crushed, but crushed roots are more distinct. Believe it, don't try it.

BLOOMS: May to August.

FLOWERS: Curious, **purplish-brown, bell-shaped flowers with 3 wide-spreading lobes ending in long, slender tails.** Usually on the ground half-hidden by the leaves.

LEAVES: Attractive, dark green, **large, heart-shaped** with 2 leaves branching from a node.

RANGE: In rich forest soils west of the Cascades. To an elevation of 1200 m (4000').

NOTES: Roots and leaves saw wide medicinal uses by Native Americans.

Chocolate lily • rice root • *Fritillaria lanceolata*

FORM: 30–60 cm (1–2') tall. Single, erect stem from a large bulb which appears covered with rice, hence "rice root."

BLOOMS: April.

FLOWERS: A cup-like, 6-petalled flower about 2.5 cm (1") across, **hangs down.** It is a **dark-brown color with green and yellow mottling**—a camouflage that hides them in the vegetation. Usually several buds and flowers to a stem, but sometimes single.

LEAVES: 1–2 whorls of 3–5 leaves on the stem.

RANGE: Grassy forest openings, bluffs. Both sides of the Cascades. From low to moderate elevations.

NOTES: Coastal Native Americans valued the large, succulent bulbs as a food item. They were steamed in pits or in later years cooked in pots.

Curly dock • *Rumex crispus*

FORM: 30–90 cm (1–3') tall. Stout, erect, ribbed stem.

BLOOMS: June to August. After blooming, plant turns russet-brown and **stands out starkly for most of the winter.**

FLOWERS: Tiny, inconspicuous, mostly **reddish-brown color.** Clustered along upper part of stems and high branches.

FRUITS: Flowers turn to seeds of almost the same color.

LEAVES: Narrow, lower leaves, to 25 cm (10") long, **curly edges.**

RANGE: Native of Europe. Wide ranging across state.

SHEEP SORREL (*R. acetosella*) is a weed under 30 cm (12") tall. Very small, reddish-brown flowers and seeds. Leaves have a sour taste—oxalic acid. Used in Europe for salads and pot herbs. Leaves are arrowhead-shaped. Poor exposed soils. Ranges low to high on the mountains.

Youth-on-age • piggy-back plant • *Tolmiea menziesii*

FORM: 30–60 cm (1–2') tall. Tall, slender flower stems.

BLOOMS: May to August.

FLOWERS: Important: An intricate design. The **4 petals branch** out from **between the sepals and are almost thread-like. Sepals are greenish with purple streaks.** Flowers, about 6 mm (1/4") long, are loosely spaced along the top half of the stem.

LEAVES: Check in late summer to see **small leaves growing from the bases of old leaf blades.** (Hence the name, youth-on-age.) When the old leaf withers and falls to the ground the new leaves have a chance to root. **Most leaves are basal,** long-stemmed and round with shallow lobes.

RANGE: Moist, shady places. Mostly west of the Cascades.

NOTES: The Latin names are derived from Tolmie and Menzies. Dr. William Tolmie was a physician for the Hudson's Bay Company at Ft. Vancouver in 1832. Archibald Menzies was the first European botanist to explore the Pacific Northwest.

• Sometimes used as a houseplant.

Seabeach sandwort • *Honkenya peploides*

FORM: 10–25 cm (4–10") tall. A sprawling, yellowish-green, beach plant forming a well-rooted mound on the sand.

BLOOMS: May to August.

FLOWERS: Tiny, pale green or greenish-white. Sepals greenish, 5 widely spaced white petals, 10 stamens. Seeds are small, oval and yellowish.

LEAVES: Stiff, yellow green and in pairs.

RANGE: Important: **Coastal beaches often among logs.** Long Beach. Often with American glehnia and American searocket, p.114.

Giant frasera • *Frasera speciosa*

FORM: To 2.1 m (7') tall. Is this our area's tallest wildflower? See **white** false hellebore, p. 54, which is about the same height.

BLOOMS: June to August.

FLOWERS: Flowers, about 2.5 cm (1") across, have **purple-spotted petals** each with a pair of **hairy glands near the base.** Flowers form in open clusters in upper leaf axils.

LEAVES: Narrow, to 23 cm (9") long, **in whorls of 3–5** and cover the stem.

RANGE: Wide ranging in eastern Washington and associated with ponderosa pine and Douglas-fir. Douglas recorded it on the low hills near Spokane and on subalpine parts of the Blue Mountains.

NOTES: A real curiosity because of its size and often random spotting in an open forest.

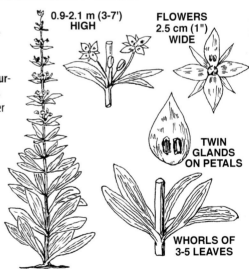

0.9-2.1 m (3-7') HIGH

FLOWERS 2.5 cm (1") WIDE

TWIN GLANDS ON PETALS

WHORLS OF 3-5 LEAVES

MITREWORTS • *Mitella* spp.

THERE ARE 8 mitreworts in the state. 5 have greenish-yellow flowers. Slender flower stems carry a scattering of tiny, delicate, symmetrical flowers whose thread-like petals separate them from the related *Heucheras* with entire petals, see pp.45–46. **Petal design and location in relation to the stamens provides identification.** Seeds disperse when the top half of the seed capsule breaks off and a falling raindrop splashes them out.

BREWER'S MITREWORT (*M. breweri*): To 15–40 cm (6–16") tall. 6–20 flowers to a stem. Flowers greenish-yellow, saucer-shaped, **petals divide into 3–5 segments, thread-thin and horizontal from the main axis. 5 stamens rise between the petals or alternate.** So are the stamens of oval-leaved mitewort (below), but Brewer's **has rounded, kidney-shaped leaves with rounded teeth.** Moist woods and meadows across the state.

15-40 cm (6-16")

FIVE-STAMENED MITREWORT (*M. pentandra*): A plant to 15–35 cm (6–14") tall. The 5 stamens are significant, but 4 more plants have the same. However, **stamens are opposite the petals.** Sepals are broad and re-curved while the **petals are hair-like or fringed.** There are several oval, basal leaves, hairy and round-toothed. Moist woods, wet meadows. Middle mountain to subalpine.

THREE-TOOTHED MITREWORT (*M. trifida*): The name says it. There are **3 teeth on each of the 5 petals** that protrude from a narrow, bowl-shaped flower. Many blooms point upward.

15-35 cm (6-14") HIGH

LEAVES AND STEMS HAIRY

FIVE-STAMENED   THREE-TOOTHED   OVAL-LEAVED

Petals may be whitish or pink instead of green. Stems and leaves very hairy. Moist areas at mid-elevations west of the Cascades.

OVAL-LEAVED MITREWORT (*M. ovalis*): Notice that the **5 stamens alternate between the petals.** See drawing for flower shape. Hairy, oblong-oval leaves.

COMMON MITREWORT (*M. nuda*): **Only to 20 cm (8")** tall. General features similar, but note that there are

7.5-20 cm (3-8") HIGH

10 stamens. That is enough for positive identification. Small kidney-shaped basal leaves, doubly toothed. Moist areas, streambanks, lower elevations of north Cascades.

LEAFY MITREWORT (*M. caulescens*): The name is the best clue for **this has several leaves on the stem while the others are leafless on the stem.** 1–3 basal leaves with maple-like look. **Flowers bloom** April to June **from top downwards**, a reversal of the usual. Broad range in moist valleys and mountain slopes. Forested areas across the state.

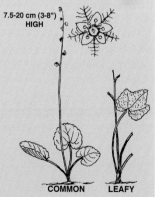

COMMON   LEAFY

Indian hellebore • green false hellebore • *Veratrum viride*

FORM: 0.9–1.5 m (3–5′) tall. Stout, erect, leafy stem.

BLOOMS: May to August depending on elevation.

FLOWERS: Small, **yellowish-green** on **thin spikes or drooping tassels.** Flower tassels resemble the rest of the plant in its greenish-yellow color.

LEAVES: Large, heavily ribbed and clasping at base.

RANGE: In damp places from coastal elevations to higher, wet meadows. Greatest abundance in the subalpine ecosystem. Olympics and Cascades.

NOTES: Native Americans, through centuries of experimentation, learned which plants were edible, which seemed to cure or alleviate illnesses, the ones best suited to make twine and which could be woven or fashioned into requirements for everyday use. Some plants like devil's club had mystic values as well. **Indian hellebore was known for its poisonous properties—all parts of it.** However, a small portion was used in various ways as a medicine and was believed potent for a great number of human ills. The lushness of the leaves create an illusion of edibility and hungry hikers have tried it with serious consequences. Enjoy it as part of the high country scene. Photograph its exotic form. But **avoid it as a food item.**

Pineapple weed • *Matricaria discoidea*

FORM: 5–30 cm (2–12″) tall. A low-branching weed **purported to smell like pineapple when crushed.**

BLOOMS: May to September.

FLOWERS: Greenish-yellow, pineapple-like flower head about 1 cm (3/8″) tall held in a cup of greenish bracts. Many flower heads because of short, branching stems.

LEAVES: Dark green leaves so divided as to appear like **carrot-tops.**

RANGE: On hard, dry ground, along roadsides and parking lots, disturbed and compacted areas. Widespread. Low elevation plant southward to Mexico. Lewis recorded it on the banks of the Kooskoosky (Clearwater River).

Silver bur-weed • sand bur • *Ambrosia chamissonis*

FORM: To 30 cm (12") tall. A sprawling, **drab olive-green, common beach plant.**

BLOOMS: July to September.

FLOWERS: Spike tops of small greenish flowers, inconspicuous because the spikes are much the same color as the leaves. Flowers form **burs with horrendous spines.**

LEAVES: **A sage color from** silvery hairs. Main stems often partially covered with sand. Leaves, alternate, divided or toothed.

RANGE: Among logs or in rocky places. Coastal beaches to California.

NOTES: *Ambrosia* refers to the food of the Greek gods while *chamissonis* is from Chamisso, California, where it was collected in 1891. This plant isn't food for gods or humans.

Wild sarsaparilla • *Aralia nudicaulis*

FORM: 20–40 cm (8–16") tall. More or less erect.

BLOOMS: May to June.

FLOWERS: Very small, 5-petalled, **greenish-white** flowers with petals turned down and 5 projecting stamens. Flowers in a 3 cluster formation. Inedible green or purple-brown ribbed berries form later.

LEAVES: Each of the 3 branches carrying from 3–5 oval leaflets 5–10 cm (2–4") long. **Turns yellow during August** and so advertises its presence.

RANGE: Semi-open forests at middle elevations. Northeastern Washington.

NOTES: The root has medicinal properties like the true sarsaparilla, a tropical plant. The unusual name comes from a tropical relative, zarzaparilla, a 'prickly vine' in Spanish.

Stinging nettle • *Urtica dioica*

FORM: 0.6–1.5 m (2–5') tall. Stout, erect stems. **Usually a thicket.**

BLOOMS: May to September. New plants keep growing.

FLOWERS: Tiny, greenish and in dense, drooping clusters at stem tips or in the leaf axils. Male and female flowers in separate spikes, the female usually uppermost.

LEAVES: Opposite, narrowly oval, **coarsely toothed and covered with stinging hairs.**

RANGE: In richer, moist soils, old habitations, pastures. A native of Europe with an early introduction to North America. Now widespread. From lowlands to high on the mountains.

NOTES: The irritation from stinging hairs results from them stabbing you with jolts of formic acid. Young nettles make excellent steamed greens. Native peoples in more recent times used the strong fibers in making cord. Some European species produce fiber for the best of linens.

Alaska rein-orchid • *Platanthera unalascensis*

FORM: To 60 cm (2') tall. Single, erect stem. **Usually in numbers.**

BLOOMS: June to August.

FLOWERS: Tiny, green flowers are spaced alternately and rather regularly up a **slender, leafless stem.** Some fragrance. **The lip and the spur are the same length.**

LEAVES: Important: **The basal location of the several leaves,** even if withered, is an identification feature. Leaves do wither by the time the plant is in bloom.

RANGE: Drier ground than most rein-orchids. Sporadic and mostly east of the Cascades. Low lands and to near the subalpine.

NOTES: These plants are subject to confusion even with the professionals. Other genus names in use are *Piperia* and *Habenaria.* For **white** rein-orchid, see p.74.

ELEGANT REIN-ORCHID *(P. elegans)* is similar to the above in **few withering basal leaves** and flower color. **Flowers rather thickly clustered** on the stem. Tiny flowers with a very **long spur, about twice the length of the lip petal.** Open woods at lower elevations. Klickitat County, Columbia Gorge.

Slender rein-orchid • *Platanthera stricta* • *Platanthera saccata*

FORM: To 75 cm (30") tall. Notice the height!

BLOOMS: June to August.

FLOWERS: Entire plant is green. Flowers scattered along a comparatively short spike. **The spur petal is a broad tongue (sac) and shorter than the lip.**

LEAVES: Important: Note that unlike the Alaska rein-orchid and elegant rein-orchid, which may only have withered basal leaves, **this rein-orchid has oval leaves** all the way to the flowers.

RANGE: Important: This is a plant of **wet, boggy places and moist forests.** Wide range in elevation and across the state.

Green-flowered bog-orchid • *Platanthera hyperborea*

FORM: 20–60 cm (8–24") tall.

BLOOMS: June to August.

FLOWERS: Green, stemless, often tinged or veined with purple. Spur is cylindrical or tube-like. Uniform spacing along stem.

LEAVES: Narrow and pointed. **4–6 on lower half of stem.**

RANGE: In moist, shady places. Mostly east of the Cascades. Wide range in elevation.

Heart-leaved twayblade • *Listera cordata*

FORM: To 20 cm (8") tall. Slender stem from creeping roots.

BLOOMS: June to August. The same for the ones below.

FLOWERS: Important: **The orchid flower has its narrow, lip petal split into 2 distinct forks.** Note **the 2 teeth at the base of this petal.** Flowers vary from **light-green to purplish to brown.** They have a bad odor that attracts pollinating insects.

LEAVES: Twayblades have **a pair near the center of the stem.**

RANGE: In moist forests, wet areas, low to medium elevations. Circumboreal. Not abundant, but widespread. Mt. Baker, Olympics.

NORTHWESTERN TWAYBLADE (*L. caurina*) is one of the 3 twayblades in the state. Very similar to the above. The orchid-like, **greenish-yellow flowers have a lip petal, not forked as above,** but in **a definite wedge-shape.** Leaves are more oval than heart-shaped. The range is the same except that this plant can be found to the subalpine.

BROAD-LEAVED TWAYBLADE *(L. convallarioides)*: **The lip petal, broadly wedge-shaped, has a noticeable notch at its tip.** The two leaves near mid-center of the stem are **almost as broad as long.** Range as above.

Subalpine terrain, Mt. Rainier

CLIFF FERNS *(Woodsia* spp.): The most common is **mountain cliff fern,** *Woodsia scopulina,* which has hairy fronds. Look for it in dry, rocky places from lowlands to subalpine heights. Coulee City and Pullman. **Western cliff fern,** *W. oregana,* is the common fern on rockslides east of the Cascades. Its bunchy tuft of fronds is from 10–30 cm (4–12") tall.

PARSLEY FERN *(Cryptogramma acrostichoides):* A densely tufted little fern 15–30 cm (6–12") tall. There are 2 distinct types of fronds, the fertile being the taller with margins rolled over to enclose the spores. Dry, rocky areas mostly in the subalpine of the Olympics and Cascades. Mt. Rainier, Stevens Pass, Chelan County.

Licorice fern

LICORICE FERN *(Polypodium glycyrrhiza):* The thickish roots have a licorice flavor. Often found on mossy cliffs, logs or tree trunks. A sparse fern with fronds to 30 cm (12") long and 2.5–7.5 cm (1–3") wide. Sori are large and round. Frond leaves are lobed to the midrib. Damp areas at low elevations along coast, higher in the Olympics and Cascades.

LEATHERY POLYPODY *(Polypodium scouleri):* Leathery leaves, pinnae rounded. Notable because of its tolerance to the salt spray zone. Coastal areas through Washington.

LADY FERN *(Athyrium filix-femina):* A large graceful fern common in damp, shady woods to 1200 m (4000′). Fronds to 1.2 m (4′) long and 25 cm (10") wide arch outwards; widest below the center, tapering in both directions. In dampish places from lowlands to alpine heights.

Leathery polypody

ALPINE LADY FERN *(Athyrium distentifolium):* A smaller, bushier edition of lady fern. Rockslides and scree slopes in subalpine and alpine terrain.

MAIDENHAIR FERN *(Adiantum aleuticum* or *A. pedatum):* The most delicate of our ferns, with each tiny leaf frond fringed along the upper edge. Strong, shiny black stems with fronds usually not more than 60 cm (2′) long. Often clings to wet rock faces or masses in shady, damp places. Coast forest ecosystem to elevations of 1500 m (5000′). Also eastern slopes of southern Cascades.

Maidenhair fern

DEER FERN *(Blechnum spicant):* Easily recognized by its distinct types of fronds. Non-fertile or vegetative fronds are evergreen and form a low rosette often flat on the ground. Leaves taper toward both ends. Fertile leaves are similar but stand upright from the center of the clump. Damp, shady, coastal forests at low to medium elevations.

SWORD FERN *(Polystichum munitum):* Symmetrical, dark-green sprays of fronds to 90 cm (3′) long. Pinnules (the smallest leaf divisions) are sharp-pointed and sharp-toothed. The underside is almost orange because of twin rows of spore cases. These attractive fronds are shipped east for use as florist's decorations. A major part of the coast forest ecosystem.

BRACKEN *(Pteridium aquilinum):* Bracken is the most widespread and luxuriant fern in the region. The stout stems, often to 2.1 m (7′) tall, grow singly instead of clustering from a compact base, as with most ferns. A line of spore cases follows the margin of each leaf division. In lower coniferous forests west of the Cascades, also in shady places from the bunchgrass ecosystem to mountain elevations. Blue Mountains.

Deer fern

REFERENCES

Davies, J. 1980. *Douglas of the Forests*. Dumfriesshire, Scotland.

Douglas, C. W, G. B. Straley and D. Meidinger. 1990-94. *The Vascular Plants of British Columbia*. Special Report Series 1-4. Victoria: British Columbia Ministry of Forests, Research Branch.

Hawke, D. F. 1980. *Those Tremendous Mountains*. New York: Norton.

Hitchcock, K. C. L., A. Conquist, M. Ownbey and J. W. Thompson. 1955, 1959, 1961, 1964, 1969. *Vascular Plants of the Pacific Northwest*. 5 vols. Seattle: University of Washington Press.

Jolley, R. 1988. *Wildflowers of the Columbia Gorge*. Portland: Oregon Historical Society.

Kirk, R., and C. Alexander. 1990. *Exploring Washington's Past: A Road Guide to History*. Seattle: University of Washington Press.

Lyons, C. P., and B. Merilees. 1995. *Trees, Shrubs and Flowers to Know in Washington and British Columbia*. Edmonton: Lone Pine Publishing.

McKelvey, S. Delano. 1991. *Botanical Exploration of the Trans-Mississippi-West*. Portland: Oregon State University Press.

Morwood, W. 1974. *Traveller in a Vanished Landscape*. Newton Abbot, Devon: Readers Union.

Pojar, J., and A. MacKinnon. 1994. *Plants of the Pacific Northwest Coast*. Edmonton: Lone Pine Publishing.

Thwaites, R. G. Reprint edition. *Original Journals of the Lewis and Clark Expedition*. 8 vols. Ayer.

Turner, N. J. 1975. *Food Plants of British Columbia Indians*. Victoria: Royal British Columbia Museum.

Willard, T. 1992. *Edible and Medicinal Plants of the Rocky Mountains and Neighboring Territories*. Calgary: Wild Rose College of Natural Healing.

INDEX

INDEX OF SCIENTIFIC NAMES

INDEX OF COMMON NAMES

About the Author

THE MOUNTAINS and streams were only minutes away from the family orchard in British Columbia's Okanagan Valley where Chess Lyons spent his boyhood. The Depression years offered little money for recreation, but hiking, camping and fishing were for the taking. Chess received a degree in Forest Engineering from the University of British Columbia, and in 1940 he became the first technical employee of the newly formed Parks Branch of the B.C. Forest Service. After Chess left government service in 1962, he produced wildlife and travel films and acted as travel guide to many foreign countries.

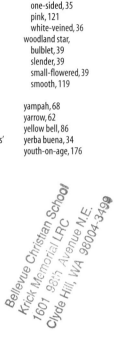

Chess' first book, *Trees, Shrubs and Flowers to Know in British Columbia*, published in 1954, was the first non-technical field guide in the province. Two years later, he wrote a similar book for Washington State. They served for many decades, through many reprints and revisions, and were finally combined into one volume in 1995.

For the past several years Chess has criss-crossed Washington, hiking the trails, photographing the plants and researching the travels of Lewis and Clark, David Douglas and other explorer-botanists, so that he could write this new book about the wealth of wildflowers in the state of Washington.